# Black
# *Lives*

# Black *Lives*

*Essays in*
African American Biography

Edited by James L. Conyers Jr.

*M.E. Sharpe*
Armonk, New York
London, England

**Library of Congress Cataloging-in-Publication Data**

Black lives : essays in African American biography / James L. Conyers, Jr.
p.   cm.
Includes bibliographical references and index.
ISBN 0–7656–0329–2 (alk. paper)   ISBN 0–7656–0330–6 (pbl. : alk. paper)
1. Afro-Americans—Biography.   2. Afro-Americans—Biography—History and criticism.
3. Afro-Americans—Biography—Study and teaching.   I. Conyers, James L.
E185.96.B5363   1998
920′.00929073—dc21        98–5996

CIP

Printed in the United States of America

The paper used in this publication meets the minimum requirements of
American National Standard for Information Sciences—
Permanence of Paper for Printed Library Materials,
ANSI Z 39.48-1984.

BM (c)   10   9   8   7   6   5   4   3   2   1
BM (p)   10   9   8   7   6   5   4   3   2   1

# Dedication

This book is dedicated to the loving memory of my Auntie Bee
(Gladys B. Cox), Dr. John Henrik Clarke, and Mrs. Frances Furman.
Your ideas and wisdom will be passed on. We mourn!

# Contents

# Foreword

## *Julius E. Thompson*

*Black Lives: Essays in African American Biography* is an important contribution to African American history, culture, and literary studies. The fifteen scholars in this academic volume offer insights into three focal areas of the black experience: first, intellectual biographical studies, with a focus on the life and work of Maulana Karenga (1941– ), Vinnette Carroll (1922– ), Daniel "Chappie" James Jr. (1920–1978), and Richard Allen (1760–1831); second, cultural biographical studies, concentrating on the careers of Malcolm X (1925–1965), Harriet Jacobs (1813–1897), Bessie Head (1937–1986), Elizabeth Ross Haynes (1883–1953), William Levi Dawson (1899–1990), and Maria Stewart (1803–1870); third, oral history narratives and biography as a teaching tool, suggesting that profound insights into black culture and life are offered in portraits of life in Trinidad, black female slave stories, in teaching black history courses, and as paths for greater understanding of Malcolm X, of the Ghanian scholar James Emman Kwegyir Aggrey (1875–1927), and of Emmett Jay Scott (1873–1957).

Collectively, then, the essays represent a panorama view of the world black community in all of its diversity and complexity, as represented in the African, African American, and Caribbean experiences of people of African ancestry. Three centuries are covered in the studies of this book—from the eighteenth century with one individual, to the nineteenth century with five major topics, to the twentieth century with seven individuals

In the initial essay, James L. Conyers Jr. notes the special significance of a very different leader in the last quarter of the twentieth century, Maulana Karenga, a philosopher, teacher, and activist, whose work represents that of a significant contemporary intellectual "renaissance" that has influenced Black African world consciousness since the 1960s.

In the creative universe of African American arts, Calvin A. McClinton suggests that the career of Vinnette Carroll, a director of black theater, must be recognized as a major contribution to the field. Carroll helped to develop a new form of teacher, "the gospel song-play," in order to capture the richness and variety of black life through music, theater, and dance. His essay also reminds readers of the limitations that gender has sought to impose on American women, that in the case of black women these limitations have been augmented by biases of race and class.

Earnest Bracey captures the legacy of General Daniel "Chappie" James Jr., the first African American to rise to the rank of four-star general in the United States Air Force. Bracey's study on James highlights the continuing theme of black service in the U.S. armed forces—often against the odds—in the twentieth century, through the age of segregation (1890–1960) and the modern Civil Rights Movement era. Perhaps General James's career helps contemporary readers to understand the reasons why African Americans have fought in America's wars and been willing to serve in the military during peacetime. One answer, as expressed in the life and career of General James, is that many blacks believed that by serving in the military they were working to help make the nature of American democracy a "real" reality for all of the people of the nation.

Mitchell Kachun's essay on the career of Bishop Richard Allen, the founder of the African Methodist Episcopal Church, denotes the historical role of black ministers and the black church in African American life in this country. Bishop Allen remains a central figure in this tradition. Yet, according to Kachun, it is the responsibility of each succeeding generation to record, interpret, and understand the historical, cultural, political, and social contributions of the leaders of the past.

Five scholars in this collection offer fresh literary insights into the careers of six significant black world figures. Gloria Randle's essay, "Outlaw Women and Toni Morrison's Communities," is a literary analysis centering on outlaws and the conceptual framework of collective black communities. The author focuses on three characters in three of Morrison's works: Breedlove in *The Bluest Eye*, Sula in the novel *Sula*, and Sethe in *Beloved*. Over all, this essay makes a valuable contribution to literary biographical studies by examining deep structural and cultural aspects of African American life and history.

Owen G. Mordaunt's study on Bessie Head, the South African–born writer, suggests the complexity of life in the world black community. He denotes the issue of the "color" factor among black people—Bessie Head was of mixed race—and the relationship of this issue to the conditions of slavery and colonialism. Mordaunt's important study also indicates the nature of the writer in society, and especially the emergence of black women writers in modern times and of the Southern African women writers in particular. Finally, this study raises some interesting observations on the nature of religion in the black world and its influences on the individual and the group.

LaVerne Gyant writes on Elizabeth Ross Haynes and Ida Young on Maria Stewart, both African American women writers who helped to make a difference in the life and social uplift of their communities. In 1923, Haynes produced the first scholarly study on the impact of domestic workers in this nation, while Maria Stewart wrote an autobiography of her life's work and was a significant speaker and activist in the abolitionist struggle. Both essays emphasize the importance of recovering the hidden history of black people from earlier times.

Ralph Anthony Russell's study on the black composer William Levi Dawson breaks new ground with an analysis of the artist's important "Negro Folk Symphony" (1934), which stresses the use of folk melodies and materials by black composers in the 1920s and 1930s. Dawson's musical contributions are evidence of the long black struggle in America for intellectual and creative growth and development while overcoming the historical burdens of racism, segregation, and discrimination in American life against black people.

Five scholars in this volume contribute studies that explore the importance of using oral history narratives and biography to reach large numbers of students and lay persons in the wider local communities of this nation.

Clement London uses oral history techniques to give a portrait of life in twentieth-century Trinidad, a significant nation in the Caribbean region. London is especially interested in gaining the impressions of senior citizens on the island, whom he allows to tell their own stories. London trained a number of young local students to help him conduct the research on their own people. Thus, he aided in the cross-communication of the generations in his native homeland.

Olga Idriss Davis and Robin Balthrope are both concerned with using African American biographies and autobiographies as teaching aids and communication devices to reach students and advance their knowledge on American life and history. Davis's study focuses on the black female slave narratives to achieve this end, while Balthrope develops a comparative perspective with the life of Nate Shaw in *All God's Danger* and Stowe's *Uncle Tom's Cabin*. These studies are able to use such works to capture the various views, issues, and conditions of black people in American society, with a focus on life under slavery and later during the Great Depression.

Andrew Smallwood is also concerned with issues of American education, and in a study on Malcolm X, he traces the role and influence of this activist on Black adult education in the United States, with a focus on the period of 1950 to 1965. In sum, with Martin Luther King Jr. (1929–1968),

Malcolm X emerges as the most significant black leader of the period. However, Smallwood suggests that this is an area for more research on the contributions of Malcolm X to black leadership in America.

The international dimensions of black education are explored in Daniel Boamah-Wiafe's article on the career of the Ghanian scholar James Emman Kwegyir Aggrey. Aggrey's work as an educator included twenty years of service at Livingston College, in Salisbury, North Carolina, where he also was a minister in the Zion Methodist Church. He later worked in the areas of education and religion in West Africa, with a concentration of his services in Ghana. Thus, his career represents the pan-African expressions of a Black person born in Africa, but who was able to offer educational and religious opportunities to Black people throughout the world.

The book concludes with Maceo Crenshaw Dailey's description of the writing of his biography on the life of Emmett Jay Scott, the important private secretary of Booker T. Washington (1857–1915), founder in 1882 of Tuskegee Institute, now Tuskegee University, in Alabama. Dailey traces Scott's leadership abilities as an aid to Washington, the most powerful black leader in America between 1895–1915. In doing so, he helps contemporary readers to view the hidden dimensions and special challenges raised by the leadership of Washington and his allies.

In summary, the contributors to *Black Lives* have helped to advance scholarly attention on the worldwide impact of the black experience. Collectively, their work helps to focus attention on the role of African American biography in (1) exploring the group consciousness of the black community, (2) fostering greater understanding on race relations, (3) creating greater diversity among scholars in American universities, (4) encouraging greater appreciation for gender roles in American society and especially of the contributions of American women to American life, history, and culture; (5) youth concerns; (6) adding to the literature on ethnic life in America; and (7) exploring the worldwide impact of biography, especially in Third World countries.

# Preface

This edited volume is devoted to studying African American biography and culture in the organizational form of (1) intellectual studies, (2) literary studies, (3) oral history narratives, and (4) autobiographical studies examining the concept of an authentic self.

As argued in the studies conducted within this volume, African Americans are too often reflected in biographical studies as objects; there is the pattern of dismissal of Afrocentric culture, memory, and ethos, which are critical variables to describing and evaluating African American history and culture. Germane to this point, these studies seek to present selected authors who have studied the genre of Black biography and culture from an African American prism. Although, this draws the implication of an Afrocentric perspective, an intersubjective lens provides readers with an alternative worldview and scheme to examine Africana diasporic phenomena. Simply put, as African American scholars write about the everyday experiences of African Americans in place and time, their historical and cultural experiences must be taken into account in order to seek balance and a critical interpretative analysis of the subject matter.

I expect readers to have an ongoing dialog in regards to alternative methods, theories, and typologies in conducting biographical studies relative to the African American experience. Moreover, whether the reader may agree or not, discourse, the exercise in creating options and open dialog, is an essential basis for explaining, enumerating, and developing a contextual analysis of black biography and culture in place and time.

# Acknowledgments

In the fall of 1995 my wife Jacqueline suggested that I strongly consider recommending to the Black Studies Department at the University of Nebraska at Omaha the idea of hosting a colloquium on African American biography. Initially, the thought of inviting scholars to brainstorm for two days seemed ambiguous. However, as the program began to organize, take structure, and crystallize, the reality became more apparent concerning the need for scholars to critically examine the genre of biography in the form of intellectual, literary, full-scale, and oral history narratives. Fortunately, the Black Studies Department was able to attract an experienced and prolific external consultant, quality faculty, advanced graduate students, and independent scholars. Reflexive from these untiring efforts, selected essays were organized for the development of this book. Again, after publishing each book, I am still astounded by seeing ideas come to print, and more important, that print articulated into a book. All of the contributors need time to be commended for their tenacity and discipline in submitting their rough draft manuscripts on time before the colloquium and responding expeditiously to galley-proof commentary. Collectively, these untiring efforts and vision have come to fruition, and hopefully this book will make a contribution to the literature on the genre of African American biography.

I would to acknowledge my mother Agnes Conyers and my wife Jacqueline I. Conyers for their support, love, encouragement, and guidance. Also my three sons Chad Anthony, Khalfani Sekou, and Kamau Abotare are my young lions who consistently test my commonsense skills and ability to articulate data and information to the common man and woman.

Mentoring is key and an essential attribute for any scholar or writer who attempts the perils of explaining the meaningfulness of the existence of humans, and more appropriately, the meaning and existence of African continental and diasporic people. I must add to this credit recognition of Dr. Julius E. Thompson, Dr. James B. Stewart, and Dr. Delores Aldridge. Their support, encouragement, vision, and kindness have enabled me to take on challenges and adversity with the attempt to describe and evaluate the Black experience from an Afrocentric perspective.

Friendship is mandatory for any scholar or individual to move from one point to another. By saying this, I am referring to the fact that I have been blessed with having as close and old friends Black men with whom I've been associated for more than two decades. Reminiscent of a line from the movie *Get on the Bus*, one cannot find or make old friends of new friends. My brothers in struggle and adversity are Qawi Jamison, Zane Corbin, Anthony Robinson, Henry Bernard Robinson, Gregory Mainor, James Mainor, Mustafa Aziz Rasool, Mustafa Harper, Joseph Taylor, and James Bullock. To these brothers much respect and thanks for our continued friendship and brotherhood.

Others to whom I would like to give a shout of thanks, whose work has impacted me and those who personally have touched my life are the following: Dr. Molefi Kete Asante, Dr. Abu Abarry, Gwen Woods, Shaheed Woods, Khalis Woods, Frederick Pierce, Inger Pierce, Elise Brandon, Shawn Pierce, Dr. Nancy Belck, Dr. John Flocken, Dr. Nancy Dawson, Professor Joye Knight, Dr. Phyliss Cunningham, Dr. John Wanzenried, Dr. Darryl Lewis, Dr. Carol Mitchell, Mr. George Dilliard, Mr. Ben Gray, Dr. Brenda Council, Dr. Earnie Chambers, Mrs. Lous Thomas, Dr. Mary Mudd, Professor Barbara Hewins-Maroney, Dr. David Hinton, Mr. Russell and Mrs. Bettye Jackson, Mr. John Brown, and to countless others who have been supportive of the mission and thrust of the Afrocentric enterprise.

# Part I

# Intellectual Biography

# 1

# Maulana Karenga, Kawaida, and Phenomenology

## An Intellectual Study

*James L. Conyers Jr.*

### Introduction

Maulana Karenga—philosopher, historian, writer, scholar, orator, and political activist—is considered by many to be one of the leading Afrocentric thinkers in contemporary times. An individual of his caliber and breadth represents the essential attributes of a renaissance person. Karenga as a philosopher has illustrated advanced intellectualism and indomitable valor in his consistent struggle and agitation for the liberation of Africans throughout the diaspora.

This essay seeks to examine Karenga's philosophical ideas concerning the plurality of Africana life, history, and culture. In the process, this essay also examines the genre of Black biography. Nathan Huggins provides a survey of this genre, saying:

> The Afro-American biography generally has a racial and social meaning larger than the particular life portrayed; the life comes to exemplify the need for reform. . . . Identity, of course, is the core ingredient in any biography. Because identity is a central problem of the Afro-American condition, in one way or another "Who am I, really?" persists as the essential question to be asked and answered. As with all blacks who were born in slavery, the problem of identity may have been "Where was I born, and who were my parents?" In another time, the central question might have had to do with the trauma of self-consciousness of race, of being black. Or, again, that trauma of self-consciousness might be at the arrival of militant commitment to the

cause of racial reform (the discovery of a truth or a strategy by which one would reorder life). Central to all of the problems is the peculiar Afro-American dilemma of being both black and an American (Huggins 1988, 175).

The ideological repertoire employed in this study constitutes an Afrocentric perspective. Even more important, this study employs a multiple articulation grid to examine the locus of mediation, conflict, dissonance, recognition, and struggle of engagement of rethinking the subject matter. The purpose of structuring this study ideologically is to provide an alternative analysis to the Eurocentric hegemonic perspective. Hence, the central issue addressed is the imposition of worldview and culture by one group onto another group. This is an imposition rationalized by racialist behavior, in which—following Franz Fanon—

> the point is not only that other races are inferior, but also that they *must* be inferior. [The racist] is caught up in the *must be* aspect of the serious attitude. He has chosen to be unreasonable. Hence evidence of racial equality must be ideal evidence—absolute, immutable, perfect—which amounts to saying that every single member of the condemned race must be without fault. The requirement is an improbable goal to achieve (Gordon 1995, 76).

Admittedly, I have presented an intersubjective analysis by interpreting the ideas and philosophy of Maulana Karenga from an Afrocentric cosmology. Germane to this issue, though, is the process of describing and evaluating Karenga's paradigmatic quest to retain the concepts of memory, history, and ethos. All of the aforementioned variables form the ontological basis of Kawaida theory; equally important is the fact that these concepts are the essential grounds for a philosophy of the liberation, organization, and structuring of a collective consciousness.

## Research Methodology and Theory

The research design used in this study is secondary analysis, with an emphasis on content analysis, extracting thematic issues of Kawaida theory and phenomenology with emphasis on Maulana Karenga. The research theory used in this study is the *ujima* paradigm. *Ujima* is a Bantu term that means "collective work and responsibility." This is a theory of culture aimed at describing and evaluating the African experience from an Afrocentric perspective. The principle issues of inquiry used to examine African phenomena are ecology, ontology, epistemology, axiology, and cosmology.

From research conducted for this study, I contend that a qualitative assessment provides a concentric axiological base to locate the writings and scholarship of Karenga in place and time. Research raises the following queries: (1) what contributions has the subject made to the intellectual history of Black Studies; (2) how has the subject positioned himself in describing and evaluating the Africana experience? and (3) how do I use the knowledge acquired from the philosophical contributions of the subject? Figure 1 is a chronological summary of historical and cultural events in the life of Maulana Karenga. Again, the purpose of this summary is to locate in contextual analysis the social ecology of the subject.

## Biographical Sketch

Maulana Karenga was formerly known as Ronald Everett Karenga. He was born in 1941 in Parsonsburg, Maryland. It is significant—to locate Karenga in place and time—to note the state of Maryland's long history of endorsing segregation. Though remaining in the Union, the state of Maryland was the last southern state to abolish the enslavement of African Americans. The year of Karenga's birth was a period of international chaos, during which African Americans were confronted simultaneously with a domestic struggle to attain liberation and social equality. Indeed, because of the war, this proved to be a turning point for the advancement of African Americans: (1) President Franklin Roosevelt issued the executive order forbidding racial and religious discrimination in defense industries (Executive order 88022); (2) Roosevelt established the fair employment practices committee through Executive Order 8802; (3) the Japanese attack on Pearl Harbor (in self-defense) precipitated an executive order requesting the declaration of war; and (4) the U.S. Army established a training school for black pilots at Tuskegee, Alabama.

The purpose for providing this chronology of historical data is to describe and evaluate the social environmental factors that shaped Karenga's ecology. Indeed, we can see that he was born during a period of both struggle and hope, undergirded by the New Deal and by attempts by African Americans to locate a niche for themselves in the social, political, and economic spheres of American society.

## Civil Rights

The Civil Rights movement was a pivotal period of protest and demonstration in the United States. Malcolm X and Martin L. King Jr., were two of the key Black leadership figures. Interestingly, there are patterns that illustrate how Karenga's nationalist perspective is aligned with the philosophical orientation of Malcolm X. Haki Mahadbuti is correct when he states that

Table 1.1

## Social Ecological Summary of Maulana Karaenga

| Year | Event |
|---|---|
| 1941 | Born in Parsonsburg, Maryland |
| 1965 | Creation of the Afrocentric paradigm Kawaida theory. |
| 1966 | Creation of the holiday Kwanzaa. |
| 1966 | Establishes the organization US, in Los Angeles. |
| 1967 | Publishes *The Quotable Karenga*, Los Angeles: US. |
| 1970 | Establishes the Pan African Studies Institute, Los Angeles. |
| 1976 | Development of Afrocentric paradigm Afro-American Nationalism; completion of doctoral dissertation in Political Science at the United States University, in San Diego, California. |
| 1976 | Publishes *The Roots of US–Panther Conflict: The Perverse and Deadly Games Police Play*, San Diego, California: Kawaida Publications |
| 1978 | Publishes *In Love and Struggle: Poems for Bold Hearts*. San Diego, California: Kawaida Publications. |
| 1978 | Publishes *Essays on Struggle: Position and Analysis*, San Diego, California: Kawaida Publications. |
| 1978 | Publishes *Beyond Connections: Liberation in Love and Struggle*, New Orleans, Louisiana: Ahidiana, New Afro-American Movement. |
| 1980 | Publishes *Kawaida Theory*, Inglewood, California: Kawaida Publications. |

1983    First publication of *Introduction to Black Studies*; this text augumented the discipline of Black Studies by providing a survey of the intellectual history of the continental and diaspora African Culture and practice.

1984    Edits and publishes *Kemet and the African Worldview: Research, Rescue and Reconstruction*, Los Angeles, California: University of Sankore Press.

1984    Edits and publishes *Selections from the Husia*, Los Angles: University of Sankore Press.

1986    Publishes *Black News Reprints on Malcolm X*, New York: Black News.

1986    Accepts position of Chair and Professor of Black Studies at California State University at Long Beach.

1989    Publishes an essay titled "Towards a Sociology of Maatian Ethics, in the *Journal of African Civilizations*, No. 10, Summer 1989, pp. 352–389.

1990    Publishes *The Book of Coming Forth*, Los Angeles: University of Sankore Press.

1990    Edits and publishes *Reconstructing Ancient Kemet*, Los Angeles: University of Sankore Press.

1994    Completes Ph.D. in philosophy and ethics at the University of Southern California; dissertation titled "Maat, The Moral Ideal in Ancient Egypt: A Study in Classical African Ethics."

1996    Publishes the book, *The Million Man March*, Chicago: Third World Press.

1998    Publishes *Kwanzaa: A Celebration of Family, Community and Culture*, Los Angeles: University of Sankore Press.

Malcolm X was a cultural hero to the younger aspirants of the Black Power movement. Even more important is that the ideas and philosophy of Malcolm X were extremely influential to the development of Black Power organizations such as the Black Panther Party, US, the Student Nonviolent Coordinating Committee, and the Republic of New Africa. However, the essential point addressed here is that the ideas of Malcolm X provide an ontological basis to locate the formation of the ideas of Karenga.

Malcolm X was assassinated in February 1965. A year later, Karenga established the organization US. He is mostly known for his activism during the civil rights movement in Los Angeles, California. The ideological repertoire employed by this organization was a global Pan-Africanist (i.e., cultural nationalist) perspective. Culture became the primary epistemological framework to examine the function of Black life and historical experiences. Karenga exclaims that the key deficiency confronting African American life is the "cultural continual." In this context, the operative term *cultural continual* represents the cosmological scope to describe and evaluate Africana history and culture in the attempt to conjunct an understanding of the creation of subordinate status, given African Americans' status as involuntary migrants.

Again the concepts of place and time are essential to operationalize an understanding of Karenga's philosophical ideas relative to Africana thought and practice. In a comparative manner, Jahienz Jahn, in his book entitled *Muntu,* uses the concept *Ntu,* which signifies African philosophy as a cultural base to explain commonalities of Africana norms, values, and mores (Jahn 1990, 96). In addition, David E. Cooper addresses this point, saying, moreover, that nothing is encountered in isolation, as an independent "substance." Rather, each thing is "sign-like," pointing to the things and people that provide the contexts that give it an identity (426). Such is the case, in this sense, for Karenga's organization of ideas in the development of Afrocentric paradigms such as the Nguzo Saba, Afro-American nationalism, and Kawaida theory.

## The Nguzo Saba: Kwanzaa

In 1966, Maulana Karenga created the cultural festival Kwanzaa. *Kwanzaa* is a Bantu term that means "the first fruits of the harvest." As such, Kwanzaa is an African American cultural holiday celebrated nationally from December 26 to January 1. This holiday is based on the paradigm of the Nguzo Saba, which identifies seven key principles. During the seven days in which the holiday is celebrated, the following principles are practiced daily: *umoja* (unity), *kujichagulia* (self-determination), *ujima* (collective work and responsibility), *ujamaa* (cooperative economics), *nia* (purpose), *kuumba* (creativity), and *imani* (faith). In general, these rituals focus on atonement, reaffirmation, and the family values that relate to the African continental and diasporic experiences.

To be straightforward, much of the celebration of Kwanzaa addresses Africana kinship, culture, and history. Again the cultural continual is addressed as one of the key aspects of confronting the function and operationalization of Africana life and history. Therefore, in examining the ideas and philosophy of Karenga, perhaps Kwanzaa can be considered the ontological base of Afrocentric cultural paradigm-making. Indeed, this would support the hypothesis of the intellectual history of Afrocentric theory illustrated in the works of Maulana Karenga.

## Afro-American Nationalism

In 1976, Karenga completed his doctoral dissertation, entitled "Afro-American Nationalism: Social Strategy and Struggle for Community," at the United States International University. Similar to Kawaida theory, the basis for Afro-American nationalism (AAN) is predicated on a theory of social and cultural change. Moreover, AAN seeks to provide an applied research approach to the critical examination of issues in the African American community.

The statement of the problem addressed in "Afro-American Nationalism" focuses on the Eurocentric cultural hegemonic interpretative analysis of studies on nationalism (Karenga 1976, 1). Karenga cogently explains the hypothesis of this study this way:

> The central thrust of this study will be to challenge these approaches and assumptions and to offer a modest but meaningful contribution toward an alternative theory of nationalism as a social strategy and struggle for community. Drawing upon basic assumptions of the sociology of knowledge and using Afro-American nationalism as the central focus and fulcrum of the study, an attempt will be made to show that nationalism is essentially an ideology and that like all other ideologies, it is an historically important form of social consciousness derivative of and determined by definite social conditions. Also, it will be argued that ideologies represent conflicting and competing definitions of reality and that the basic criticism of nationalism are in essence reflective of this conflict and competition, regardless of the scientific neutrality and validity of vision each might claims. (Karenga 1976, 2–3)

Paradoxically, the central theme of this study is to provide an alternative epistemology for examining issues and schema of race, gender, and class, using the nationalist model. Equally important is that *alternative* is the operative word, which implies that the model is nonhegemonic and seeks to query the plurality of culture from a black perspective. Furthermore, T.J. Jackson Lears offers a general descriptive analysis, focusing on the ideas and philosophy of Antonio Gramsci, whose concept of hegemonic consensus acknowledges differences in wealth and power even in "democracies" and seeks to show how those inequalities have been maintained or challenged in the sphere of culture. Gramsci provides a convenient vocabulary for beginning to identify those elements in the dominant culture that serve existing power relations and those that subvert them. Unlike liberal notions of consensus, Gramsci's vision acknowledges the social and economic constraints on the less powerful and then aims to see the ways that culture collaborates with those constraints (Lears, 572).

The shape and formation of Karenga's "Afro-American Nationalism" is critically significant—because Karenga has worked outside the realm of the "dialectic of the either or controversy seeking to establish a *new Black historiography,* which sets into motion the process of redefining, reconstructing, and reclaiming" the historical experiences of Africana phenomena from an Afrocentric cosmology (Karenga 1976). Therefore, he explains how "The Afro-American national community is in fact a 'unity-in-itself,' a community of people with a common and distinguishing history (kinship in time and space); a common and distinguishing culture (kinship in life chances and activities); and a common distinguishing collective self-consciousness (kinship in collective self-apprehension and self definition)."

In other words, the commonality that exists among the three descriptions is that the African American community evolved with subordinate-group status, promoted by the fact that African Americans are involuntary migrants who have replicated and maintained their history and culture as a consequence of subordinate-group status.

The central point again in providing this descriptive analysis of Afro-American nationalism is to locate this ideological and philosophical repertoire within the structural analysis, building upon the foundations of Kawaida theory.

## Kawaida Theory

In 1980, Maulana Karenga published the research theory of Kawaida. Although Asante identifies the inception of this theoretical construct began in the 1960s (1988, 122). In addition, Karenga specifically points out that Kawaida was created in 1965, so that this Afrocentric paradigm is the antecedent to Kwanzaa and Afro-American nationalism. Nevertheless, with the publication of *Kawaida Theory* in 1980, and from the experience of

articulating Kwanzaa and Afro-American nationalism, he refined this paradigm in the intervening years to use culture as the central basis for a descriptive and evaluative analysis of African American life and history.
Karenga defines Kawaida as a theory of social and cultural change. There
are three basic activities concerning the function of Kawaida: a redefinition
of reality; a social corrective; and a collective vocation of nation-building,
using the fifth concept of Kwanzaa, *nia* (purpose).

Again, the central thrust of Kawaida is to examine Africana phenomena
from an Afrocentric perspective. This theory of social and cultural change
attempts to describe and evaluate Pan-Africanism from a global perspective. The seven core variables of inquiry that shape and format Kawaida
theory are mythology, history, social organization, economic organization,
political organization, creative motif, and ethos. All of these attempt to
examine the sacred and secular components of Africana life and spirituality.
Furthermore, Karenga describes the intellectual tradition of this Afrocentric
paradigm:

> Kawaida, as an ongoing self-conscious thrust toward synthesis of the best
> nationalist, Pan-Africanist, and socialist thought, approaches the problem of
> Black self-consciousness within the framework of several fundamental as-
> sumptions. First, Kawaida argues that the problem of self consciousness is, in
> fact, a problem of ethos, which is defined as the sum characteristics and
> achievements of a people which define and distinguish it from others and
> give it collective self-consciousness and collective personality. Secondly,
> Kawaida posits that the problem of ethos or collective consciousness is in
> essence both a problem of culture and task of cultural and social struggle.
> (1983, 212)

Interestingly, Karenga's analysis on culture has some overlap with the
ideas and philosophical orientation of Frantz Fanon and Amilicar Cabral.
Fanon, in an essay titled "Racism and Culture," queries whether racism can
be an element of culture. Indeed, if Fanon's analysis is accurate, the concept
of racism, to some extent, would then have to be examined as an element of
culture. Thus, Africana Studies scholars would examine the patterns of
culture, practiced, defended, and reaffirmed on a national and popular level
relative to a Eurocentric-hegemonic perspective.

Primarily, Karenga points out that the three basic activities of Kawaida
are the redefinition of reality, focusing on the image and interest of African
people; the socially corrective, focusing on creating alternatives for critical
thinking; and the collective vocation of nation-building, emphasizing family, community, and national consciousness to develop an alliance to address African American issues. Nevertheless, how does Kawaida transcend

the dialectic created by cultural hegemony? This can be explained in a twofold manner by its redefinition of history and culture and by its reinterpretation of historical information based on an Afrocentric cosmology and ecology. In any event, the process of critically examining the social, political, and economic conditions of African Americans provides an alternative context of locating African American history and culture in place and time. Primarily, there is a correlation between the ideological repertoires of Kwanzaa and Kawaida.

## Phenomenology

Phenomenology can be explained as the study of events and occurrences that shape and format the structure of society. This cognitive field of specialization is located within the discipline of philosophy. David Cooper discusses the intellectual foundations of this field of study in the following manner:

> The above mood, with modulations mentioned, was fully expressed during the first third of the century by Edmund Husserl, the father of phenomenology. Empirical science, he argued, can at best apprise us of facts, not of essential being, and anyway must take too much for granted to exhibit the rigor of a truly fundamental and objective account of the world. Such rigor belongs only to the style of philosophical examination of experience which Husserl calls Phenomenology or—borrowing his teacher, Franz Brentano's, misleading term—descriptive psychology. In old age, Husserl's attention turned to the crisis of European existence evident in a new barbarian hatred of spirit and reason, of the kind displayed by fascists and some of the writers discussed in the previous section. Dreadful as this hatred was, it was an inevitable revulsion against the mistaken rationalism of the positivists. (1996, 420–21)

There are research tools of analysis that can be borrowed from phenomenology to examine the ideas and philosophy of Karenga in place and time. On the other hand, Asante provides an Afrocentric analysis:

> *Edmund Husserl's Ideas: General Introduction to Phenomenology* provoked discussion around the issue of methodology in European social sciences. Husserl's introduction of phenomenology was a major advance for the social sciences. In fact, taking many of his ideas from continental African philosophy, Husserl posited a holistic view rather than a detached, isolated, disparate, reality. The phenomenologist's search for essence by questioning all assumptions about reality is similar to the Afrocentricist's search for essence by questioning all assumptions about reality that are rooted in a particularistic view of the universe. (1990, 26)

Essentially, what has been addressed is that within the conceptual thought of the creation of subordinate group status, African antiquity and philosophical thought have been relegated to the margins of history. Moreover, the ideological repertoire of the Eurocentric-hegemonic perspective scientifically justifies and implies that Africans are either non-human or underdeveloped, in order to substantiate a perspective that subordinates Blacks in a collective and historical manner.

Asante goes on to add,

> All methods of doing research have philosophical roots with specific assumptions about phenomena, human inquiry, and knowledge. The Africanists frame of reference has too often been Eurocentric, that is, flowing from a conceptualization of African people developed to support the Western version of Africa. The problem exists because so much of the Western tradition is firmly grounded in Hegel's conception of history. Hegel elaborated three histories, or three ways of writing history original, reflective, and philosophical. . . . Reflective history may be universal pragmatic, critical, or fragmentary. In its so-called universal form it seeks to survey an entire people, country, or the world. (1990, 23)

David Stewart and Algis Mickunas supplement this analysis by stating:

> Phenomenology does not limit the term "social sciences" only to the study of the structures of society but includes all areas of human life—education, literature, business and economics, history, as well as anthropology and sociology. In all these areas of inquiry, phenomenology's method of approach is rooted in the notion of the lived-world. . . . The social world is primarily the lived-world as understood by common sense. Thus, we act in the world rather than observe it as disinterested scientists, and in the lived-world questions of epistemology, ontology, or the meaning of the world do not arise. In fact, they cannot even be admitted since they are not recognized as part of the lived-world. . . . Within the lived-world the reality of the world is never called into question, neither is any theoretical foundation given for it. Daily life is *ours* from the outset in that all elements of the world are taken as real for you as well as for me. The real is not based on empirical or logical inference or a predicative judgment but on a prepredicative understanding of the world. Therefore the social sciences, phenomenologically considered, deal not with the question of the reality of the world but rather with human relationships within this world. Thus intersubjective relations and the question of knowledge of the other person are of primary importance for phenomenology. (1974, 126–27)

Moreover, Drew Faust discusses that dichotomy of the sacred and secular from a Eurocentric hegemonic perspective:

> In an earlier, less secular age, man had lived within a web of sacred meaning that had influenced every aspect of his life. But the emergence of conflict

between reason and revelation had undermined not only the integrity of this earlier conceptual world but the legitimacy of all knowledge. [George Frederick] Holmes proposed to re-establish "an entire harmony between the speculative and active life" of man by reconciling science and religion. In this manner, he hoped to find the foundation for a "practical and operative belief" that would demonstrate that philosophical speculation remained essential in guiding men and society and would satisfy his own longing for religious certainty. (1977, 63)

The central thrust of this study will be to challenge these approaches and assumptions and to offer a modest but meaningful contribution toward an alternative theory of nationalism as social strategy and struggle for community. Drawing upon basic assumptions of the sociology of knowledge and using Afro-American nationalism as the central focus and fulcrum of the study, an attempt will be made to show that nationalism is essentially an ideology and that like all other ideologies, it is an historically important form of social consciousness derivative of and determined by definite social conditions.

At the base of describing and evaluating his ideas, Karenga advances an alternative epistemology to examine Africana culture. There exists the underlying variables of culture and kinship that extract a conceptual foundation from phenomenology. In developing a paradigm to measure the pattern of systematic oppression and subordination, Ani coins three variables to describe and evaluate European thought and praxis. Therefore the concept of the *asili* and the variables of *utamawazo* and *utamaroho* are essential bases in creating order in the attempt to understand retention factors of Africana history and culture. Ani defines the aforementioned concepts and variables in the following manner:

*Asili*      The logos of a culture, within which its various aspects cohere. It is the developmental germ/seed of a culture. It is the cultural essence, the ideological core, the matrix of a cultural entity which must be identified in order to make sense of the collective creations of its members.

*Utamawazo*  Culturally structured thought. It is the way in which cognition is determined by a cultural *Asili*. It is the way in which the thought of members of a culture must be patterned if the *Asili* is to be fulfilled.

*Utamaroho*  The vital force of a culture, set in motion by the *Asili*. It is the thrust or energy source of a culture; that which gives it its emotional tone and motivates the collective behavior of its members. Both the *Utamawazo* and the *Utamaroho* are born out of the *Asili* and, in turn, affirm it. They should not be thought of as distinct from the *Asili* but as its manifestations. (1994, xxv).

To discuss this issue in a general context, Cooper states that:

> [m]any philosophers this century have construed their job to be the establishing of "conceptual" truths through examination of the meanings of the words we employ for talking about the world. That is not Husserl's view, but only because he sees no reason to restrict "meaning-conferring acts" to the utterances of words. If hoping, believing and perceiving are also to be viewed as such acts, whereby objects are "intended," the kinship between "conceptual analysis" and pure phenomenology is close. (1991, 423)

These points are relevant to this study, which demonstrates that Karenga's philosophical ideas take shape and form in examining the psychology and ethos of the Africana historical and cultural experiences. Moreover, the essential thrust of Karenga's ideas in formulating Afrocentric paradigms around Kawaida, Kwanzaa, Afro-American nationalism, and *Maat*, which refers to the balance of ethical and moral equity of humans, regarding the moral ideal in ancient Egypt—is the correlation and dialectic between the sacred and secular formation of African spirituality. In a comparative manner there is some commonality between Karenga's ideas and *hermeneutic phenomenology,* which Herbert Spielberg describes thus:

> Suffice it to point out that there is at least a possibility of extending the conception of phenomenology in such a way that it can give us access to meanings of the phenomena which are not directly perceived. Such an extension would clearly make a significant addition to our insight.
> What could such an interpretation add to the human uses of phenomenology? Hermeneutic phenomenology, insofar as it should be really in the position to interpret for us the meaning of human existence (*existenzielle Analytik),* could clearly change not only our outlook upon life but our actual living. (1970, 30)

Again in reviewing and examining the social and philosophical ideas of Karenga, I identify how one can adapt research tools of analysis in hermeneutic phenomenology to his cultural nationalist perspective. Spielberg defines hermeneutic phenomenology as "a special kind of phenomenological interpretation, designed to unveil otherwise concealed meanings in the phenomena." (1970, 19)

## Conclusion

The objective set forth in this study was to conduct an intellectual study of Maulana Karenga, in the way of extracting thematic schemes of the social ecology of the subject, Kawaida theory, and the use of phenomenology as a research tool of analysis in locating the ideas and philosophies of Karenga.

Indeed, Karenga has made a prolific contribution to the body of scholarship in Black Studies. Paradoxically, Karenga has been able to infuse technology and contemporary Afrocentric theories, while simultaneously synthesizing a paradigmatic quest to describe and evaluate Africana phenomena from an Afrocentric perspective. He describes this methodological approach in the following manner:

> If conceiving and building our cultural future rests with the rescue and reconstruction of Egypt, and if the research required for this depends on the development and ongoing expansion of an African world view, then it is critical to identify and begin work at the source of Egyptian culture most conducive to the self-conscious reconstruction of this world view. (1990, 182)

Finally, the purpose of this study is to examine how place and time are critical variables in examining the social context and ecology of a biographical figure. Such is the case with Karenga. What is learned through this investigative analysis of secondary sources is that there is a consistent pattern and theme of African American searching for the higher ground. Even within the face of adversity and struggle, Black intellectuals have remained steadfast and tenacious in transcending ideology and critical thought. Maulana Karenga is a testimony to that intellectual tradition. The concept of the "sacred" and the "secular" remain as the essential base of African American perseverance and advancement. Indeed, as one studies the conceptual foundation of phenomenology, spirituality becomes a variable of analysis to synthesize, enumerate, describe, and evaluate African Americans. In closing, I offer Rkhty Amen's prophetic and philosophical analysis of Kemetic spirituality:

> Spirituality is above religion, above science, above social creeds (holy books). Spirituality is about the Amen, the infinite unknown, and Atum, the infinite known. Spirituality is about a love of and understanding of the entire universe, an understanding that life is more than just what is here on Earth, but includes the entire Universe and the infinite dimensions thereof. All life is animate, all life is intelligent. We exist because everything else exists. Everything is One. Therefore Spirituality is about love and respect for all life. Spirituality is about understanding oneself so that one can maintain harmony with nature and self. The Universe itself is the Supreme life form. All life is

animate everything is alive. All life is intelligent (intelligence is relative). There was no word in the language (Medu Netcher) for Spirituality, perhaps because all aspects of life were "Spiritual." (1988, 115)

Ani expands on this concept:

The idea of *spirit* is especially important for an appreciation of the African-American experience. Spirit is, of course, not a rationalistic concept. It cannot be quantified, measured, explained by or reduced to neat, rational, conceptual categories as Western thought demands. Spirit is ethereal. It is neither touched nor moved, seen nor felt in the way that physical entities are touched, moved, seen and felt. These characteristics make it ill-suited to the analytical mode most favored by European academics. We experience our spirituality often, but the translation of that experience into an intellectual language can never be accurate. The attempt results in reductionism. . . . Our spirit symbolizes our uniqueness as a people, or we could say that the African-American ethos is spiritual. The ethos of a people is related to special characteristics which identify them as a group, setting them apart from other groups. Our ethos refers to our emotional responses and reactions. It does not refer to consciousness or to self-conscious responses and reactions. It has to do with the way in which certain things make us feel good and others displease us. It is the bedrock of our aesthetic. (Richards 1985, 208).

The genre of Black biography, through the cultural ascension of an Afrocentric perspective, will seek to transcend the historical and cultural experiences of Africana diasporic people to the higher ground. *Nzuri Sana!*

## References

Amen, Rhkty Wimby. 1990. "The Philosophy of Kemetic Spirituality," in Maulana Karenga, ed., *Reconstructing Kemetic Culture*. Los Angeles: University of Sankore Press, 115–30.

Ani, Marimba (Dona Marimba Richards). 1994. *Yurugu*. Trenton, NJ: Africa World Press.

Asante, Molefi K. 1988. *Afrocentricity*. Trenton, NJ: Africa World Press.

———. 1990. *Kemet, Afrocentricity, and Knowledge*. Trenton, NJ: Africa World Press.

Asante, Molefi K., and Kariamu Welsh-Asante, eds. 1985. *African Culture: The Rhythm of Unity*. Westport, CT: Greenwood Press, 1985.

Cooper, David E. 1996. *World Philosophies*. Oxford: Basil Blackwell.

Fanon, Frantz. 1995. "Race and Culture," in Fred L. Hord and Jonathan Scott Lee, eds., *I Am Because We Are*. Amherst: University of Massachusetts Press.

Faust, Drew Gilpin. 1977. *A Sacred Circle*. Baltimore, MD: Johns Hopkins University Press.

Gordon, Lewis R. 1995. *Bad Faith and AntiBlack Racism*. Atlantic Highlands, NJ: Humanities Press.

Huggins, Nathan I. 1988. "Uses of the Self: Afro-American Autobiography." In *Historical Judgements Reconsidered,* ed. Genna Rae McNeil and Micheal R. Winston. Washington, DC: Howard University Press, 173–79.

Jahn, Jahienz. *Muntu.* 1990. New York: Grove Weidenfeld.

Kambon, Kobi K. K. 1992. *The African American Personality in America.* Tallahassee, FL: Nubian Nation.

Karenga, Maulana. 1976. "Afro-American Nationalism: Social Strategy and Struggle for Community." Ph.D. diss., United States International University, San Diego, CA.

———. 1980. *Kawaida Theory.* Los Angeles: University of Sankore Press.

———, ed. 1990. *Reconstructing Kemetic Culture.* Los Angeles: University of Sankore Press.

Lears, T. J. Jackson. 1985. "The Concept of Cultural Hegemony: Problems and Possibilities." *American Historical Review* 90, no. 3 (June): 567–93.

Mahdhubuti, Haki R. 1994. *Claiming Earth: Race, Rage, Rape, Redemption: Blacks Seeking a Culture of Enlightened Empowerment.* Chicago: Third World Press.

Richards, Dona (aka Marimba Ani). 1985. "The Implications of African American Spirituality, "in Molefi Kete Asante and Kariamu Welsh-Asante, eds., *African Culture: The Rhythms of Unity,* Westport, CT: Greenwood press.

Speigelberg, Herbert. 1970. "On Some Human Uses of Phenomenology." In *Phenomenology in Perspective,* ed. F.J. Smith. The Hague: Martinus-Nijhoff, 16–31.

Stewart, David, and Algis Mickunas. 1974. *Exploring Phenomenology.* Chicago: American Library Association.

Williams, Michael W., ed. 1993. *The African American Encyclopedia.* Vol. 4. New York: Marshall Cavendish.

# 2

# Vinnette Carroll

## African American Director and Playwright

### Calvin A. McClinton

While there has been considerable scholarly research on the development of the American musical, minstrels, vaudeville, and early Black musicals, there has been minimal research done on the development of the African American musical, which has its roots in the gospel tradition of the African American church. The expression of identity through gospel music in the African American theater experience is very clearly delineated in the development of the *song-play,* as shaped and realized by Vinnette Carroll.

Carroll's contributions to theater, musical theater, and Broadway are impressive— especially her work as developer of the song-play through her collaborations with writer Langston Hughes, composer Micki Grant, and choreographer Talley Beatty. She is also known for her outstanding work with New York's Urban Arts Corps and as the first woman of color to direct on Broadway. Despite her achievements, there has not been a serious comprehensive study of her work. This study endeavors to rectify that neglect and to examine the reinvention of the song-play as presented in her work.

In acknowledging her contributions as an actor, director, playwright, and administrator, I have concentrated my research on her attempt to revitalize the spirit of the African American theater experience through her directing, on the development of the gospel song-play, and on her innovative administrative style.

In my own search for identity in the theater as a musical theater artist and director, I have always tried to find some balance between music, theater, and dance—something that would identify my style as a director and also associate me with musical theater.

In discovering the works of Vinnette Carroll, I have a musical theater innovator—both actual and theoretical—to mirror my own search for identity as a total theater artist. Additionally, Carroll's work reaffirms my own belief that the director is there to serve the audience and community and to provide a unity of vision.

After looking at Carroll's legacy, I was able to see a strong connection between the African American musical and its roots in the gospel music of the African American church experience and its celebratory nature. It is the gospel music and the church experience that are at the heart of the gospel song-play, and it is this genre that Carroll pioneered.

The importance of this research to other scholars is that it documents (1) Carroll's legacy as the first African American woman director to work on Broadway, exploring her journey from actor to director; (2) her unique contributions in codifying an interdisciplinary approach to theater training, especially in musical theater as it was developed at the Urban Arts; and (3) Carroll's pioneering vision in identifying and synthesizing the principles of performance as they apply to the development and production of the song-play, through her collaboration with Langston Hughes, Alex Bradford, Talley Beatty, and Micki Grant.

Carroll's entrance into theater is atypical of most African Americans of her period—and even of today. Her parents wanted her to pursue a "real" profession such as medicine, but Vinnette was more interested in the arts; she wanted to be an actor. However, she compromised for a while and studied as a clinical psychologist. Her father was disappointed but supported her for being at least in a related field. After receiving her master's degree from New York University in 1946, she took a job with the New York Bureau of Child Guidance as a psychologist. Because of pressure from her father, she again enrolled into a doctoral program at Columbia University in psychology. She took classes in her spare time and completed all course work. It was just before she was to start her dissertation that she became totally disenchanted with her studies and dropped out of the program and went into acting. Of course, she was disowned by her father; but with her mother's support, Carroll began her study of study theater at the New School for Social Research in 1946. There she studied acting with Lee Strasberg and Stella Adler. Carroll gives credit to Erwin Piscator, with whom she studied directing, for being a major factor in her development of a theater aesthetic. However, Carroll's primary goal at the New School was to become an actress.[1] She performed in many of the school's productions, as Clytemnestra in *Agamemnon,* the Nurse in *Romeo and Juliet,* and the Duchess in *Alice in Wonderland.* In 1947 Carroll made her first professional stage debut as a Christian in a summer stock production of *Androcles and the Lion* at the Southold Playhouse on Long Island. She also appeared in several other productions—*The Little Foxes, Deep Are the Roots,* and *Outside the Door*—while she studied at the New School. But it wasn't until after she left the New School in 1950 that she received her big break and was cast as Ftatateeta in the national tour of *Caesar and Cleopatra* with Paulette Goddard and Hurd Hatfield. Carroll hoped that getting this role would open the door to more acting opportunities and a chance to perform more positive roles beside the servant or maid roles she was then getting. Unfortunately this did not happen. She went on to create work for herself, developing roles she liked, such as Lady Macbeth, Hedda Gabler, Sojourner Truth, and Medea. She put together a one-woman show, which she intermittently toured throughout the United States and the West Indies from 1952 to 1957, while still performing on and off Broadway in minor roles. She found that trying to sustain a living on acting was a major challenge, especially for an African American woman. In 1955 Carroll joined the faculty of the High School for the Performing Arts in New York, where she taught acting and directing. It was during this period of 1958–1967 that she found greater satisfaction in directing than in acting. However, Carroll continued to perform on and off Broadway in minor roles—though she, like most African American actors, felt that the roles offered to Blacks often lacked in dignity and promoted a particular stereotype of black people. It was this perception that lead Carroll into creating and directing new works that positively and artistically presented people of color in theater and art. She was also prompted by the fact that there were even fewer avenues for Blacks to have a career in directing.[2]

The turning point for Carroll was in 1957, when she formed her first all-black cast to present *Dark of the Moon* at the Harlem YMCA. Some critics contend it was after this production that Carroll discovered her talent for directing. But it is for certain that this production launched several major careers—Roscoe Lee Browne, Cicely Tyson, Isabell Sanford, and Clarence Williams III, to name a few. Three years later Carroll would revisit this work, which would also establish a three-year relationship with the Equity Library Theatre, which installed Carroll on the roster as a guest director. The second production of *Dark of the Moon* also launched the careers of several young African American actors—James Earl Jones, Shauneille Perry, and Harold Scott.[3]

Much of Carroll's directing philosophy is shaped by the training she received at the New School with Erwin Piscator. The presentational style and theatrical nature of her work seemed to follow the principles and theories of the German school of theater directors, primarily those tenets of the epic theater popularized by Bertolt Brecht and Piscator. Michael Patterson, a scholar on the emergence and development of drama in the German theater, stated, "In addition to the political influence exercised by Piscator, Brecht shared with him an enthusiasm for the entertainment of the common people and wanted to enliven the theater with their colour and vitality."[4] Carroll, like Brecht and Piscator, believed in a theater that not only educates its community historically, socially, and politically, but one that provides entertainment that is endemic to the ethnicity of its community's origins.

Carroll's theater is about life and the reaffirmation of life and its people. Ideas presented in her works are drawn from the everyday dialogue and concerns of the common man. Her main interest is in giving voice to African Americans or to minority communities that have been culturally and artistically silent. This is not to say that the church (the central focus in most African American communities) has not been active or given voice to its community, but that through the use of a particular folk or communal activity Carroll was able to enliven a spirit that spoke to a community's needs in a theatrical manner.

Carroll would join the New York State Council on the Arts upon the request of the executive director, John B. Hightower, in 1968. She had been appointed director of the Ghetto Arts Program for the State of New York. She was to develop programs that would foster "positive self-images" and also "involve the community in the art of the community" through arts workshops and programs at community centers and day camps. These training programs and workshops were designed to enhance not only theatrical and artistic skills but personal, business, and social skills, as well. Carroll made it very clear that this specially targeted, state-funded program had as its main agenda to serve ghetto communities.

The Ghetto Arts Program was the brainchild of Governor Nelson A. Rockefeller, founded in 1966. Its intent was to create a training program that would develop and encourage young talent from the African American and Hispanic communities. Carroll considered such a program to be much needed and long overdue. The program would help provide role models and positive images of people of color. It would also present the community with works performed by, about, and for people of color. Carroll believed that youth who were involved in a program of this caliber would develop a confidence they otherwise would not receive from the streets.

This lack of confidence and self-identity in youth was something Carroll found very disturbing. She understood that confidence did not happen overnight and that acting is not inherent. The group worked with the communities to develop programs that were taken to local schools, universities, and local prisons throughout the state. This new approach to helping heal some of the social wounds through community arts was just the thing Carroll knew how to do best. Her background from the New School with Piscator and the German school of social realism, plus her own rich ethnic experience, gave her an edge that was most timely. She also simultaneously developed a small group of twenty-five African American and Hispanic performers between the ages of seventeen and twenty-two into a company that would perform and help communities find material that would express and identify their desires and needs. This group she started, known as the Urban Arts Corp, was a pilot program funded by the state arts council. The Urban Arts Corp, later to be known as the Urban Arts Theatre, was a summer pilot project. The group performed their own material: songs, poetry, dramatic readings, and dance to audiences in minority communities. Carroll later proposed to the Arts Council that the project be expanded from a summer project to a year-round institution. After serving for approximately three years as director of the Ghetto Arts Program, Carroll resigned her $12,000-a-year position to become artistic director of the Urban Arts Corps, where she would devote all of her talents to developing a repertory company that would foster minority talent and provide a place for them to train, grow, and have an entrance to a professional career. It is here that Carroll's career as a director, playwright, and teacher really comes full circle. Her development of the song-play in collaboration with Micki Grant and others really helped define her own directing style. The Urban Arts Corps presented a philosophical concept of a humanistic art, an art that is both specific and universal in addressing the human condition and the spirit of humankind through a multicultural theatrical expression. Carroll's vision is one that is rooted in "truth" of spirit. The work of the Urban Arts Theatre is both expressionistic and theatrical, with emphasis on didacticism and reason. Carroll's ensemble worked from a spiritual and moral Afrocentric base, using all of its cultural mediums of expression and communication. The well-being of the community was always of importance to Carroll and the work she presented. She challenged white American society, whose black autonomy of "art" diminished the acceptance of cultural differences and prevented the growth of a deeper social value that would be more trusting and accepting in the common pursuit for excellence. She also called for the same kind of commitment in recognizing the responsibility for excellence in the African American community.

Carroll's philosophy of theater echoes the celebration of life and the African American experience in the New World: a theater of experience that has presented in the past the pain of its existence and the hope that its joys may be dealt with in the future. Carroll believed that in order for African American theater to be totally complete, it must first be rooted in its communities, it must take pride in its unique history, it must remember and embrace its past, and it must use its own talents. Establishing a strong and complete theatrical presence in the community, Carroll nevertheless believed we must not stop there. We do not live in a vacuum. We must interact with other cultures in order to become a part of the mainstream. This does not mean we have to assimilate; however, in order to have a wider range and variety of theatrical material, we must be willing to integrate our work and theater. It is through this sharing of ideas and experiences that Carroll sensed we "begin to develop a greater sense of style"[5] These values of an African American theater reverberate through all of Carroll's work, affirming and reaffirming the idea of a universal experience—one that shows our similarities more than our differences.[6] Carroll stated in an interview with Loften Mitchell:

> [T]he more we are economically and artistically secure, the more we will be able to share our experiences with others, and the more people get to know us. . . . I am very optimistic about that, because the more trained actors and the more trained artists we have, the more they'll be used in just any play. . . . there will be lots of places where Black artists can develop and their work will have a value in the society as a whole.[7]

Carroll also reiterates these same ideals in another interview to columnist Bill Hutchinson of the *New York Sunday News*. She commented:

> In the '60s, we were all so busy trying to work through our identity crisis. We wanted to talk about our hurts and our Blackness. It was a very introspective time, and out of that anger and pain came serious theater that dealt with what it means to be Black. Now that some of our anger has diminished, Black artists are turning to more universal themes. We're talking about what it means to be alive, and we're finding out that the similarities between people are far deeper than any difference resulting from race.[8]

The development of Carroll's folk canon of theatrical material began with *Black Nativity* in 1961. *Black Nativity* was her first attempt at creating a style of folk dramas that incorporated elements that come directly out of the African American experience. She interwove the narrative with music and dance that was Afrocentric in its origins. This technique of directing and developing theatrical stage works became Carroll's trademark. *Prodigal Son* by Langston Hughes was the second work in which Carroll used her technique for interweaving Afrocentric themes, text, music, and dance into one seamless theatrical experience.

This new form of African American "folk" musical theater, which combined traditional African American church elements with popular jazz, gospel, and other ethnic music idioms would later canonize Carroll as "The Earth Mother of black musical theater."[9]

Carroll's philosophy of directing and her technique for creating her folk dramas reflect many of the same theories, ideas, and aesthetic principles as those expounded by Brecht. However, she also promoted the principles of Piscator's "objective style" of performance. The juxtaposition of these two opposite styles is a technique that Carroll created in forming her new style of folk drama. She agreed with Brecht, who stated:

> [Folk] theater . . . demands . . . an entirely new art of theatrical representation. Yet, like it or not, this demand has got to be made; our whole repertoire calls for a new kind of art which is quite indispensable for the performance of the great masterpieces of the past and has to be developed if new masterpieces are to arise. . . . The folk play is a type of work that has long been treated with contempt and left to amateurs and hacks. It is time it was infected with the high ideals to which its very name commits it.[10]

Carroll also recognized the need for new masterpieces in the African-American canon. She began to create works drawn from the "folk" community. However, these works were so innovative and different that it was hard to categorize them. In her attempt to combine the two styles to create a new form, Carroll found that her directing technique had to be very technical in order to foster an art that dared to create theater—and not simply to recreate reality. Carroll believed in three basic fundamentals: (1) the total picture, one that is perfect in design and execution; (2) the total artist, the performer who can present ideas physically, intellectually, and artistically through dance, music, and poetry; and (3) the total theatrical experience, which not only seeks to entertain but to inform, inspire, and elevate the human spirit.

Carroll's directing technique resonates with many of the fundamental theories of Gordon Craig, the English actor and designer, and Adolphe Appia, the Swiss scenic and light designer. Much of Carroll's directing style coincides with their theories. Craig, who saw the theater as an independent art with all of its elements working towards a harmonious whole, felt the director-artist to be the supreme visionary, who creates a unified theatrical event. He sought to find a unit set capable of expressing the thought of the entire work. Appia also felt the artist to be the interpreter of the work and that every movement and gesture needed to present this event could be found in the rhythms of the text.[11]

Another aspect of Carroll's directing was her keen vision of what a theatrical production would become. She knew from the very first moment of conception, when the idea for a production came to her, how the world of the play would look and how the performers would portray the characters. She believed the value and endurance of a piece of art was determined by the quality of material with which you begin. Carroll said:

[Y]ou really have to find really good material to work with. A good piece of fabric, because if you're going to invest in making this suit, you better have good fabric to do it, if it's going to endure. You have to have faith in the product, in that piece you're going to do.[12]

Carroll's efforts were spent in upholding a quality of work that could endure, while at the same time developing artists who possessed some sense of "standards." She abhorred ignorance, complacency, vague and apathetic complicity, and tasteless vulgar presentations. However, Carroll at times appeared to some theater practitioners to be in contradiction with her own principles and theories—mainly because of her varied approaches in working with performers. Moving between the superficial and the specific or the improvisatory and the meticulously orchestrated, Carroll continued to forge a theatrical form that established its own aesthetic principles, even as it simultaneously communicated and enlightened the community from which it sprang. In his book, *The Artist of the Theater,* Gordon Craig provided a statement that aptly illuminates this interesting paradox. He wrote, "What the theater people have not yet quite comprehended is *the value of a high standard and the value of a director who abides by it.*"[13]

Carroll's dissatisfaction with the quality and standards of commercial theater along with the images and types of roles portrayed and offered to African Americans are two of the major factors in her perceived need to develop plays.

In an interview with Nelson George, a reviewer for the *New York Amsterdam News,* Carroll said, "I don't want to contribute to any negative images . . . I want to show Black people that there's dignity and beauty in our art. That's my goal."[14]

Carroll's creations for the stage did not reflect the current trends in the theater. She had little interest in promoting the European paradigm of recreating reality (naturalism) in the theater—for the simple fact that the theater was not a reality that most African Americans could positively identify with culturally. The most important aspect of her creations for the theater were the projection of "positive images for Black people." She said, "That's more important for me than almost anything; that Black people like themselves, to walk with pride and like their work. That drives me a lot."[15] Carroll also stated, her conception of the theater is "to take the richness of Black life. The strong fabric of Black people and contribute to getting it on stage."[16]

Carroll's talent and passion to create positive black images made her both a pioneer and a very respected director-playwright. Carroll's directing career grew directly out of her acting career. Indeed, her desire to perform roles that portrayed Blacks with dignity and the shortage of such roles led her to create her own works for the theater. Thus, her acting, playwriting, and directing careers are inexplicably tied together.

Many of Carroll's associates also agreed that her collaborations and playwriting were a direct result of her success as a director. Impressed by her direction, John Patterson, reviewer for *The Villager,* observed that some of her most notable strengths are her "directorial brilliance and fidelity":

> At the center of . . . success is the heart, mind, and imagination of director Carroll. . . . She has, for example, always managed to combine, with great success, both the roles of playwright and director in her past work. . . . She applies them with complete success and . . . creates a [work] which is clear, clean, and as carefully structured and balanced as the best straight drama. Song, dance, and movement are . . . seamlessly interwoven.[17]

Patterson goes on to enumerate other strengths of Carroll's directing in relationship to her creations for the stage. He pointed out "her unparalleled instinct for matching performers with vehicles, and, more important, her uncanny ability to render a distinctive Black voice and performance style in positive dramatic terms.[18]

Carroll's approach to directing did not include the Broadway theater tradition of casting "stars" in roles to make a box office hit. She believed in casting actors because they are right for parts, and because they understand and are familiar with her directing style, not because they are big names. Because of her views on casting, Carroll and her producers did not always see eye to eye. She showed little concern with the casting policies of producers who dominate the "Great White Way" with their philosophy of "big stars, big bucks." However, Carroll was very much aware of the Broadway stamp of approval and of its importance as set by society. She commented, "Stars do bring in money and that makes a difference in terms of your bankability. That's really where that is. It makes a show easier to sell later."[19]

Carroll recognized the difficulty of finding backers for black theater productions. For her, it is a "double edged sword," being a black female, which to producers was financially risky.[20]

Sydné Mahone of Crossroads Theatre agreed that the theater industry as an art form is directly impacted by race, gender politics, and social conservatism.[21] In an article from the introduction of her book *Moon Marked and Touched by Sun,* reprinted for *American Theatre* magazine, she wrote:

> America is a profit-driven, racist, sexist and homophobic society. Black women playwrights are not included in mainstream American theater because their work in some way challenges or simply does not reflect the images and interests of the financially dominant culture. The Black female

playwright presents an alternative viewpoint to the White patriarchy and is therefore more likely to be embraced in those venues that serve alternative, progressive artistic agendas.

. . . These playwrights thrive on artistic risk and aesthetic adventure. To the commercial and nonprofit producer alike, artistic risk represents an inflation of financial risk.[22]

Nevertheless, throughout the course of Carroll's career, she fostered the careers of many young artists who have gone on to become well known to the general public. These talents include Micki Grant, composer of *Don't Bother Me I Can't Cope;* Jennifer Holiday, the star of *Dreamgirls;* Cleavant Derricks, featured in *Moscow on the Hudson* and the current TV series "Sliders"; Sherman Hensley of the *Jeffersons;* Phylicia Rashad of the *Cosby Show;* and Cicely Tyson, Debbie Allen, and a host of other talented actors.

Langston Hughes, the poet and dramatist has generally been credited with the creation of the gospel song-play.[23] However, not until Hughes' collaboration, if you want to call it that, with Carroll as director of *Black Nativity* in 1961 does the song-play begin to take shape and become a viable art form. Structurally, Carroll had always worked with music and the spoken word, but in her work she combined them with dance and mime to express some of the aesthetic beauty she found in her own culture. Carroll was especially interested in the new "gospel" music that had begun to emerge in the African American church. This new music was alive and vibrant, fully rhythmical and drawing from an ancestral spirit. She felt this music expressed the basic qualities of black life—its sorrows, its joys, and most of all, its magnificent wonder at being one of God's creatures. Carroll understood the gospel roots to be germane to the African American experience in America. The use of gospel music in the theater, however, was a new concept that Carroll incorporated easily and early in her career. The Broadway theater was very familiar with musicals whose background were either in jazz or ragtime, but never with the gospel-style musical. Hughes may have coined the term "gospel song-play," but it was Carroll who developed the style and paved the way for a distinct black American musical.

The song-play, as Jerry Campbell, Carroll's assistant describes it, is "a tapestry of interaction woven together using poetry, dance and music whereas the weight and color of that tapestry changes with the energy of the moment." Most of the early song-plays that contain religious material are taken from the Bible, such as *Black Nativity* (1961), *Trumpets of the Lord* (1963), *The Prodigal Son* (1965), and *Your Arms Too Short to Box with God* (1976). These plays usually follow a traditional plot or story line. Later applications of the song-play to Carroll's work were in the form of collages or montages. According to Jerry Campbell, "she was one of the first people in the sixties who experimented with nonlinear ways of doing things." He stated:

> Even the people who created *Hair* (when that was originally done it was very specifically not a plot show) attribute a lot of their inspiration to Vinnette, as being one of the very first people who create a theatrical format that was not based on plot.[24]

The placement of ideas or events in a nonlinear sequence was probably one of Carroll's most unique devices—"the juxtaposition of opposites." Carroll was thrilled in working with a play in which all of a sudden things would shift 180 degrees because of placement. The juxtaposition of opposites increased the value of a moment or emotion just because it was right next door to something totally different than itself. Nevertheless, Campbell claimed this technique was not always found in all of Carroll's work that used the song-play format. He stated:

> [A] lot of pieces like *When Hell Freezes Over I'll Skate* and *Don't Bother Me I Can't Cope* really aren't plot driven, it's sort of an impressionistic thing. It's totally about the feeling. She wants this kind of feeling, then you segue to this kind of feeling and then abruptly we'll shift gears into this kind of feeling. So pieces like that are really extraordinary because the running order of them changes 14,000 times during the course of the rehearsal.[25]

The song-play is an ensemble work in structure, composition, and execution. One element is not more important than another; however, there are moments within the work when one element may take precedence, but only to enhance or give energy to the moment through a different perspective. This combining of two different elements gives new meaning to the moment and a heightened understanding of the intangible emotion. This constant shifting and sharing of the same moment through song, dance, and dialogue creates "the duality of being." This duality is what in Carroll's vision holds the ensemble together. In the ensemble, Carroll always presents two juxtaposed ideas that occupy the same moment without conflict. She uses the ideas to amplify each other, making the sum of the moment more than the individual parts. It is a synergistic use of the four elements basic to the genre: music, dance, mime, and text.

The form Carroll used in creating the song-play was not based on structure in which text in a linear fashion reigns supreme, but in a nonlinear form in which the expression of ideas from multiple perspectives synthesize to create a new hermeneutic level. Carroll's training allowed her to find, through her development of the "duality of being," a heightened moment of understanding. This theatrical exegesis of biblical and secular text—combined with music, dance, and mime—are the fundamental components of the gospel song-play as understood and articulated in Carroll's directing aesthetic.

In recent years, an increasingly large number of musicals have appeared on Broadway, off-Broadway, and regional stages that employ the use of gospel-style music. Scholar and historian Samuel A. Hay cites in *African American Theatre* such works as *Mama, I Want To Sing, Part I* (1982), *Don't Get God Started* (1987), *Abyssinia* (1988), *Let the Music Play Gospel* (1989), *Beauty Shop* (1989), and *Mama, I Want To Sing, Part II* (1990), which all follow the gospel style. This new trend of musical presentation takes its inspiration from the song-play introduced by Langston Hughes and developed by Vinnette Carroll as the gospel song-play in the early 1960s. Carroll's unique blend of music, dance, and classic theatrical material can also be seen as the inspiration for the 1983 musical adaptation of the Greek tragedy, *Gospel at Colonus*.

Carroll considered the song-play form to evoke the classical Greek theater. She said:

> [I]t's really Greek theater. A song-play is really Greek theater, you always have use of the chorus, so I always like to have a chorus or something, or maybe it's a narrator used in my works. . . . [B]ut before *Black Nativity,* they [the chorus] were just treated like you have a chorus and they stand there, they move there and they dance here.[26]

Carroll's use of the chorus in the song-play followed the same principles as those applied to the choruses of the Greek plays: they presented information about prior events, commented on past and present action, and moralized on the possible fate or outcome of the preceding events. The chorus also gave insight to the emotional and spiritual well-being of individual characters along with setting the mood of the event.

After a long and distinguished career in directing, playmaking, and administrating the Urban Arts Theatre, Carroll went into semiretirement in Fort Lauderdale, Florida, where she established permanent residency. But because of her theatrical reputation, she was persuaded by members of the Broward County Arts Council to establish a group like the New York Urban Arts Theatre in South Fort Lauderdale. And in 1982, in her sixties, when most artists are thinking of retiring, Carroll took on the challenge of creating a new theater company. Two years later the group's name was changed from the Urban Arts Theatre South to the Vinnette Carroll Repertory Company.

Despite age, changing fads, and finances, Carroll continues into the millennium to produce excellent dramatic and musical theater that never forgets that its community and audience are at the heart of her success.

# References

1. Tanner, J. A. 1989. "Vinnette Carroll." In *Notable Women in the American Theater: A Biographical Dictionary,* ed. Alice Robinson, Vera Mowry Roberts, and Milly Barranger, p. 111. New York: Greenwood.

2. Mortiz, C. 1983. Vinnette Carroll. *Current Biography Yearbook 1983,* pp. 54–57. New York: H. W. Wilson.

3. Anderson, A. 1994. "Vinnette Carroll." In *Theatrical Directors: A Biographical Dictionary,* edited by John W. Frick and Stephen M. Vallillo, pp. 70–71. Westport, CT: Greenwood.

4. Patterson, M. 1981. *The Revolution in German Theatre 1900–1993,* p. 152. London: Routledge and Kegan Paul.

5. Carroll, V. 1996. Personal papers and transcripts of the Vinnette Carroll Repertory Theatre and Urban Arts Corps. Unpublished raw data.

6. Mitchell, L. 1975. *Voices of the Black Theater,* pp. 189–207. Clifton, NJ: James T. White.

7. Ibid., p. 209.

8. *New York Post,* July 3, 1968. Clipping file, Vinnette Carroll. New York Performing Arts Library, Billy Rose theater Collection.

9. Erstein, H. 1984. "The Earth Mother of Black Musical Theater." *Harlem Weekly,* May 31–June 6, p. 6.

10. Willett, J., ed. 1964. *Brecht on Theater: The Development of an Aesthetic,* p. 156. New York: Hill and Wang.

11. Brockett, O.G. 1987. *History of the Theater.* 5th ed, pp. 565–67. Boston: Allyn and Bacon.

12. Carroll, V. 1996. Personal papers and transcripts of the Vinnette Carroll Repertory Theatre and Arts Corps. Unpublished raw data.

13. Craig, G. 1985. "The Artist of the Theater." In *Directors on Directing,* edited by Toby Cole and Helen Krich Chinoy, pp. 158–59. New York: Macmillan.

14. George, N. 1977. "Ms. Carroll Brings Back Richness to the Stage." *New York Amsterdam News,* March 5, D9.

15. Erstein, H., p. 6.

16. George, N. See note 14.

17. Patterson, J.S. 1978. "*Black Alice,* Lewis Carroll Via Vinnette, Broadway Bound Sensation." *The Villager,* September 21, p. 14.

18. Ibid.

19. Greene, M. 1967. "Negro Director: A Hit with Two Strikes on Her." *Sunday Times,* October 29, p.N.

20. Mahone, S. 1994. "Seers on the Rim: African-American Women Playwrights Battle Avoidance and Neglect to Bring their Visions to the Stage." *American Theatre* (March): 22–24.

21. Ibid.

22. Ibid.

23. Woll, A., ed. 1983. *Dictionary of the Black Theater,* pp. 218–19. Westport, CT: Greenwood.

24. Campbell, J. 1996. Personal interview, February 20. Unpublished raw data.

25. Ibid.

26. Carroll, V. 1995. Personal interview, January 2–6. Unpublished raw data.

# 3

# Higher than the Eagle

## The Legacy of General Daniel "Chappie" James Jr.

*Earnest Norton Bracey*

This essay focuses on the personality growth and character development of General Daniel "Chappie" James Jr., rather than with a play-by-play account of his life. Hence, this narrative is not the definitive word, nor does it give exhaustive detail, but it does try to appraise James's stature as a Black leader and to assess his place in American military history.

This work also takes the general format of a biography, though some aspects of this paper are selected purely by the since curiosity of the author, since the narrative is the product of my long-time interest and extended scholarly research into the life of General James. In this story we shall see that General James had a lot in common with another famous Black American military officer—Lieutenant General (Retired) Benjamin O. Davis Jr., the World War II pilot and flying ace, who became the nation's second and the air force's first Black general. James, a star football athlete, was the product of the Reserve Officers' Training Corp (ROTC) at Tuskegee Institution, whereas Davis, all spit and polish, graduated from the military academy at West Point. And perhaps because of the background differences between them, Davis might have resented James's rise to military stardom. According to James's biographer, J. Alfred Phelps:

> James recognized Benjamin Davis Jr.'s success and ability as a career officer [however], he [James] partially blamed him for his slow advancement. In return, Davis had reason to wonder if Chappie would ever really become a soldier. The two were of different stripe. James's nature was effusive and outgoing; Davis was taciturn, conservative, and, above all, proper. (1991, 165)

At one time, Davis outranked James in the Air Force, reaching the coveted three-star rank; however, Davis never achieved four-star rank, like James. Was Davis upset or jealous because of this? After all, Davis had actually been James's instructor in the ROTC program at Tuskegee.

James, however, achieved what no other had ever done at the time—that is, he was the first Black American to attain the rank of four-star general in the U.S. Air Force. Moreover, later as commander of the North American Air Defense Command (NORAD), General James was the only U.S. military officer with emergency authority to deploy nuclear weapons without presidential approval. Journalist Ralph Novak, in the July 18, 1977 issue of *People* magazine, wrote that: "It was an awesome right no other American commander had in the event the President is unreachable—to fire nuclear-armed defensive missiles" (1977, 78).

The riddles General James leaves us concern why James —supposedly a radical—developed the way he did and why he succeeded in winning four stars, his greatest achievement. How did James become what earlier Black officers could not? What was so special about him? Maureen Mylander in *The Generals* wrote, "by 1973, when James rose to three-star general, circumstances had changed and the services—chafing under accusations of racial tokenism—were ready to promote a "radical" (1974, 171). However, a *Washington Post* (1978b) editorial put it this way: "There are only 36 officers of four-star rank in the entire military, so Chappie James is the outstanding exception rather the rule among black and white." There are no easy answers to our questions, of course, but the following brief account will shed some light on James's success. One thing is certain: promotion of Black Americans to general, officer, or "flag rank" today is no longer a rarity in the U.S. armed forces. And as military sociologist, Charles C. Mosko has written, "It occassions little comment" (1986, 71).

About being the first Black four-star general in the U.S. Air Force, James once made his position thusly:

> My mother used to say, and I agree with her philosophy, that there are two negroes we can do without—the *only* one to do this and the first one to do that. Black people are doing some outstanding work in many lines of endeavor, making many fine contributions to their country. I look forward to the day when there will be so many negroes accomplishing so much, that their blackness will not be newsworthy. I qualified for my promotion across the board—I earned my star[s]." ("A Study in Success," 1970–71, 40).

The events that shaped General James's life and military career were extraordinary in the sense that in his early days as a young, neophyte lieutenant, he was considered a rebel and labeled a malcontent, which would have destroyed a lesser man, but after diligently serving years in the U.S. Army Air Corps, and later in the U.S. Air Force, he escaped certain ruin and destruction by being persistent and resilient and by never giving up.

However, because of his early background and having to fight past prejudices, General James did not seem like a very strong contender for advancement or promotion. Indeed, as the *Pacific Stars and Stripes'* senior writer, Hal Drake, pointed out, "James seemed a poor candidate for a military career—unable to accept posted racial rule of that day" (1994, 8).

Morever, many of James's Black military friends, following World War II, could not stand nor tolerate the *outright* and sometimes overt and blatant racism in the Army Air Corps; many simply gave up, resigning their hard-earned officer commissions—though in fairness to the military, some "were lost to postwar discharges" (Phelps 1991, 163).

James, on the other hand, was able to look beyond the petty efforts of his white comrades-in-arms to degrade and force him out of the military. Hal Drake explained it in this way:

> James stayed in after the war, locked in the rank of first lieutenant for five years—gaining no significant notice until the Korean War, when he flew 101 missions and showed himself to be a first-class fighter pilot and leader. (1994)

Nick Thimmesch in *People* magazine speculated that James realized perhaps, that at 6'4" and 230 pounds he was too big to be ridden out of anywhere on a rail" (Thimmesch 1975, 24). James once remarked after pinning on his coveted stars, "When I came into this men's Air Force I vowed to be a general officer and a leader of men, and I've got news for you, I am" (1973, 534). These words typified this eminently qualified military officer, who successfully combined a pragmatic approach to leadership with an unwavering vision of the future for Blacks in the U.S. armed forces.

In the course of his life, James became a legend; and although on the surface he seemed like a simple, affable man, he nevertheless was quite complex. James certainly understood the complicated *mechanics* and difficulties of running the sophisticated North American Air Defense Command (NORAD). Moreover, many of the traits he exhibited in later life in the military were manifested even before he became an officer. He often spoke eloquently and tearfully about the harsh episodes in his early days as an impoverished young Black boy, growing up in Pensacola, Florida, about his trials as a young cadet and student at Tuskegee Institute in Alabama, and about his struggles as a young officer in the Army Air Corps. But the endearing way, as an adult, in which he often spoke of his mother, Mrs.

Lillie Anna James, was heartwarming, for he mentioned her positive guidance and influence constantly.

Almost a reluctant American hero, James believed in the virtues instilled in him by his mother: Never quit! Be the best! Be competitive! Later in his life these things are what shaped and sustained him. In retrospect, his parents had a lot to do with molding his character, inculcating in him his staunch determination and will to excel in every endeavor he undertook. And this attitude was life-long.

Excellence, hard work and competiveness are words that James believed in, even if he did not always, in some instances, live up to them. Nonetheless, through hard work, merit, heroism, and professional competence, James rose to the highest ranks of the air force. And as John Huey of the *Wall Street Journal* once observed, "He was one of the most powerful men of any color, in or out of the military" (1976, 1).

Air Force Colonel William B. Horne, II, who once commanded the famous 374th Air Force Support Group recalled "an optimistic and positive Chappie James—the against-the-odds underdog who did it all on sheer ability and drive" (Drake 1994, 8). James served his country during three American wars. However, his heroic and pathbreaking deeds have almost been forgotten. Richard G. Capen Jr., has written, "Lamentably, the memory of Chappie James is fading fast ... [And] if the recent past is any pattern, most will overlook the legacy of General James, and that's a disgrace"(1984, 3E).

General Daniel "Chappie" James was a highly decorated fighter pilot and the recipient of many honorary degrees and civilian honors. He also received twenty-four military medals, which even exceeded General Douglas MacArthur's twenty-two (Manchester 1979, 15; Phelps 1991, 345; *United States Air Force Biography* 1977, 3). The only military medal of significance that eluded him was the Congressional Medal of Honor.

James was an enigma, but he was popular among higher military circles and particularly well liked by people from all sectors of life; although he did have his critics—both Black and white. And even though he held the rank of general later on in his air force career, with some higher-ranking government civilians and top military brass, he could never have an effective dialogue.

When commanding, James was extremely competent, leaving no task unturned until it was perfected, but he too suffered the agonizing price and responsibilities of leadership. By nature—or rather through first-hand experience and training—however, he became an outstanding and first-rate military leader.

General James has been compared with such great American generals as

Patton, Pershing, and MacArthur. Former conservative senator and presidential candidate Barry Goldwater once said, "You cannot put down in black and white what it is in one man that makes other men want to follow him. But I've seen it in Curtis LeMay and General George Brown and Douglas MacArthur. Chappie [James] has that same unexplainable quality" (Novak 1977, 79).

James was brilliant and irascible and stood vehemently against prejudices and injustices of any kind. Having no patience with bigots and racists, he also became a passionate champion of nonviolent activism and a proponent for equal rights for Blacks in the armed forces. A dominant figure in the Army Air Corps and later in the newly established air force in 1947, James "waged a relentless battle against racial segregation in the military throughout his career" (*Parade,* October 24, 1982, 17).

Of course, during its segregated years, the military services suffered greatly—it was a disastrous state of affairs—and it took the air force many years to come to terms with the extreme and terrible prejudices it had against Black airmen. With overwhelming odds, James risked career ruin, along with other Black servicemen who bravely fought racism and discrimination to help bring about change in the armed forces. An example of James's tenacity and persistence in the fight against discrimination during World War II is provided by Hal Drake: "James and other black officers first went into a white club at Selfridge Field, Michigan—not once, but many times. The club was closed. The black pilots were sent to Godman Field, next to Fort Knox, Kentucky, turned away by direct-order authority as they again marched on clubs that wanted no blacks" (1994, 8).

Therefore, General James should always be remembered in American military history as one individual who stood fast and in the forefront of trying to bring our nation out of the darkness of racial segregation into the light of equality. In this respect, answers to the problems of discrimination in the U.S. armed forces, as early as 1940, were found not in "one-sided" solutions, but in the compassion of those who loved justice and equality and wanted to do what was right.

James came to say out of modesty that he was not the only one responsible for the changes in the integrated or desegregated military, but then humility was also characteristic of this general, for he tended not to be caught up unnecessarily in his own importance; although it has been claimed that he relished the publicity and notoriety. Retired Brigadier General Robin Olds stated:

> In a very real way, Chappie [James] basked in the sunlight of public notoriety, and to an extent, fed the furnace of legend, not by misstatement, but by

innuendo, and by allowing the enthusiastic bombasts to go unchecked and uncorrected (personal letter to the author, September 10, 1981).

It is difficult to tell exactly the direct effect James had upon the military's integration policies, but integration might not have come about as quickly as it did if not for his staunch support and the efforts of other like-minded Black and white officers. Yet, it is even more conceivable that "integration" in the armed forces, as well as in our society, was imminent— and even predestined.

Similarly, the *Washington Post* wrote: "A large measure of the credit for this progress must go to those black soldiers and airmen whose demonstrations against segregation in the armed forces during World War II forced the military down the right road on this matter" (1978a).

General James's contributions against racial segregation in the military were notedly tremendous. The main point is that General James paved the way for other Black officers—including General Colin Powell, the former and first African American chairman of the Joint Chiefs of Staff. James was first to break the traditional stereotype that Blacks could not make "competent" general officers.

It is also important to remember that not many Blacks in the segregated past had a chance of attaining the rank of general. Now it is not only conceivable, but in the combined armed forces today, we have at least one Black "flag" rank officer in each branch of the military services.

It has also been claimed that James was more controversial than any other general in modern military history. Indeed, he was formidable, a different "breed of cat," such as the black panther emblem he so proudly emblazoned on his fighter pilot helmet and on many of his other personal effects. "I wore the panther on my helmet all through Korea and Vietnam and I still wear it," James once boldly stated, "mine started long before the infamous Black Panthers [referring to the militant Black separatist group of the 1960s] came into being" (*Ebony Success Library* 1973, 124).

As the story of his life and military career unfolded, James established himself as quite a remarkable man. James provides an excellent case history of a general of strong and moral character. He was a man who hated war, yet strove to be a warrior of notable repute. Often remarking how the warrior loathed war, James once said, "Some people say it is the warriors who cause war. I tell you nobody hates war more than the warriors. They are the ones who get shot at, they are the ones who die. I am a warrior" (Novak 1977, 80).

As a warrior and fighter pilot, James was often applauded for his fierce position on using American military force and might to resolve regional conflicts throughout the world. In fact, he was a one-man crusade for Americanism. And during the later period of his life, he received a national reputation as an unflinching American warrior and patriot. Also during this time, as J. Alfred Phelps has pointed out, James was "known internationally as an eloquent advocate of the American way of life" (1991, 345).

Moreover, James's achievements as a fighter pilot in two wars (Korea and Vietnam) were widely praised in the government and military, especially in the air force hierarchy; however, it has been claimed that he did not deserve many of these accolades. Olds has written that "after Thailand [at Ubon Air Base], Chappie started referring to us as 'Blackman and Robin.' While I was amused at the humor of the phrase and knew it to be a part of Chappie's gusto and laughter—still it bothered me. It bothered me because over a span of time, the phrase had the unfortunate effect of transfering my reputation to Chappie" (personal letter from Brig. Gen. Ret., Robin Olds to author, September 20, 1981). In this respect, "Chappie" James was never free from such criticism. Olds, however, loved and admired James, as they remained friends while he lived, and never did Olds think James deserved less attention and praise, nor was he resentful of his continuing success.

Again, General James served in the armed forces during three American wars and did extremely well when given the opportunity, excelling by virtue of his ability to adapt and his flexibility. He was bright and had a lot of common sense, with a good instinct for survival. As an inexperienced young officer in Korea, his reputation as a "rabble-rouser" preceded him, because he "led sit-ins at whites-only officers clubs during World War II, when separate clubs, barracks and squadrons were regarded as the natural order of things" (Drake 1994, 8).

During these young, lean years, fighting and jousting with Jim Crow laws—especially designed to separate public facilities and private accommodations by races—was a way of life for James. In fact, it was James's willingness to stand up for what was right that made him so audacious and flamboyant.

General James, perhaps, realized that the air force was less than perfect—that it was, for a time, separate and unequaled—forged as it was in a sort of unworthy compromise with American Black service members, as well as with most African American citizens, prior to total integration. Indeed, James was among the most ardent supporters of equal and fair treatment in the military for Blacks, believing that the alternatives were bloodshed and total chaos.

Promoted to the rank of general, James found himself propelled to the top, and in close proximity to the highest military and civilian powers on Capitol Hill. Indeed, he was finally in the "limelight," a position of high authority and visibility, and it seemed nothing or no one scared, intimidated, or truly bothered him. A *Washington Post* editorial stated that James was "a fervent patriot who wasn't afraid to speak his mind without worrying about the possible unfavorable consequences to himself and to his future" (1978b, 30).

There were so many fascinating things to remember James by: his booming voice and deep-set, almost penetrating eyes or his engaging, warm, and friendly smile. He was also a handsome man, a grizzly bear of a man, and his "bull-like" facial features were enhanced by a thick mass of wooly, black hair, styled in a fashionable Afro—always neatly trimmed—as well as by a precisely clipped moustache. He was also a gregarious man, awesome and impressive. In the eyes of the nation, James was flamboyant, a swashbuckler of sorts, but fiercely patriotic, emitting an appealing style and charisma that complemented his stern, yet sensitive personality.

James has often been described as a man of commanding physical presence, forceful and dynamic—the personification of a top-notch military officer who loved his country, enjoyed life, and genuinely cared about others. In a sense, James was bigger than life itself. General James's real and ultimate passion, perhaps, was his ability to speak to anyone, anytime and anywhere. Indeed, the intensity of his concern for America's young people—of all races—during the late and turbulent 1960s and 1970s was marked more by his famous speeches than by anything else. According to journalist Neil Super, for instance, "One of Chappie James's duties was to visit high schools and colleges to convey the president's views about the [Vietnam] war to young people. He encountered demonstrators who protested his speeches on many college campuses" (1992, 65). Nontheless, James, at great personal risk and peril continued to speak at such forums.

James, of course, talked smoothly, bravely, and freely, always acting friendly. One television correspondent admitted: "Chappie never conned me or lied. He knew how far he could go, but in tough decisions, he came down on the side of the public's right to know" (Novak 1977, 85).

James was a brilliant public speaker. Indeed, his oratorical skills were as legendary as exemplary, for he spoke with unflinching assurance about military matters as well as about controversial social and political issues of the time. Specifically, he gave speeches with conviction and great passion, regarding POWs in Vietnam and of American defense. The celebrated flying ace of World War II and Vietnam, Retired Brigadier General Robin Olds wrote: "As for his [James] speeches—find a copy of one and you've got them all. Chappie talked patriotism and spoke it well. Always the same, always eloquent, and audiences loved it" (personal letter to author, September 20, 1981).

James was not only an articulate, lucid speaker, but he could write brilliantly as well. Often candid with his comments, he twice won the prestigious American Freedom Foundation Award for his essays on "Americanism." Moreover, as a man whose ancestral heritage included African slaves, James was his own man first. He had come from a world of bitterness and pain—the child of impoverished parents—but he never did let this affect him adversely, for he still had great respect and unceasing love for both his parents and his country.

James's salient characteristics and his countenance—of the brave, proud, and noble warrior—was evidenced everywhere he visited. Later, James was highly regarded, loved, and admired by Americans of all races for his dogged stance on their country's defense and for his fighting prowess, although it has been claimed that he "wasn't the warrior he was made out to be" (personal letter from Brigadier General Robin Olds to author, September 20, 1981). According to Retired Brigadier General Olds, James did not fly many of the missions reported in the press. Olds writes, "Chappie used the editorial 'we' with the result that he was credited with an aura of fighting prowess he hadn't earned. The missions he described were those I flew. The press, and others, were happy to translate and transfer" (personal letter to author September 20, 1981). However, the *Air Force Magazine* accurately pointed out that James "flew seventy-eight F-4C Phantom [combat] missions over North Vietnam. He [also] led a flight in the 'Bolo' MIG sweep on January 2, 1966, during which seven Communist aircraft were destroyed—the highest total kill for a single unit in any day of the war" (1968, 178).

General James was inspiring and his leadership was charismatic. For Black troops in any branch of the armed forces, to see him was enough, for it arouse a great sense of hope, pride, and inspiration. As a role model he embodied the spirit of all Blacks in the military services.

Lieutenant General David Adamson, the top-ranking Canadian officer at the North American Air Defense Command (NORAD)—the central agency for the air defense of both the United States and Canada—during the period of James's command, summed it up once by saying of him, "He is an old-line, form-a-wedge-and-follow-me leader. He can lose his temper and get on someone, but nobody is quicker to apologize when he's wrong" (Novak 1977, 85).

The military was "Chappie" James's life. He was never misplaced as a warrior or leader. And that meant he was exceptional whether standing up to the despotic ruler and dictator Colonel Muammar Gadaffi as commander of Wheelus Air Base in Libya, once America's largest air base in North Africa—that is, before it was closed down—or fighting the enemy from a jet-fighter cockpit in unfriendly skies during times of war. And although

James had his weak points and setbacks in his early career, his notable qualities of character and showmanship were expansive as he forged ahead rapidly in front of his peers and associates. James was definitely military-minded; but out of all his contemporaries, he was, as already stated, considered the one most unlikely to succeed. After his appointment as a one-star brigadier general, James gained even greater fame.

James was also a sagacious general and politician. In his role as deputy assistant secretary of public affairs, he won favorable national publicity and continued to be in demand as a speaker at social and political functions across the nation. Excerpts from some of these famous speeches on Americanism and patriotism have even been read and written into the *Congressional Record.*

Because General James attained such a rank, cynics and critics have claimed that he was an "Uncle Tom" or—as he on several occassions put it—he was thought of as an "Oreo Cookie." Moreover, as Neil Super tells us, "there were some . . . who insisted that Chappie [James] was promoted because he was black" (1992, 65). But former Acting Deputy Assistant Secretary of Defense for Civil Rights and former municipal judge Howard L. Bennett explained it thus, at the time when James pinned on his stars: "I am gratified that the Air Force has selected and the President has nominated Chappie. He's a outstanding officer and has had extensive experience. But it had been hoped that he would have been named one or two years ago" (*New York Times* 1970).

Furthermore, some say that without former Secretary of Defense Melvin Laird's insistence and intervention, James could not have been promoted to the coveted rank of general. But this is entirely a fabrication. Secretary Laird, who indeed became James's friend and mentor, had been instrumental in giving James the boost that propelled him into stardom—a fact James always readily admitted—but Laird always made it known that James basically got there on his own merit. Although it was mostly, perhaps—as pointed out in the July 28, 1975 issue of *People* magazine—James's "unabashed happy warrior boosterism [that] helped propel him to four-stars" (Thimmesch 1975, 25).

Still there were those who were passionately opposed to General James, perhaps because of his patriotism and because of the way that he spoke out in support of America, without given in to dissent and to the rhetoric of revolution and violence to effect social changes. One must also remember that "as the highest-ranking black in the military [at that time], Chappie James walked with Presidents" (Capen 1984, 3E). And as Retired General Robin Olds said in 1981 in a personal letter to the author, "he made everyone feel good about our country, past, present and future."

Perhaps the most tragic of James's duties were his final days as the head of NORAD. General Daniel "Chappie" James was ailing and tired when he finally relinquished command of the cherished North American Air Defense Command. Some critics claim that he was relieved in shame, for he had been extremely outspoken about a reorganization plan and critical of the former chairman of the Joint Chiefs of Staff, Air Force General David C. Jones, and the budding efforts and policies to disband NORAD.

However, in a personal letter in 1981 to the author, Jones stated that "When General James retired from the Air Force on January 26, 1978, it was due to reaching his mandatory retirement time rather than any conflict over a NORAD reorganization."

Can we say that Daniel "Chappie" James was a great American general and military leader? Did he really get the chance to prove it? Although James served in three wars, he never saw combat during World War II. One thing is certain: while most generals become obscure and unknown in retirement and death, General James remains fondly remembered by many— in and out of the military. So we must never forget his legacy. For those would-be historians and scholars, I pose this question: Was there something missing in his military career as it passed under review? More importantly, was General James given appropriate justice and recognition?

General James's life is a story of perserverance and determination; however, because a severe heart attack robbed him of his health, he died on February 25, 1978, shortly after his celebrated retirement. But he was a fighter to the bitter end. Respected and loved by many, perhaps the world will *never* know a man quite like him.

## References

*Air Force Magazine.* 1968. Introduction to General Daniel "Chappie" James's "My Freedom—My Heritage, My Responsibilty." (April).

Capen, Richard G. 1984. "Excellence: Nobody Cares About Its Color." *Miami Herald,* February 12.

*Challenge.* 1970–71. "A Study in Success." (Winter): 40.

Drake, Hal. 1994. "Yokota Remembers General Chappie James, Jr." *Pacific Stars and Stripes,* February 27.

*Ebony Success Library.* 1973. "Despite Racism, He Became One of America's Highest-Rated Flying Aces." Vol. 2. Chicago: Johnson.

Huey, John. 1976. "Black Four-Star General Is a Man Accustomed to Tough Assignments." *Wall Street Journal,* November 24.

James, Daniel. 1973. *Daughters of the American Revolution Magazine* (June–July): 534.

Manchester, William. 1979. *American Caesar: Douglas MacArthur, 1880–1964.* New York: Dell.

Moskos, Charles C. 1986. "Success Story: Blacks in the Army." *Atlantic Monthly* (May): 71.

Mylander, Maureen. 1974. *The Generals.* New York: Dial Press.

*New York Times.* 1970. "Black Colonel Getting General's Rank." Editorial. January 26.

Novak, Ralph. 1977. "General 'Chappie' James is the Boss of America's Defense Business and its Four-Star Salesman." *People* (July 18).

*Parade.* 1982. "Four-Star General." October 24, p. 17.

Phelps, J. Alfred. 1991. *Chappie: America's First Black Four-Star General—The Life and Times of Daniel James, Jr.* Novato, CA: Presidio Press, 1991.

Super, Neil. 1992. *Daniel "Chappie" James.* Frederick, MD: Twenty-First Century Books.

Thimmesch, Nick. 1975. "Super Patriot: 'Chappie' James Earns Unprecedented Fourth Star." *People* 4, no. 4 (July 8): 24.

*United States Air Force Biography on General James.* Office of Information, United States Air Force. Current as of March, 1977.

*Washington Post.* 1978a. "The Career of 'Chappie' James." Op-ed page. January 23.

———. 1978b. "Daniel 'Chappie' James, Jr." Editorial. March 1.

# 4

# The Shaping of a Public Biography

## Richard Allen and the African Methodist Episcopal Church

*Mitchell Kachun*

Richard Allen (1760–1831), founder and first bishop of the African Methodist Episcopal Church (A.M.E.), embodied the assertive free-black culture that was maturing in the North by the 1830s. Despite criticisms of his domineering manner and personal ambition, Allen had attained by the time of his death in 1831, a position of respect among his people that was rivaled by very few of his contemporaries. But between the 1830s and 1870s little formal effort was made to perpetuate the memory of this great leader. In the two decades after the 1870s, A.M.E. leaders began to use both written biographical materials and public commemorations of Allen's life to instill a sense of history and tradition among the largely nonliterate masses. Their complementary use of public commemorations and written accounts of Allen's life during this period suggest a more general attempt among Black leaders to bridge the overlapping worlds of orality and literacy in order to establish a sense of tradition, an empowering historical memory, and a pantheon of Black heroes who might one day gain their rightful place in the national pantheon.

The construction of historical memory through commemorative activity is important, both to those doing the constructing and to those of us who would understand our heritage. Commemoration—whether of an event or of the life of an individual—is never undertaken "naturally," as a matter of course. It is always the result of conscious organization and always is made to serve some social, cultural, political, or economic interests. Richard

Allen, founder and first bishop of the African Methodist Episcopal Church, undeniably was revered by his spiritual descendants. But it was not a foregone conclusion that his memory would be perpetuated through either published biographies or organized commemorative activities. When A.M.E. leaders began, in the late-nineteenth century, to commemorate the life of their founder, they were impelled by a complex of motives involving (1) the denomination's financial status and missionary work, (2) efforts to expand literacy within the race, and (3) the construction of a racial collective memory that would both honor Blacks' distinctive identity and history and legitimize their inclusion in the American national family.

Biography—defined narrowly as a written account of an individual's life—was only a small part of the Church's attention to Allen as they engaged this project. African Methodist Episcopal leaders, cognizant of the particular challenges involved in reaching out to a largely nonliterate population, worked within an established commemorative tradition that relied upon the written word, the spoken word, and the performance of public rituals. In their efforts to celebrate and publicize the life of their founder, A.M.E leaders used all these techniques to construct a public historical memory of Richard Allen that they intended to serve the Church, the race, and the nation.

The Church's attention to Allen's public biography and his legacy was part of an emergent tradition of commemoration among nineteenth-century Black Americans. The most important African American commemorations during this period celebrated the emancipation of slaves in the British West Indies on August 1, 1834. West Indian Emancipation celebrations became important public rituals that fulfilled a variety of functions for the Black community. Sometimes attended by several thousand people, these celebrations of Black freedom provided a vital forum for Blacks to galvanize intraracial communication and organizational networks, to assert their right to use public space, and to publicly articulate a Black-centered interpretation of American society and history that emphasized both Blacks' essential American-ness and their participation in a distinct historical and cultural tradition that must be preserved and passed on. By the 1850s annual August 1 observances had become the cornerstone of a maturing commemorative tradition. A large part of their purpose was to instill a sense of pride in history and tradition among their Black auditors and to articulate their distinctive historical interpretation to both the minority and the majority in the expanding public sphere of mid-nineteenth-century America. These early Black leaders recognized that a knowledge of their history was essential to Black Americans' comprehension of their present and future condition in the United States (see Fabre 1994; Gravely 1982; Kachun 1997; White 1994).

In their attempts to establish a viable heritage, antebellum activists were extremely conscious of the importance of commemorations as cultural rituals that publicly demonstrated the legitimacy of a people's collective identity. Northern Blacks, of course, had numerous vehicles for organization and mobilization by mid-century, including religious denominations, fraternal orders, voluntary associations, schools, the convention movement, and the press. The regular participation of all these groups in August 1 commemorations itself suggests that the annual rituals filled a need that other institutions could not address. One of their most important functions was to mediate between the overlapping oral and literate elements of the Black community. After the 1830s Black newspapers served as written vehicles for attitudes and feelings that previously had been expressed primarily in the oral forms of spoken poems, folk songs and tales, orations, and sermons (Wolseley 1990, 28). But their reach was limited. Up to the end of the eighteenth century, Americans of African descent had left scant written expressions of any kind. Over 90 percent of Black Americans were still nonliterate at the time of the Emancipation Proclamation in 1863. Nineteenth-century Blacks lived a predominantly oral culture (Levine 1977, 155–58, 177). With a foot in each of the intermeshed and overlapping worlds of orality and literacy, African Americans experienced Emancipation Day orations as crucial educational and mobilizational tools, especially at a time when literacy and access to education were denied all but a few Black Americans. After having reached large numbers of auditors upon their public delivery, orations often found their way to a larger audience through publication in newspapers, which were frequently read aloud and disseminated throughout the Black community. The orations thus moved back and forth between oral and written forms of expression and promulgation. In this way the celebrations fit into the emerging impulse among community leaders to educate the masses, to instill in them a sense of history and tradition, and to mobilize the community toward political action (Finnegan 1988, 175).

African American leaders used these events to construct a set of historical traditions for Black Americans and a distinctive reinterpretation of American history that was intended to inform the understanding of all Americans. Black speakers at commemorative events could reach hundreds or even thousands of their fellows. They took advantage of this powerful forum to provide Blacks with vital information on the legacies of their past and the exigencies of their present; to reiterate the words of previous orators, thus reminding audiences that the day's event was part of a tradition reaching back into the past and forward toward a more hopeful future; to instill a sense of unity and cultural potency; and to incite action toward positive social change. They spoke to reach their entire audience with a message of freedom, knowledge, uplift, self-respect, and belonging.

An important component in constructing a viable heritage and an empowering collective memory involved identifying a legitimate pantheon of African American heroes. Frederick Douglass used an 1857 address to assert that the exaltation of Black heroes was necessary not only to rectify the race's erasure from dominant interpretations of history, but also "to stimulate us to the execution of [further] great deeds of heroism worthy to be held in admiration and perpetual remembrance." Douglass claimed that "Virginia was never nearer emancipation than when General [Nat] Turner kindled the fires of insurrection at Southampton [in 1831]." The increasingly bellicose Douglass often called attention to the deeds of Joseph Cinque, who led the 1839 *Amistad* uprising, and Madison Washington, who led a similar revolt aboard the *Creole* in 1841. Douglass was so inspired by the latter incident that he perpetuated its memory in a fictional account, pointedly entitled *The Heroic Slave,* which he published in *Frederick Douglass' Paper* in 1853 (Blassingame 1985, 201, 206–8; Takaki 1972, 17–77).

It is in this context—the essential illiteracy of the majority of the race, the effort to establish a history, a heritage, and a commemorative tradition that would legitimize the race's inclusion in American society, the search for heroes to inspire noble deeds—that the A.M.E. Church's attention to the life of Richard Allen becomes significant and instructive.

Richard Allen was born a slave in Philadelphia on February 14, 1760. As a teenager Allen embraced the teachings of Methodism, helped convert his master, and was able to purchase his freedom around 1780. After several years as an itinerant preacher, Allen returned to Philadelphia in 1786, where he rapidly assumed a leadership role in the city's growing African American community. Almost immediately he organized Black Methodists into a separate congregation, which would become Philadelphia's Bethel African Methodist Episcopal Church (Allen 1833; Nash 1888). Black Methodists throughout the region faced recurrent problems within white denominations, and in 1816 representatives from several states met in Philadelphia to establish their own denomination. Richard Allen emerged as African Methodism's first bishop (Allen 1833; Nash 1888; Walker 1982). From the late-eighteenth century until his death in 1831, Richard Allen arguably "had greater influence upon the colored people of the North than any other man of his times" (Bennett 1968, 46). In addition to his spiritual leadership, Allen was a successful businessman and property owner, leaving an estate of some $40,000. He was active as a humanitarian, a political activist, an educator, and an organizer throughout the early national period. In the year before his death he helped to organize, and presided over, the inaugural National Negro Convention in Philadelphia (Nash 1888).

But Allen was hardly unchallenged as a community and religious leader, and his admirable life was not without its controversies and blemishes. There is ample evidence to support historian Clarence Walker's observation that Allen "often alienated other Blacks because of his aggressive and domineering behavior" (1982, 4–11). In 1787 Allen helped to found the Free African Society, a nondenominational mutual aid society in Philadelphia. But when a rift developed between Quaker and Methodist members, Allen was censured "for attempting to sow division among us." When this had no effect on his behavior, it was declared in 1789 that "he [had] disunited himself from membership" in the society (Nash 1888, 111).

Similarly, despite his credentials as a pioneer of individual and racial religious self-determination, Allen's position at the top of the A.M.E. hierarchy was not a foregone conclusion. At the 1816 organizational meeting Daniel Coker of Baltimore was in fact the first elected bishop. Coker, however, was persuaded to resign, with Allen elected in his stead, ostensibly because Coker's complexion was too fair (his mother was white) for him to be an acceptable first bishop for an African denomination (Walker 1982; Nash 1888, 232). Along the same lines, historian Milton Sernett observes that, when the A.M.E. Zion Church was formed in New York in 1820, a "strong-willed and zealous" Bishop Allen "declared that he would not ordain clergy for the Zionites unless they subordinated themselves to his authority" (1975, 125). A historian of the inaugural National Negro Convention notes that Allen participated in "an undignified scramble for leadership," during which "some leaders in high places . . . considered self and community above the interests of the race" (Bell 1969, 14–15). As late as 1887, when Allen was emerging as a venerated and esteemed hero, he still had to be defended against the assertion that he was a "strong-willed" and "exceedingly ambitious" man who "has been charged with having been a malcontent who found pleasure in sowing seeds of sedition to awaken rebellion" (*Christian Recorder,* February 17, 1887).

Notwithstanding these criticisms, Richard Allen, by the end of his life, had attained a position among his people that could be rivaled by very few of his contemporaries. In 1829, in his famous "Appeal to the Coloured Citizens of the World," David Walker considered himself unworthy to communicate adequately "the labors of this man and his ministrations among his deplorably wretched brethren. . . . When the Lord shall raise up coloured historians in succeeding generations," Walker predicted, "the Holy Ghost will make them do justice to the name of Richard Allen of Philadelphia" (Stuckey 1972).

Upon his death in 1831, Allen's admirers and rivals alike could not wait for future historians to acknowledge the signal accomplishments of their departed colleague. A tribute in the *African Sentinel* treated Allen's demise not as the exclusive loss of African Americans, but rather as a universal tragedy. Not solely African Americans, but "humanity throughout the world becomes a mourner." Allen "walked like the Saviour upon troubled waters, in favor of African Religious Independence," and "his noble deeds will remain, cherished in the memory of mankind, imperishable monuments of eternal glory" (*Liberator*, April 9, 1831). White abolitionist and editor Benjamin Lundy predicted that Allen's "surviving colored brethren" would long lament "their great, if not irreparable loss" (Mathews 1963, 151).

Though Allen's loss was particularly great for the A.M.E. Church, the denomination continued to thrive. Between the 1830s and the 1870s little effort was made either by Allen's co-religionists or by other Blacks to pay tribute to the departed leader. But by the end of the century, the name of Richard Allen was beginning to receive the recognition predicted in 1829 by David Walker. Historian Roger Lane, in his study of Black Philadelphia in the late-nineteenth century, identified Allen as "the most revered single individual in the history of the [city's] Afro-American community" (1991, 100).

It is hardly surprising that Richard Allen has been accorded a prominent place in the pantheon of African American heroes. His many personal accomplishments are only magnified by his assertive race leadership. Biographers have been consistent in their recognition of Allen's signal achievements in asserting Blacks' independence from white religious administration and for setting an example of personal and group advancement in the realms of education, economics, and political action. It is also not surprising that Allen's apparent contentiousness and personal ambition have received little attention from his panegyrists. The most enduring aspect of Richard Allen's legacy, even today, is his example of self-determination, social activism, community service, and race pride.

What is interesting and worthy of closer scrutiny, however, is the appropriation of Richard Allen's memory by A.M.E. leaders as they began actively to construct a public biography of the Church's founder through commemorations of his life in the last quarter of the nineteenth century. The reverence for Allen noted by Lane may be as much a result of A.M.E. commemorations as a reason for them. The fashioning of Allen's legacy demonstrates that the construction of historical memory through commemoration involves more than mere adulation; commemoration also serves functionalist and utilitarian ends. When the leaders of the A.M.E. Church, over a generation after Allen's death, began devoting considerable energy to the commemoration of his life, their efforts fit into the broader project of constructing a viable African American sense of history and tradition. But they also addressed several more narrowly denominational concerns: the A.M.E. mission to proselytize and expand the denomination's reach; the movement within the Church to enlighten the masses and establish stricter educational requirements for the clergy; and the related effort to maintain a denominational publications department.

The origin of the A.M.E. Book Concern and Publications Department was virtually simultaneous with the founding of the denomination. Richard Allen himself served as the first general book steward, a position that, by the end of the century, had "proved to be one of the most important offices of the Connection." Before the 1840s, however, the Book Concern's power and influence in the denomination were negligible, and it was also rather poorly and inefficiently run (Payne 1891, 17–18, 189).

The book agent in the early 1850s, M.M. Clark, was one of the few college-educated African Americans of his time. Clark, Bishop Daniel A. Payne, and a few other Church leaders were persistent in their efforts to raise the general educational level of both the ministry and the members of the Church. Upon his resignation Clark made a plea for the Book Concern. He cited the great need for printing not only disciplines and New Testaments, but also biographies of Bishop Allen and other "fathers of our Church, whose lives and labors have perished from the eyes of the Church, but which ought to live on the enduring pages of history for the encouragement of the rising generations." (Payne 1891, 191). Thus, very early in the denomination's journalistic experiment, at a time when Black attention to historical memory was expanding, an explicit connection was made between the Book Concern's publications and the development African American heroes and historical consciousness. But widespread illiteracy among the potential readers of A.M.E. publications proved an obstacle for many years to come.

The Church's use of history and Black heroes in reaching out to the people in a largely oral culture was expanded during the Civil War era. Methodism is an evangelical denomination, and the African Methodists were no less enthusiastic than other branches regarding the mission to spread both the gospel and denominational influence. When the Church acquired denominational status in 1816, it claimed about 400 members in the states of Pennsylvania, New Jersey, Delaware, and Maryland. In the 1850s the A.M.E. Church could boast of about 20,000 communicants as far west as Missouri and as far south as Louisiana. But expansion in the South, where the vast majority of Blacks resided, was virtually impossible until after the Civil War. The A.M.E. Church was by far the largest and most successful of the various Black denominations that competed for these newly liberated Black souls. By 1865 the Church's southern missionary field included every state of the former Confederacy. The opening of the South allowed its membership to jump to 73,000 in 1866, to 300,000 a decade later, and to over half a million by the end of the century (Montgomery 1992; Walker 1982; Wright 1916).

In reaching out to the freedpeople, A.M.E. missionaries found their knowledge of the race's history a useful tool. The spoken word—delivered through sermons, Freedom Day orations, and political speeches—provided a fundamental mechanism for disseminating historical knowledge. William Henry Heard, an ex-slave later to become an A.M.E. bishop, recalled a sermon by Henry McNeal Turner, delivered in Augusta, Georgia, in 1867, when Heard was just seventeen:

> He spoke on "The Negro in All Ages." He spoke for two hours. I was so impressed with the pictures and historical facts he presented of the Race in the past ages, and of the men of the present, that my life is largely what it is because of the impressions made at that meeting. (1969, 90).

As historian Reginald Hildebrand has observed, "the missionaries wrapped themselves in the mantles of tradition and heritage" dating from Civil War heroism back to Hannibal and Aesop in their efforts to attract converts (1995, 56).

In addition to the power of the spoken word, another central component of the A.M.E. strategy in the postwar competition for souls was the spreading of the printed word through the pages of the *Christian Recorder*. The expansion of missionary work during the 1860s corresponded with a boom in the business of the Book Concern: between 1864 and 1868 the Concern's income surpassed the total from the preceding sixteen years combined (Wright 1916). The paper became "a silent, but most efficient missionary, operating in an enlarged field of usefulness" during the 1860s (Payne 1866, 124). Even in wartime, the *Recorder* was obviously reaching the Black troops and the freed people in Union-held areas, where it was "received . . . the same as bread is received by a hungry man" (*Christian Recorder,* July 23, 1864).

The A.M.E.'s use of written and oral techniques to reach out to a Black population making the transition between oral and literate orientations was a conscious strategy to expand denominational influence and elevate the race amidst the tumultuous transformations of Reconstruction. The West Indian Emancipation Day tradition expanded to incorporate the reality of U.S. emancipation, and Blacks participated with particular zeal in a national trend of increased attention to the nation's past, its heroes, and its traditions.

It was during this exciting and optimistic period that Richard Allen was presented to the race and the nation as both an important African American hero and a legitimate American hero who epitomized Blacks' distinctive heritage as well as their right to an unqualified American identity.

The first attempts to honor Allen came earlier, in the mid-1850s, a quarter-century after the bishop's death. At that time Allen's remains lay in Philadelphia's Mother Bethel Church, "without even a marble slab to cover them." Church leaders solicited donations for a suitably engraved stone (*Christian Recorder,* December 3, 1874; the Philadelphia *Press,* June 12, 1876). At about the same time the *Christian Recorder* reported a "very good attendance" at the first recorded celebration of the birthday of Richard Allen at Mother Bethel. But these early commemorations of the founder were ill-fated. The grave marker was not placed, and Allen's birthday was observed only intermittently over the next thirty years.

For several decades after his death, Allen lived on primarily in the memories of those who had known him. Perhaps the exigencies of life in an increasingly hostile, racist environment made such commemoration a low priority. Perhaps commemoration was seen as unnecessary since the bishop's erstwhile acquaintances could pass on his memory through reminiscences. Or perhaps no earlier movement to perpetuate Allen's legacy took hold because no one could agree just what that legacy was. As one eulogist noted in 1866, Allen "had his friends and his foes in this world (*Christian Recorder,* December 15, 1866). At that first birthday observance it was clear that not all held Allen's name in equal esteem. In his oration on the life of the founder, the Rev. Dr. J.J.G. Bias praised Allen's love for his people, his influence, his antislavery activism, his "moral honesty," and his efforts toward "the elevation of his race." But Bias also lamented that "there are a great many men in the ministry, and eminent ones too, standing at the head of the list, who think the sainted Allen too ignorant to mention his many virtues" (*Christian Recorder,* March 4, 1856). In the mid-1850s at least, despite his considerable accomplishments, Richard Allen's lack of formal education seems to have made him a dubious role model in the eyes of churchmen who sought more stringent educational requirements for the clergy.

As the years passed, the blemishes on Richard Allen's image—his lack of formal education, his contentiousness—began to fade from public view. By the denominational expansion of the 1870s, the fathers and founders were long in their graves. Even the second generation of A.M.E. leaders, those who worked during the antebellum era, were dwindling in number. Third-generation Church leaders took note of the passing of their spiritual progenitors and expressed concern that the memory of their accomplishments be preserved.

In January 1874 Benjamin T. Tanner, the thirty-nine-year-old editor of the *Christian Recorder,* challenged "the popular thought that we colored Americans have not contributed anything to the moral grandeur of the common country—anything in the shape of heroes." In a column entitled "Our Heroes," Tanner commented on the recent funeral of an early Church father, noting that, these religious leaders—"heroes of a higher type," he called them—deserved national recognition (*Christian Recorder,* January 22, 1874). Foremost among those heroes, of course, was Richard Allen. Over the next several months Tanner devised a plan to perpetuate Allen's memory within the denomination and advertise it to the rest of the race and to the nation.

This incipient desire to honor the heroes of African Methodism fit into a larger pattern of commemoration and historical consciousness among Blacks and in American culture generally (Bodnar 1991; Glassberg 1990; Heard 1959; Kammen 1991). Tanner was well aware that the whole nation was preparing for the national Centennial Exposition, to be held in Philadelphia in 1876. With plans for the Centennial accelerating, Tanner and other A.M.E. leaders proposed to celebrate Richard Allen in conjunction with the celebration of the nation by erecting a statue of the A.M.E. founder among the other commemorative sculptures on the Centennial grounds.

In his initial entreaty, Tanner appealed to Black Americans' sense of national belonging. A monument to Allen, Tanner felt, would "tell mightily in the interest . . . not only of our Church, but of our whole race" (*Christian Recorder,* March 5, 1874). He challenged Black Americans to fuse pride of race with pride of nation in claiming their rightful place among the celebrants at Philadelphia. On another level he appealed very specifically to the members of the A.M.E. Church. Tanner believed that the Allen monument would help to assuage the internal dissension that had intensified within the Church after the Civil War allowed A.M.E. expansion into the South. In particular, debate over the education of preachers became increasingly divisive when hundreds of southern congregations were forming. Most religious leaders among the former slaves were illiterate, and they, as well as their congregations, resented the attempts of highly educated Northerners to alter their religious observances and replace their preachers. Refusing to relax its literacy requirements for the clergy, A.M.E. leaders engendered the enmity of not a few southern converts (Walker 1982, 76–77).

Tanner must have been especially gratified when his monument plan received its most enthusiastic support from the South. Scant public attention had been given to Tanner's proposal before November 1874, when the Church's Arkansas conference resolved to raise funds to erect "a monument to the memory of Richard Allen[,] first Bishop of the A.M.E. Church . . . to be unveiled on the centennial anniversary of the nation." Like Tanner, Bishop John M. Brown and Rev. Andrew J. Chambers emphasized the monument's significance for African Methodists as a denomination, for Blacks as a race, and perhaps most fundamentally for African Americans as U.S. citizens and patriots. The Arkansans called particular attention to the fact that "the Negro race has figured so conspicuously in the history of the United States." Blacks, they argued, had to join in the celebration not as a separate people, but as an integral part of the American national family. Recognizing that many whites might take exception to such a claim—and again fusing literary and nonliterary approaches—they called for the "publication of historical pamphlets" to edify the public as to the role of African Americans, and of African Methodists in particular, in the nation's history. The African Methodist leaders saw their denomination as "the noblest represented body of the Negro race on this continent," and felt it proper and fitting that a statue of Allen stand for the achievements of all African Americans (*Christian Recorder,* November 5, 1874).

Andrew Chambers provided a definitive statement of the monument movement's ideals in the pages of the *Christian Recorder.* In doing so he responded directly to the objections of A.M.E. business manager William Hunter, who argued that until the Church was financially solvent and could claim success in its missionary, educational, and mutual aid endeavors, intangible gains based on myth and tradition would have to wait (*Christian Recorder,* November 12, 1874). Chambers agreed that the goals Hunter emphasized were indeed proper ones. But, he countered, "we claim our [monument] idea to be a middle ground pointing our illiterate race toward these loftier institutions." An unlearned people, he asserted, needed visual displays like statues and monuments in order to "arouse the masses" to support the more high-minded enterprises like publishing houses and universities. In assessing the practical value of the monument, Chambers emphasized the bolstering of race and denominational pride, the educative value for the present generation, and particularly the importance of leaving a legacy for subsequent generations. "This generation," he claimed, "intends to leave traces of its existence for posterity to look upon." The erection of the monument "shall work an epoch in the history of our race. It shall be a stepping stone to the colored men of America to rise higher in self esteem and the esteem of all nations." Future generations would "gather around the Monument in question, shed tears of gratitude for the example we have left them, and call us blessed" (*Christian Recorder,* December 3, 1874).

Supporters maintained a steady defense of the monument plan. Future bishop William Dickerson demanded that "we should be represented at [the nation's] first centennial celebration of independence and liberty" in order to provide "justice to ourselves and our history." James A. Handy asserted that "We owe it to ourselves, and to our children. We owe it to the race. To make this mark, and to make it at this period in our country, and in our church's history, that the world may know of the magnificent and glorious legacy bequeathed to us by Allen" (*Christian Recorder* December 31, 1874, and January 7, 28, 1875).

The culmination of this drive to mobilize popular support came with the celebration of Richard Allen's birthday in February 1875, an event that proved to be a key turning point for the development of A.M.E. commemorations of the founder. In promoting the birthday event, Tanner interlaced his attention to historical memory with William Hunter's fiscal concerns. "It has always seemed to us," he suggested, "that [the birthday of Bishop Allen] could be made to do good service." Two weeks later Tanner reported with approval that the Sunday school students had resolved to set aside February 14 as " 'Father Allen's Day,' whereon the children of all the Sunday Schools of the connection, may be brought together and instructed in its history and its work; and we the little ones be allowed at the same time to contribute our mites in furtherance of the common cause." Church leaders were beginning to recognize the potential for fusing their commemorative impulse, and the name of Richard Allen, with the financial problems of the denomination (*Christian Recorder,* February 11, 25, 1875).

Allen's name and legacy were also kept before the readers of the *Christian Recorder* with a series of front page extracts from Allen's autobiography, *The Life, Experience and Gospel Labors of Rev. Richard Allen,* which ran through the summer and fall of 1875. This slim memoir was first published in 1833, two years after Allen's death, but had not been widely circulated. It contained a compressed overview of Allen's life, followed by several documents related to key developments in the Church and Philadelphia's Black community. Once again A.M.E. leaders worked on two fronts—through public commemorations and in the pages of the *Recorder*—in their efforts to keep the name and accomplishments of Allen in the minds of both their literate and nonliterate constituencies.

After innumerable delays, on Thursday, November 2, 1876, barely a week before the Exposition closed its gates, a marble bust of the Right Reverend Richard Allen, first bishop of the African Methodist Episcopal Church, was unveiled "with appropriate ceremonies in the presence of several hundred colored people" in Philadelphia's Fairmount Park. In the absence of John Mercer Langston, who was to deliver a historical oration on the life and times of Bishop Allen, Howard University professor and A.M.E. bishop John M. Brown was called upon to speak. Brown compared Allen with the likes of Luther, Wesley, and George Whitefield in the lasting effects of his "Christ-like" work for the religious liberty of his people. Brown did justice to the varied achievements of the honored prelate, highlighting Allen's integrity, benevolence, moral courage, and love of freedom and education (*Christian Recorder,* November 9, 1876; the Philadelphia *Press,* November 3, 1876). Langston eventually did deliver his own paean to Allen a month later before two thousand people at Allen's own Mother Bethel Church. Like Bishop Brown, Langston uncompromisingly praised the Founder of African Methodism and called attention to the significant fact that the Allen monument was the first ever erected by Black Americans to honor one of their own (1969, 123–40).

The enthusiasm generated by the Allen monument attenuated but had not fully extinguished by the early 1880s. Richard Allen continued to hold an esteemed place in the memory of the A.M.E. Church, even if the commemoration of his natal day was undertaken only sporadically and locally. But by 1884 Benjamin Tanner noted with satisfaction that "[g]radually the annual celebration of the birth-day of Richard Allen is becoming generally observed." In that year many of the Church leaders who were involved in the Centennial monument movement participated in a "grand commemoration of Bishop Allen's birthday" in Boston that was designed to raise money for a church mortgage. Part of the week's proceedings involved historical and inspirational addresses, including J.T. Jenifer's "very interesting and instructive sermon . . . 'Who Was Richard Allen? What Did He Do?'" and Tanner's "Richard Allen and His Place in History." The estimated attendance of "at least four thousand" people assured not only that the fundraising drive would be a success, but also that Allen's place in A.M.E. history might be reaffirmed (*Christian Recorder,* February 21, 1884). The Boston affair represents a key transitional moment, during which the fundraising potential of the founding prelate's birthday became clear to several influential Church leaders.

Most Februarys through the 1880s found some acknowledgment in the *Recorder,* noting the observance of Allen's birthday and urging readers to familiarize themselves with, and to emulate, the great leader's life. The centennial of the Free African Society in 1887 prompted a lengthy essay that paid homage to the founder, comparing him variously with Moses, Martin Luther, Jan Hus, George Whitefield, George Washington, and Thomas Jefferson (*Christian Recorder,* February 17, 1887). Further literary homage to Allen appeared with the publication of two separate editions of his autobiography and of J.F. Dyson's pamphlet, *Richard Allen's Place in History: A Commentary on the Life and Deeds of the Chief Founder and First Bishop of the African Methodist Episcopal Church.* These 1887 centennial publications suggest an increasingly literary approach to honoring the founder. But the acceleration of Allen Day exercises across the nation also indicates the continued use of nonliterary forms for disseminating historical and biographical knowledge about this increasingly recognized African American hero.

The A.M.E. Church's commemorative spirit, its desire to aggrandize its founder, and its economic and missionary needs coalesced more fully over the next several years. In a half-page appeal featuring a large portrait of Allen in the *Christian Recorder* in January 1889, Book Concern manager J.C. Embry promoted a cause that would fulfill these overlapping missions: the Allen Press. Embry described the project by first calling attention to the "custom of civilized people to revere the names and illustrious deeds of their heroic dead." The American people, for example, honored Washington, "not by the mighty monument [completed in 1885] they have built to pierce the sky, but by crowning with his name the Nation's citadel" and by "set[ting] apart . . . the day of his birth as a legal holiday." Richard Allen, Embry contended, "did even more for the Church than Washington for the Nation. . . . Our church should in all her coasts meet and celebrate in some fitting way, the birth of our noble founder."

This established, Embry turned to the cause which Allen's name would be made to serve. The 1888 general conference had reaffirmed its commitment to "perpetuate the Publishing House" in the particular interest of strengthening its foothold in the South, where "[r]ecent incidents of persecution and horrid wrong" threatened both African American rights and African Methodist influence. The plan required that the entire Church and ministry, "while celebrating the birth of Allen on the 14th of February, contribute from five cents to five dollars to aid the Book Concern and the ALLEN PRESS." Two weeks later *Recorder* editor Benjamin F. Lee claimed that the new press would "extend the honors of the great Allen" and should have the support of every pastorate in the connection (*Christian Recorder,* January 24, February 7, 1889). Over the next several years the bond between Allen's name and A.M.E. publications grew even stronger.

In 1891 Lee stressed that Allen Day was to be both a sincere homage to Allen and a profitable enterprise for the Book Concern. "While we do not make the collection feature paramount to all others, we do hope that every church will celebrate the day with enthusiasm and real praise, and that no church will fail to make a nice remittance to the Publishing House." The broad reach of the event is attested by the participation of churches as far afield as Texas and Colorado. By 1891 annual Allen Day celebrations across the Church's ever-expanding territory provided both a solution for the financial woes of the Book Concern and a valuable tool in spreading knowledge of Allen's accomplishments (*Christian Recorder,* February 12, 1891).

Allen Day drives intensified in 1893 and 1894. In 1893 Benjamin Lee stressed that it should be a great day, not just for the Church, but for the whole race: "It is to foster in the hearts of our people—especially in the young—a loving respect for the men of our own race and blood who have demonstrated the inherent power of the race to rise in spite of oppression, to achievements which rank them among the great" (*Christian Recorder,* February 2, 1893). By the next year the A.M.E. "Publishing House [had] connect[ed] itself firmly, prayerfully[,] lovingly, with the name and character of Richard Allen, and with the institutions, enterprises and energies founded in pursuance of his great purpose." The fusion of practical necessity, historical consciousness, and commemorative impulse was now complete. The publications of the A.M.E. Book Concern would keep alive the legacy of Allen's institutional monument—the A.M.E. Church—and the annual Allen Day exercises would preserve the race's collective memory of the founder of African Methodism in America (*Christian Recorder,* January 25, 1894).

In 1894 Allen's one hundred thirty-fourth birthday was marked by a special "memorial edition" of the *Recorder* that celebrated Allen's life and legacy in page after page of poetry and prose from a wide array of Church and race leaders. The various essayists noted multiple aspects of Allen's life and legacy: his overriding faith, his "independence and manliness," his broad public-spiritedness, his race pride, his simple dignity, and his commitment to "religious liberty and human brotherhood." In marked contrast to some early commentaries about the founder, by the 1890s there remained little public evidence that Allen possessed any faults whatsoever. He had become cloaked in the mantle of myth.

At a time when African American aspirations toward inclusion in the national family and unfettered exercise of basic civil and political rights were, perhaps, at their lowest point ever, educator William H. Councill used the occasion to drum up pride and the spirit of self-support among his people. In particular he emphasized the example Allen provided for the "young men" of the race. Allen refused to let his ambitions be "cramped by the Anglo-Saxon prejudice around him." He would never "have accepted a position in which he would have been forced to serve all other races except his own. . . . He recognized the fact that no Negro . . . who does not read Negro literature as found in Negro journals, periodicals and books can . . . be in sympathy, and interest with the negro race. . . . It takes Negro song, Negro music, Negro history, Negro literature to build Negro manhood." Allen, in his day, had used "the full height of manhood" to exemplify the "race love" that Black Americans in the 1890s needed to foster among themselves.

*Christian Recorder* editor H.T. Johnson was more nationalistic than race-centered in his contribution. He noted that February contained the birthdays of the country's "triple saviors"—Washington, Allen, and Lincoln—whose names "will be affectionately remembered by a grateful posterity. The first for delivering his country, the second for rescuing his people, the other for saving the Union." The "memories of these champions of truth and freedom" should be perpetuated by all Americans "until patriotism, devotion and loyalty cease to be honored by men." Reminiscent of the rhetoric of the 1870s monument drive, Johnson presented Allen not as an African Methodist hero, not as a race hero, but as a national hero, a legitimate Founding Father. Elsewhere the editor acknowledged that, indeed, "the great and good founder is much more venerated, known and celebrated than ever before." But the denominational recognition that was now so far reaching was insufficient homage to one whose memory should be "honored throughout the land." The recognition of the nation was not forthcoming, but the objective of placing Allen's name firmly in the historical memory of the denomination and the race had been realized. Book Manager Embry claimed to "have succeeded in bringing the life and character of Allen before a wider circle of people, old and young, than ever before in our history" (*Christian Recorder,* February 22, 1894).

Even as African Methodists congratulated themselves for establishing Richard Allen as one of the early stars in the firmament of African American history, the United States was in the process of defining its own pantheon of heroes to be honored in a national hall of fame. In 1900 a long list of contenders was compiled by soliciting nominations from one hundred selected editors, scholars, and national leaders. Of the dozens of patriots, inventors, explorers, politicians, reformers, authors, and religious leaders suggested by these experts, not one African American's name was put forward (Banks 1902). This is not altogether surprising, given the racial climate of turn-of-the-century America. Allen's elevation as a race hero in a "separate but equal" pantheon underscores the cruel irony of the age of Jim Crow. The 1896 *Plessy v. Ferguson* decision, it would seem, applied to historical memory as well as to streetcars.

In the early 1900s more written biographies of Richard Allen began to augment the annual Allen Day commemorations. In 1905 Rev. John T. Jenifer published a short pamphlet based on his 1884 lecture, "Who Was Richard Allen? And What Did He Do?" In 1910 the A.M.E. Sunday School Union published another short work jointly honoring Allen, his wife Sarah, and Rev. Daniel Coker (Welch 1910). Five years later George Freeman Bragg published a slim pamphlet on Allen and Absalom Jones. These works emerged along with a wave of publications relating to Black history. By the 1920s it was clear that the growing Black middle class and expanding literacy rates among African Americans were beginning to shift the focus of Black activists concerned with preserving a distinctive African American historical memory. The growing corpus connected with Carter G. Woodson and his various publishing enterprises alone provides ample evidence of the increasing power of the printed word in reaching out to both Black and white audiences. At the same time the once-vibrant Emancipation Day commemorative tradition was losing its potency and its usefulness in mobilizing Black activism and disseminating Black history.

In the 1920s and 1930s longer treatments of Allen's life began to appear. In 1923 the A.M.E. Book Concern lived up to part of its mission by publishing a 107-page biography, *Bishop Richard Allen and His Spirit,* by Daniel Minort Baxter. Eleven years later the same publisher and author combined to produce a theatrical drama based on Allen's role in founding the Church. In 1935 the first truly scholarly biography of Allen appeared with Charles H. Wesley's *Richard Allen: Apostle of Freedom.* The past half-century has also seen numerous biographical works, including juvenile literature, historical fiction, social commentary, and scholarly analysis. Allen Day has continued to be observed in the A.M.E. Church, both to serve as a fundraising vehicle and to perpetuate the memory of this great African American hero.

But most Americans today have never heard of Richard Allen. He has never been fully accepted into an American pantheon of heroes. While the efforts of nineteenth-century Church leaders helped establish Allen's recognition within the race, the commemoration of Richard Allen did virtually nothing to convince white America of Blacks' cultural belongingness and rights to full inclusion. Not until the 1980s would Whites begrudgingly accept an African American into that pantheon of American heroes who rated a special day set aside for their remembrance. And even now the observance of Martin Luther King Day meets with considerable resistance in some quarters. Among those with some familiarity with African American history, the name of Richard Allen has immediate recognition and conjures up images of self-determination, independence, religious liberty, and race pride. What most do not actively consider is that the construction of our memory of Richard Allen has its own history, a history that can enhance our understanding of the uses of historical memory and the process through which it is constructed.

In their efforts to commemorate the life of Richard Allen in the late nineteenth century, A.M.E. leaders were sincere in their assertions that Allen was a noble ancestor who deserved to be revered by Black and white Americans alike. They were, in one sense, participating in a national trend—a general rise in historical consciousness and commemorative zeal in American culture. And they were clearly in step with other African Americans who were struggling to construct an empowering sense of history and tradition. African Methodists' particular engagement with this project worked on several different levels. Most fundamentally, the movement served the Church by addressing the serious financial problems of the Book Concern. In addition, calling attention to Allen's role as the father of Black religious liberty was explicitly designed to win converts, especially in the post-emancipation South. Second, commemorating Allen served the race by celebrating the considerable accomplishments of a Black man to foster a sense of race pride and historical consciousness among all (and especially young) African Americans in order to inspire further accomplishments. Third, it at least attempted to serve the nation by seeking to expand the pantheon of American heroes by including a Black Founding Father in their ranks.

This movement to honor Richard Allen illustrates the power of historical memory. A.M.E. leaders recognized the importance of maintaining a claim on the past. They used commemoration and the creation of Allen's public biography both to address contemporary concerns and to shape the legacy they passed on to future generations. Their constructions of historical memory and their contributions to a commemorative tradition were part of an important cultural struggle that was shouldered by numerous Black intellectual and political leaders in the late-nineteenth century. These efforts to maintain a continuity with the past represent a vital component in African Americans' challenge to establish a sense of history, a set of traditions, and a pantheon of heroes that would legitimize, to the nation and to themselves, their inherent worth as a people and as American citizens.

## References

Allen, R. 1833. *The Life and Gospel Labors of the Right Rev. Richard Allen*. Philadelphia: Martin and Boden.

———. 1887. *The Life and Gospel Labors of the Right Rev. Richard Allen*. Philadelphia: A.M.E. Book Concern.

———. 1887. *The Life and Gospel Labors of the Right Rev. Richard Allen*. Philadelphia: Lee and Yeocum.

Banks, L.A. 1902. *The Story of the Hall of Fame*. New York: n. p.

Baxter, D.M. 1923. *Bishop Richard Allen and His Spirit*. Philadelphia: A.M.E. Book Concern.

———. 1934. *Richard Allen: From Boy to First Bishop of the African Methodist Episcopal Church, 1760–1816. A Drama in Four Acts*. Philadelphia: A.M.E. Book Concern.

Bell, H.H. 1969. *A Survey of the Negro Convention Movement, 1830–1861*. New York: Arno Press.

Bennett, L. 1968. *Pioneers in Protest*. Chicago: Johnson.

Blassingame, J., ed. 1985. *The Frederick Douglass Papers*. Series 1, vol. 3. New Haven: Yale University Press.

Bodnar, J. 1991. *Remaking America: Public Memory, Commemoration, and Patriotism in the Twentieth Century.* Princeton: Princeton University Press.

Bowers, D. 1992. *A Strange Speech of an Estranged People: Theory and Practice of African-American Freedom Day Orations.* Ph.D. diss., Purdue University.

Bragg, G.F. 1915. *Richard Allen and Absalom Jones.* Baltimore: Church Advocates Press (serialized in the *Christian Recorder*).

Dyson, J.F. 1887. *Richard Allen's Place in History: A Commentary on the Life and Deeds of the Founder and First Bishop of the African Methodist Episcopal Church.* Nashville: Cumberland Presbyterian Publishing House.

Fabre, G. 1994. "Nineteenth Century Emancipation Celebrations. In *History and Memory in African American Culture,* ed. G. Fabre and M. O'Meally. New York: Oxford University Press.

Finnegan, R. 1988. *Literacy and Orality: Studies in the Technology of Communication.* New York: Blackwell.

Glassberg, D. 1990. *American Historical Pageantry: The Uses of Tradition in the Early Twentieth Century.* Chapel Hill: University of North Carolina Press.

Gravely, W.B. 1982. "The Dialectic of Double-Consciousness in Black Freedom Day Celebrations, 1808–1863." *Journal of Negro History* 67: 302–17.

Heard, W.H. 1969. *From Slavery to the Bishopric in the* A.M.E. Church. New York: Arno Press.

Hildebrand, R. 1995. *The Rimes Were Strange and Stirring: Methodist Preachers and the Crisis of Emancipation.* Durham, NC: Duke University Press.

Jenifer, J.T. 1905. *Who Was Richard Allen and What Did He Do?* Baltimore: n. p.

Kachun, M. 1997. " 'The Faith That the Dark Past Has Taught Us': African American Commemorations in the North and West and the Construction of a Usable Past, 1808–1915." Ph.D. diss., Cornell University.

Kammen, M. 1991. *Mystic Chords of Memory: The Transformation of Tradition in American Culture.* New York: Random House.

Lane, R. 1991. *William Dorsey's Philadelphia and Ours: On the Past and the Future of the Black City in America.* New York: Oxford University Press.

Langston, John Mercer. 1968. *From the Virginia Plantation to the National Capitol.* New York: Johnson Reprint Corp.

―――. 1969. *Freedom and Citizenship: Selected Lectures and Addresses.* Miami: Mnemosyne.

Levine, L. 1977. *Black Culture and Black Consciousness: Afro-American Folk Thought from Slavery to Freedom.* New York: Oxford University Press.

Mathews, M. 1963. *Richard Allen.* Baltimore: Helicon.

Montgomery, W.E. 1992. *Under Their Own Vine and Fig Tree: The African-American Church in the South, 1865–1900.* Baton Rouge: Louisiana State University Press.

Nash, G. 1988. *Forging Freedom: The Formation of Philadelphia's Black Community, 1720–1840.* Cambridge: Harvard University Press.

Payne, D.A. 1866. *The Semi-centenary and the Retrospection of the African Methodist Episcopal Church.* Baltimore: Sherwood.

―――. 1891. *History of the African Methodist Episcopal Church.* Baltimore: Sherwood.

Sernett, M. 1975. *Black Religion and American Evangelism: White Protestants, Plantation Missions, and the Flowering of Negro Christianity, 1787–1865.* Metuchen, NJ: Scarecrow Press.

Smith, C.S., ed. 1891.*History of the African Methodist Episcopal Church.* Nashville: A.M.E. Sunday School Union.

Stuckey, S., ed. 1972. *The Ideological Origins of Black Nationalism.* Boston: Beacon Press.

Takaki, R., ed. 1972. *Violence in the Black Imagination: Essays and Documents.* New York: Putnam.

Walker, C. 1982. *A Rock in a Weary Land: The African Methodist Episcopal Church during the Civil War and Reconstruction.* Baton Rouge: Louisiana State University Press.

Welch, I.H. 1910. *The Heroism of the Rev. Richard Allen, Founder and First Bishop of the African Methodist Episcopal Church in the United States of American and Rev. Daniel Coker, Co-founder and First Missionary to Africa from Said Church: With a Brief Sketch of Sister Sarah Allen's Heroism.* Nashville: A.M.E. Sunday School Union.

Wesley, C.H. 1935. *Richard Allen: Apostle of Freedom.* Washington, DC: Associated Publishers.

White, S. 1994. " 'It Was a Proud Day': African Americans, Festivals, and Parades in the North, 1741–1834." *Journal of American History* 81, no. 1: 13–50.

Wolseley, R.E. 1990. *The Black Press, U.S.A.* 2nd ed. Ames: Iowa State University Press.

Wright, R.R., ed. 1916. *Centennial Encyclopaedia of the African Methodist Episcopal Church.* Philadelphia: A.M.E. Church Book Concern.

# Part II

# Cultural Biography

# 5

# Outlaw Women and Toni Morrison's Communities

## Gloria T. Randle

Depictions of community in Toni Morrison's work are powerful not only as literary portraits but also as reflections of shared group experience as a crucial aspect of community self-identity. In language both subtle and explicit, the author exposes the empowering and uplifting aspects of *communitas* and the isolation, tensions, and schisms that can and do occur, particularly among a historically disenfranchised group, as its members attempt, through varying methods, to establish a coherent sense of self. At the same time, Morrison's novels are peopled with what I call "outlaw women"—women whose behavior, in some fashion, goes against the grain of group ethos and practice. An analysis of interactions between these outlaws and their respective communities suggests how the collective and the individual—especially the female individual—can impede or uplift one another's goals and provides implicit critiques of certain belief systems at work within the culture. For these inquiries, this essay focuses on Pecola Breedlove in *The Bluest Eye,* Sula in the novel by the same name, and Sethe in *Beloved.*

*Song of Solomon* opens in the 1930s, in a community surrounding Not Doctor Street, so named by its residents in honor of the first black medical practitioner in the area. The street name both embraces culture and signifies on history with its the proud self-naming ("Doctor Street") in rejection of official name designation and its response to town authorities who mandate that residents cease referring to the neighborhood as "Doctor Street." It also gives a nod to the exclusionary institutional racial practices of the time: the daughter of the now-deceased doctor had once been refused admittance into nearby Mercy Hospital (predictably dubbed "No Mercy" by the residents).

For reasons of status, and because the physician's presence ensures that no ailing resident will be denied medical care, "a doctor in the house" is important to this neighborhood. The name "Doctor Street" is a proud symbol for residents that one of their own has gained the prize to the benefit of the common good. "Not Doctor Street," a communal act of reappropriation, carves a presence from an absence, recognizing—and mocking—the limits of community authority while situating the agency of repression on social authorities and reaffirming a group holding that City Hall would deny.

While individual self-development—like that of *Song of Solomon*'s doctor—is essential to the perpetuation and prosperity of community, individual methods are often at odds with group philosophy. Although male characters also mirror such dissonance, Morrison's texts, it is with her striking female reprobates that the author most effectively probes the dynamics between the individual and the collective. From the prescient, navel-less Pilate in *Song of Solomon* to the exotic, fearful Jade in *Tar Baby* and the elusive Wild in *Jazz,* to name but a few, Morrison's novels abound with outlaw women—not criminals necessarily, but misfits and miscreants, women who situate themselves decidedly *outside* the *law* of the community. For their part, Morrison's communities are also flawed; they are not safe always safe havens overflowing with warm group experience but, at times, intolerant, censorious, small-minded, and oppressive. In other words, they are real. These novels do not idealize; instead, they problematize the individual/communal relationship in ways that challenge the reader to reexamine traditional behaviors.

## Black e Mo

> *Pretty eyes. Pretty blue eyes. Big blue pretty eyes. Run, Jip, run. Jip runs, Alice runs. Alice has blue eyes. Jerry has blue eyes. Jerry runs. Alice runs. They run with their blue eyes. Four blue eyes. Four pretty blue eyes. Blue-sky eyes, Blue-like Mrs. Forrest's blue blouse eyes. Morning-glory-blue eyes. Alice-and-Jerry-blue-storybook eyes.* (34–35)

The power of blue eyes, for Pecola Breedlove, is reflected in her nightly prayer. Its italicized format, repetitious-compulsive rhythm, primerlike story line, and deft characterization of the desired eyes as "storybook" all suggest the depth of Pecola's fantasy life and the extent to which she has internalized European concepts of beauty.

Pecola's desire for blue eyes is not such an aberration in her insular community. Although they do not openly acknowledge the self-loathing that creates such a desire, Pecola's family, like many in her community, is afflicted with a negative sense of self.

> The Breedloves lived [in a storefront] because they were poor and black, and they stayed there because they believed they were ugly. . . . [They] wore their ugliness, put it on, so to speak, although it did not belong to them. . . . You looked at them and wondered why they were so ugly: you looked closely and could not find the source. Then you realized that it came from conviction, their conviction. (28)

Unable to love themselves, Pecola's parents are ill equipped to love her. Pauline's emotional distance is reflected in Pecola's calling her mother "Mrs. Breedlove," while the child of the white family for whom Pauline Breedlove works is free to call her "Polly." Cholly Breedlove, once a kind and confident man, has been beaten down by life until he has "nothing more to lose" (126). If anything, he is contemptuous and angered by what he feels is his ungainly daughter's shy affection: "How dare she love him?" (127).

Such profound self-loathing has actually been nurtured in the northern community to which Pauline and Cholly relocated when they married. They came to Lorain, Ohio, "young, loving, and full of energy" (90), their southern natures open to the new experiences and opportunities that the North professed to hold for people of color in the 1940s. What they found was cold condescension and isolation. Pauline recalls:

> Northern colored folk was different. . . . Dicty-like. No better than whites for meanness. They could make you feel just as no-count, 'cept I didn't expect it from them. That was the lonesomest time of my life. (91)

In this pre–civil rights era, Black is anything *but* beautiful in America, and Pauline's unaffected nature is mocked by community women who have embraced the larger culture's message. They are "amused by her because she [does] not straighten her hair," and their "goading glances and private snickers" at her dress and speech lead her to adopt their demeanor, not because she likes it, but because she wants to be accepted (92).

Pauline also begins a movie career ("The onliest time I be happy seem like was when I was in the picture show" [95]), which, ironically, compounds rather than mitigates her discomfort in her own skin. Even as she notes the differences between herself and the silver screen beauties, she fails to realize that by worshipping them, she is contributing to her own self-contempt. What she blames on a lost tooth is in fact a consequence of her failure to mirror the white feminine ideal:

> I 'member one time I went to see Clark Gable and Jean Harlow. I fixed my hair up like I'd seen hers on a magazine. A part on the side, with one little curl on my forehead. It looked just like her. Well, almost just like. . . . I taken a big bite of that candy, and it pulled a tooth right out of my mouth. . . . There

I was, five months pregnant, trying to look like Jean Harlow, and a front tooth gone. Everything went then. Look like I just didn't care no more after that. I let my hair go back, plaited it up, and settled down to just being ugly. (96)

It would hardly be possible for a woman filled with self-hatred to produce a beautiful child. At the moment of Pecola's birth, Pauline's critical inspection of her newborn bears out the self-fulfilling prophecy: "Head full of pretty hair, but Lord was she ugly" (98).

Thus begins the subtle but relentless destruction of a psyche as everyone, including her family, alternately mocks and dismisses Pecola, who, as Michael Awkward maintains, "represents for the entire community the literal embodiment of the shadow of blackness."[1] At the corner grocery the (blue-eyed) clerk regards her with a gaze like "a vacuum . . . because for him there is nothing to see" (36). On the playground, classmates taunt her:

> Black e mo Black e mo Ya daddy sleeps nekked
> Stch ta ta stch ta ta
> stach ta ta ta ta ta. (50)

In class, she is the only student who sits alone at a double desk. Her teachers "tried never to glance at her, and called on her only when everyone was required to respond" (34). Pecola's nemesis is Maureen Peal, devilishly renamed "Meringue Pie" by the young narrator, Claudia, and her sister Frieda, signifying not only her light skin but also her insubstantial character. In sharp contrast to Pecola, Maureen Peal, the "high-yellow dream child with long brown hair . . . enchanted the entire school" (47).

> When teachers called on her, they smiled encouragingly. Black boys didn't trip her in the halls; white boys didn't stone her, white girls didn't suck their teeth when she was assigned to be their work partners; black girls stepped aside when she wanted to use the sink in the girl's toilet, and their eyes genuflected under sliding lids. (48)

Privileged for no reason other than her appearance, Maureen routinely accepts such deference as her due. When her initial (and insincere) attempts at friendship with Claudia, Frieda, and Pecola are rebuffed, Meringue Pie reverts to type, screaming, "I *am* cute! And you ugly! Black and ugly black e mos. I *am* cute!" (56). Unlike her friends, who have been nurtured into a well-developed sense of self, Pecola, unable to withstand such an attack, "seemed to fold into herself, like a pleated wing" (57).

Similar scenes of insult and humiliation that occur throughout the novel lead inevitably to a dangerous ego fragility. Pecola's consequent obsession with eyes—her own and, especially, those of others—reflects classic double consciousness.[2]

> "Please, God," she whispered into the palm of her hand. "Please make me disappear." . . . Almost done, almost. Only her tight, tight eyes were left. They were always left. (33)

> Long hours she sat looking in the mirror, trying to discover the secret of the ugliness, the ugliness that made her ignored or despised at school, by teachers and classmates alike. (34)

> . . . she would never know her beauty. She would see only what there was to see: the eyes of other people. (150)

Pecola responds to the external gaze by first questioning, then rejecting, her own perception; finally, by desperately wishing to be, and to be seen *as,* someone entirely different. One rare delight has been her relationship with the dandelion: "Why do people call them weeds? She thought they were pretty" (35). In her mind, Pecola owns the ones that she has blown away, and "owning them made her part of the world, and the world part of her" (36). Finally unable to sustain her own opinion against the burden of the world's judgment, she surrenders one of her very few touchstones.

> Dandelions. A dart of affection leaps out from them to her. But they do not look at her and do not send love back. She thinks, "They *are* ugly. They *are* weeds." (37)

Not coincidentally, the candy that Pecola has bought at the grocery store carries a picture of her blue-eyed ideal; in unwitting parody of her mother, who "becomes" Jean Harlow while at the movies, Pecola internalizes the image, both physically and psychically:

> Smiling white face. Blond hair in gentle disarray, blue eyes looking at her out of a world of clean comfort. . . . She eats the candy, and its sweetness is good. To eat the candy is somehow to eat the eyes, eat Mary Jane. Love Mary Jane. Be Mary Jane. (38)

Pecola's impossible wish for blue eyes is hardly inconceivable. Whatever the character of her physical challenges, she is *not* blind: the Mary Janes and the Maureen Peals of the world are the noticed, the accepted, the beloved; such is the immense power of idealized beauty that it commands love. And this, at bottom, is of course what Pecola so desperately desires. She believes that the unexpected beauty of blue eyes will bring her love, making "Cholly . . . different, and Mrs. Breedlove, too. Maybe they'd say, 'Why, look at pretty-eyed Pecola. We mustn't do bad things in front of those pretty eyes' " (34).

While Pecola is marginally aligned with two rather loosely structured communal groups—her childhood friends Claudia and Frieda and a trio of friendly prostitutes—both units are suspect, to say the least, in the larger community's eyes. Claudia's narrative skills and mature insights give the lie—as is surely Morrison's intent—to the popular idea of the era that children are nonpersons who should be seen and not heard; nevertheless, Pecola's associates have neither voice nor validity in the general scheme of community affairs. Further, they are not equipped to nurture, guide, or affirm her adequately. For the all-important question that gives rise to her desire for blue eyes, her friends cannot help.

> Then Pecola asked a question that had never entered my mind. "How do you do that? I mean, how do you get somebody to *love you*?" But Frieda was asleep. And I didn't know. (23)

> "I never seen nobody with as many boyfriends as you got, Miss Marie. How come they all *love you*?" . . . What did love feel like? she wondered. (43–44 [emphases mine])

The irony of the Breedlove name is not lost on the reader. Pecola's ignorance about that emotion is evidence that this family does *not* love. Worse, what the bitter, defeated father calls love is in fact perversion: Cholly propels his vulnerable daughter into insanity when, like an animal, "crawling on all fours toward her," he breeds with her (128). After this "unspeakable thing, unspoken," Pecola lives totally inside herself, her community reduced to two, her alter ego representing another part of her severely fragmented ego.

Roberta Rubenstein notes a metaphorical link between character and community in Morrison's work, wherein certain "divisions and splits within individuals . . . mirror their cultural situation."[3] In spite of its professed morality and cultural rootedness, the community reveals *its* fragmented self by privileging European ideals and neglecting the needs of its young. This depiction of a disinterested community bears critiquing. Certainly, *The Bluest Eye* is apparently more a family than a communal story, but Morrison makes clear that crucial issues of communal self-image are also involved. Residents are complicit in making Pecola feel ugly because so many of them feel ugly themselves. The apparently blameless community has accused Pecola with eyes that say "Black e mo" until she has disappeared from view. Its failure to embrace her is not merely benign behavior but a deliberate act of negligence and even, in some cases, malice. Always an outcast, Pecola becomes an outlaw when she refuses, ultimately, to remain invisible. Walking along the streets in animated conversation with herself, her child's body grotesquely extended with her father's baby, the profound obscenity of her condition forces her community to know its guilt and its failure. The lessons they share are poignant; Pecola's community has taught her to despise and deny herself in marvelous fashion. She, in turn, has shown them that beyond the next unloved child is, at best, a damaged sense of self, and at worst, disaster.

**An Excess in Nature**

The opening pages of *Sula* relate the history behind a bizarre community ritual: Traumatized during World War I, Shadrack is unable to locate anything substantial in or around him: there are "loose cords in his mind"; the doctors and nurses are "paper people"; "he [doesn't] know who or what he [is]" (10–12). His hands are grotesquely elongated and deformed and he cannot perceive boundaries within his physical self.

> . . . his huge growing hands . . . the monstrous hand . . . his terrible fingers . . . fingers of each hand fused into the fabric. (9, 13)

He finally neutralizes his condition by instituting National Suicide Day. The annual ritual, wherein no one commits suicide, creates a fail-safe, especially for Shadrack, by ensuring that the other 364 days will be *non*suicidal. The preeminent issue in this community is containment, and containment is accomplished through the establishment of boundaries.

The community in Medallion, Ohio, aptly called the Bottom, represents a broken dream constructed on yet another broken promise (of the classic forty-acres-and-a-mule variety) from white America through which residents in the early part of the century could access the American Dream. One does not have "fun" in the Bottom; its people are about the serious business of work, responsibility, and survival. Sula Peace, town pariah, does not share in Suicide Day festivities nor, for that matter, in much else that goes on in the community. Her only companion is her best childhood friend, Nel. Nel conforms to communal standards as fiercely as Sula ignores them, and it is this attitude that brands Sula an outlaw. Like the sweeping flock of birds that herald her return after a ten-year absence, Sula, now presumably aligned with the dark forces, is an "excess in nature" (86).

> The people in the Bottom shook their heads and said Sula was a roach . . . a bitch. Everybody remembered the plague of robins that announced her return. . . . (112)

And her crimes? Almost immediately upon her return she dispatches her grandmother Eva to a nursing home; she sleeps with Nel's husband, Jude; she also sleeps with white men, against the town's credo that "unions between white men and black women [had to be] rape" because willingness on the woman's part would be unthinkable (113). For all their notoriety, Sula's violations overlay a more fundamental, unspoken crime to which the community responds on a purely visceral level. Her censure is a consequence of other 'excesses' that point directly to the community itself, especially to its women.

Whereas even Eva has always seen Nel and Sula as "just alike. . . . Never was no difference between you" (169), the matronly Nel, twenty-five years after Jude's infidelity and abandonment, has comfortably settled into "a tiny life" (165). She is both respected and respectable, unmindful of the self-imposed constraints within which she exists. The narrative exposes not only Sula's disregard for boundaries but also Nel's excessive need for them. The women *are* alike in the sense that they both need to get the balance right.

In the 1920s and 1930s young black women rarely left home to attend college; instead, they met their familial and communal responsibilities and expectations; they did not drink of life's deep cup, fulfilling themselves while their families waited patiently at home. Sula is an outlaw not so much for forsaking the Bottom for college and big-city life but for returning *home* to flaunt unorthodox ideas and behavior that fly directly in the face of community women, who have always dutifully known and kept their place. Her defiance threatens the residents' complacency and forces them to confront their own learned inadequacies and untapped potential. Finally and unforgivably, Sula, who neither seeks nor needs approbation, "acknowledged none of their attempts at counter-conjure or their gossip and seemed to need the services of nobody" (113).

The stalemate between Sula and the townspeople forestalls the communication that could otherwise benefit the collective, for Sula and her community have much to learn from one another. The townspeople would profit from a discriminating relaxation of their many restrictions, and Sula would gain from an awareness that some boundaries are necessary. To her credit, Sula believes that the human spirit has limitless potential and that society's imposed boundaries or biologically determined faculties, particularly those of race and gender, should not affect one's ambitions, accomplishments, or worldview; she especially rejects the idea that a woman is incomplete within herself. And while the Bottom finds comfort in conformity, Sula's independent nature might prove exemplary for a community accustomed to discouraging, rather than uplifting, individual differences. Still, if some of the town's values are objectionable, at least it *possesses* a moral code, as well as a sense of community—two elements sorely lacking in Sula.

Sula has come honestly by her moral deficiencies. Her grandmother, deserted by her husband but determined to ensure her children's survival, literally sacrificed her*self* (a leg, at least, for insurance money) to supply their most basic material needs. In her intense focus on their physical welfare, however, she seriously neglected their emotional needs, even abandoning them in order to put the insurance plan into effect. Eva had left her children with a neighbor, "saying she would be back the next day. *Eighteen months later* she swept down from a wagon, two crutches, a new black pocketbook, and one leg" (34; emphasis mine). This long-term maternal absence would profoundly affect the characters Hannah and Plum into adulthood. Sweet, gentle, drug-addicted Plum dies by Eva's own hand to end his suffering but also to avert her fear that "he wanted to crawl back into my womb" (69). Hannah owns the reputation of town whore. "It was manlove that Eva bequeathed to her daughters" (41). Manlove, yes; but sadly, not self-love. Biased toward the male gender, Eva invariably takes the man's part when she involves herself in others' private affairs. Hannah has internalized her mother's philosophy of romantic relationships ("those Peace women loved all men" [41]) and compensated for her mother's failure to nurture her during childhood by indiscriminately "loving" and "playing" with men as an adult.

The transgenerational cycle of deficient mothering from grandmother to mother to daughter has wrought profound psychic damaged upon the beautiful Peace women.

> "Mama, did you ever love us?" She sang the words like a small child. . . .
>     "No. I don't reckon I did. Not the way you thinkin'."
> . . . "Did you ever, you know, play with us?"
> "Play? Wasn't nobody playin' in 1895." (69)

The *only* legitimate answer to a child—whatever her age—who asks if a parent loves her is "Yes." Instead, Eva recalls the meanness of black life in those days—the starvation and deprivation, the sickness and disease, the loss of spirit and soul to the relentless elements, both natural and societal. There was "no time. They wasn't no time. Not none" to play. Eva's job was to keep her children alive, and she did so by any means necessary. "Don't that count? Ain't that love?" she angrily demands, missing the real point of her daughter's question (69). History repeats itself after a fashion when Sula overhears her mother saying to friends, "I love Sula. I just don't like her" (57).

As a child, Sula had twice witnessed a death—that of the character Chicken Little, for which she and Nel are indirectly, inadvertently responsible; and of her mother, who walks into a yard fire shortly after Eva concedes that she had not loved Hannah. A loveless upbringing, coupled with the eyewitness observation of these two deaths, has engendered in Sula an emotional deadness. Eva recalls that during her frantic (and fruitless) effort to reach her burning daughter, she had seen Sula "standing on the back porch just looking."

> When Eva, who was never one to hide the faults of her children, mentioned what she thought she'd seen to a few friends, they said it was natural. Sula was probably struck dumb, as anybody would be who saw her own mama burn up. Eva said yes, but inside she dis-agreed and remained convinced that Sula had watched Hannah burn not because she was paralyzed, but because she was interested. (78)

The emotional boundaries that Sula has erected to protect herself from psychic pain are the only boundaries she observes. They are so steep that, with the exception of her feelings for Nel and later for Ajax, they amount to almost total alienation of affect. She sleeps with her best friend's husband because, like a child, she acts purely on her own desires without regard for others. Besides, Hannah had taught her that sex was a simple, "unremarkable" act of pleasure (98); finally, Sula recognizes no boundaries with Nel.

> She had clung to Nel as the closest thing to both an other and a self. . . . She had no thought at all of causing Nel pain. . . . They had always shared the affection of other people (119).

When Nel finally confronts her, twenty-five years after the fact, Sula is unrepentant and genuinely perplexed, as though *she* were the injured party. "I didn't kill him, I just fucked him. If we were such good friends, how come you couldn't get over it?" (145).

Sula's callousness is neither intentional nor malicious. Under severe emotional handicap, she is simply trying, as she tells Eva, "to make myself"; but she "had no center, no speck around which to grow . . . no ego" (119). Given her parental disinterest, her only source of affirmation early on would have come from others among whom she lived. While it is arguably not the responsibility of the community to provide intimate nurturing to its young, the African proverb that "it takes a village to raise a child" is clearly applicable here. Communal support and acceptance, rather than censure, might have contributed in some small way to Sula's emotional needs. By scapegoating her, the community fails to truly *learn* from her, although she is the catalyst for a good deal of posturing: Teapot's run-in with Sula prompts his abusive mother to become "devoted . . . sober, clean and industrious"; Sula's indiscriminate use of the men in the community causes the women to "cherish their men more [to soothe] the pride and vanity Sula had bruised" (115).

> Once the source of their personal misfortune was identified, they had leave to protect and love one another. They began to cherish their husbands and wives, protect their children, repair their homes and in general band together against the devil in their midst. (117–18)

In short, the community becomes virtuous only to the extent that it perceives Sula to be wicked; it exercises virtue not for its own sake but to justify its assessment of Sula as outlaw. Sula's influence has no lasting effect, for once she dies, "the tension is gone," and the residents fall back into their old ways (153).

Lost opportunities on both sides. Sula's self-styled "experimental life" (118) has caused untold distress, but that life might have been both enriched *by* and instructive *to* her community had the Bottom and Sula but taken note of one another's needs and gifts. Nel, for one, is moved to reassess her own "tiny life" by Sula's eternally resolute dying words: "Me, I'm going down like one of those redwoods. I sure did live in this world" (143).

## Too Thick

One can barely approach the surface of a text as dense and deep as *Beloved* in one essay; there is room here only to sketch a brief rendering of Sethe as outlaw in her Ohio community of ex-slaves. The irony of her case, especially in view of the two prior profiles, is that it is her *provision* of mother love that violates community ethos. While Pecola and Sula both suffer a damaging lack of maternal nurturing, Sethe fiercely embraces her children, her arms the motherwings with which she would shield them against pain and harm. The community's disapproval of her parenting signifies not a lack of humanity but communal reconfigurations of family values necessitated by the extreme circumstances of postslavery life in America.

The incalculable effects of slavery—and the rampant racism that succeeded it—on the African American family and community cannot be overstated. The fragmentation of both units after the Civil War is graphically depicted in *Beloved:*

> Odd clusters and strays of negroes wandered the back roads and cowpaths from Schenectady to Jackson. Dazed but insistent, they searched each other out for word of a cousin, an aunt, a friend. . . . configurations and blends of families of women and children, while elsewhere, solitary, hunted and hunting for, were men, men, men. . . . so stunned, or hungry, or tired or bereft it was a wonder they recalled or said anything. . . . Move. Walk. Run. Hide. Steal and move on. (52–53, 66)

That such extreme physical displacement would find its psychic counterpart in the mind of the newly freed slave is inevitable; in fact, a major concern for Morrison in penning the novel was to probe the "severe fragmentation of the self"[4] that characterized slave culture. Slavery was an institution *devised,* it seems, to breed insanity, if not severely damaged egos: at Sweet Home Plantation, Baby Suggs locates her sadness "at her center, the desolated center where the self that was no self made its home" (140). Given their extraordinary situation how, then, would the nearly and newly freed construct new lives, new families, new communities? *Beloved* explores this question in exquisite detail, with great sensitivity to the subtleties of the psychic processes of a beleaguered people. The answer, in short, is that they survive largely by constructing powerful defense mechanisms —repression, denial, isolation, and alienation of affect.

In Ohio, Sethe's mother-in-law, Baby Suggs, is spiritual leader in the community to which Sethe flees with her four children, including a newborn, after escaping from slavery. But freedom is an elusive concept to a people who have lived a lifetime in bondage. They are severely compromised not only by the laws and practices of the land but also by the awful experience of slavery itself, which has resulted in a psychological enslavement that persists long after Emancipation. For these reasons, Ella, like Baby Suggs, finds little improvement in her circumstances: "Slave life; freed life—every day was a test and a trial" (256).

Sethe's warm welcome into the community does not prepare her for the censure she will soon experience by collective decree.

> . . . twenty-eight days of having women friends, a mother-in-law, and all her children together; of being part of a neighborhood; of, in fact, having neighbors at all to call her own . . . twenty-eight happy days . . . twenty-eight days of unslaved life. . . . Days of healing, ease and real-talk. Days of company . . . of feeling their fun and sorrow along with her own, which made it better. One taught her the alphabet; another a stitch. All taught her how it felt to wake up at dawn and *decide* what to do with the day. (173, 95)

The level at which they "decide what to do with the day," however, is largely defined by their history. These newly freed, having emerged from a culture defined by privation, separation, pain, and loss, decide only on safe bets and sure things. They are better prepared for death than for life, more familiar with lacks than with endowments, finer versed in reacting than in acting. Baby Suggs, like others, had even initially resisted emancipation: "What does a sixty-odd-year-old woman who walks like a three-legged dog need freedom for?" (141).

In the central, stunning scene of the novel, Sethe kills her daughter Beloved when the slavemaster she had eluded in Kentucky tracks her down in Ohio. The murder, for which she is tried (and pardoned under abolitionist pressure), is not what alienates her from her new community; instead, the community condemns the perceived presumption and audacity that *enable* such conduct. Proactive behavior that calls attention to the community— whatever its nature—suggests unacceptable passion, a lack of control; even desperate measures taken to save a child from slavery indicate an excessive and inappropriate attachment to the child. The residents are of one mind with regard to its ruling imperative: one must observe restraint in all things."'Everything depends on knowing how much,' [Baby Suggs] said, and 'Good is knowing when to stop' " (87). Clearly Sethe who, given time, would have killed all four of her children, does not know when to stop.

So deeply have the other slaves and ex-slaves ingrained self-imposed prohibitions that they are able to rationalize them in philosophical, almost cavalier, fashion, concealing the history of anguish and defeat that underlies their expression. Sixo stops speaking English because "there was no future in it" (25); "Paul D had only begun" when he stopped talking. "Just as well" (72); Sethe recalls her mother's hanging as "something she had forgotten she knew" (61). In no other instance is such apparent detachment more remarkable, however, than with interpersonal relationships, especially between mothers and their children. Ella, a highly regarded voice in the community, counsels Sethe, who, holding one-day-old Denver in her arms, frets over her baby's chances for survival: "If anybody was to ask me I'd say, 'Don't love nothing.' " Sethe's declaration that she "wouldn't draw breath without [her] children," so alarms Baby Suggs that she "got down on her knees to beg God's pardon for [Sethe]" (203). Paul D's attitude follows suit.

> Risky, thought Paul D, very risky. For a used-to-be slave woman to love anything that much is dangerous, especially if it is her children she had settled on to love. (45)

Paul D and Baby Suggs are eloquent on the cause behind the effect of the emotional distance that slaves and ex-slaves maintain from others, including their children; their almost indifferent tone signals the power of the coping mechanism at work:

> The best thing, he knew, is to love just a little bit. Everything, just a little bit, so when they broke its back, or shoved it in a croaker sack, well, maybe you'd have a little love left over for the next one. (45)

> The last of [Baby Suggs'] children . . . she barely glanced at when he was born because it wasn't worth the trouble to try to learn features you would never see change into adulthood anyway. Seven times she had done that; held a little foot; examined the fat fingertips. . . . All seven are gone or dead. What would be the point of looking too hard at that youngest one? (139)

The sole exception to the communal ban against excess is the religious service that Baby Suggs, "with her great heart," leads in the Clearing every Saturday afternoon. All boundaries are relaxed on this ritual ground—children are welcomed, men and women are encouraged to laugh, to dance, to cry, to shout, to love—openly and joyfully. Outside this sacred space, however, all such behavior is firmly checked.

Sethe is already different from the others. After a brief month of freedom, she has found the answer that they still seek. "[S]he had claimed herself. Freeing yourself was one thing; claiming ownership of that freed self was another" (95). Her mother's example and her slave career are largely responsible for her singular nature. On the one hand, painful memories of the plantation fields that had claimed all her mother's time and attention inspires Sethe to love her children without restraint.

> Sethe lay in bed under, around, over, among but especially with them all. . . . Sethe's laugh of delight. . . . She kept kissing them . . . it was the boys who decided enough was enough. . . . (93)

On the other hand, it is not incidental that Sethe's mother, who was hanged for insubordination, "used different words" from the other slaves and that Nan—who spoke that same language—had come to America with Sethe's mother "from the sea" (63). Sethe's mother recalls the folktale "All God's Chillen Had Wings" wherein the most recently enslaved Africans remained closest to their culture and were thus the strongest and most powerful—the ones who were able to fly away from bondage.[5] When Sethe arrives at Sweet Home Plantation at age thirteen, she is "already iron-eyed" (10), her mutinous spirit reflected in the windows to her soul. Also, her Sweet Home experience is an uncommon one for a slave woman in at least two respects: her family unit remains intact, and she is not routinely sexually abused.

> Sethe had the amazing luck of six whole years of marriage to [Halle] who had fathered every one of their children. A blessing she was reckless enough to take for granted. . . . (23)

These small mercies have enabled her to express emotion openly. When Paul D warns that her love is "too thick," she counters, "Love is or it ain't. Thin love ain't love at all" (164).

Having learned in slavery to temper, but not to repress, feelings, Sethe is unable to exercise even temperance in times of desperation. As Schoolteacher rides up to reclaim Sethe's family into slavery, she does not think but instead acts upon pure impulse. "She saw them coming and recognized schoolteacher's hat. . . . And if she thought anything, it was No. No. Nono.

Nonono. Simple. She just flew." Sethe's intent is not to kill her children but to gather them "through the veil ... where they would be safe" (163). Firmly believing that "nothing ever dies" (36), her conviction overpowers the apparent contradiction in her reasoning: "If I hadn't killed [Beloved] she would have died and that is something that I could not bear to happen to her" (200).

The community, however, sees in Sethe a dangerously prideful woman who presumes to circumvent communal law, behaving like a hysterical mother in her excessive attachment to her children. She achieves outlaw status not only by the killing but by placing herself, like Sula, above the need for community authorization and support. "Just about everybody in town was longing for Sethe to come on difficult times. Her outrageous claims, her self-sufficiency seemed to demand it" (170). The community is pitiless and its censure is total, isolating Sethe completely for eighteen years and punctuating her life with a catalog of lacks. Paul D describes her as a woman "junkheaped for the third time because she loved her children" (174).

Even given its interdiction against excess, the "shunning" imposed upon Sethe and her family by the community is, ironically, excessive, and it puts into serious question the validity of group practice. Further, the issue of communal creditability involves behavior even more complex than its response to Beloved's murder: unacknowledged is its direct complicity in the tragedy itself. On that fateful twenty-eighth day of Sethe's freedom, a totally spontaneous gesture on Baby Suggs's part had gradually developed into a communitywide celebration marked by unrestrained indulgence. This inexcusable lapse breeds intense guilt the next morning in the celebrants, who blame Baby Suggs.

> [The house at] 124, rocking with laughter, goodwill and food for ninety, made them angry. Too much, they thought ... ice and sugar, batter bread, bread pudding, raised bread, shortbread—it made them mad. (137)

> She got proud and let herself be overwhelmed by the sight of her daughter-in-law and Halle's children ... and have a celebration of blackberries that put Christmas to shame. Now she stood in the garden smelling disapproval, feeling a dark and coming thing. ... (147)

Ostensibly, the dark thing that Baby Suggs senses is Schoolteacher closing in on "his" escaped slaves; subtextually, the dark thing is the coldheartedness that overwhelms the community after the party. The result is imposed silence on the neighborhood pipeline so that witnesses to the slaveowner's approach the morning after the party deliberately withhold that information, thereby depriving Sethe of crucial advance warning and forcing her to act with no support and no time to consider her options.

Instructive to contemporary communities is the fact that in *Beloved*, eighteen years after the killing, both Sethe and her community are provided the opportunity to reconsider their behaviors, replay their scenes, and find redemption in mutual strength, support, and caring. When the reincarnated Beloved reenters Sethe's life, the community's formerly deaf ear becomes attuned to the needs and the threat facing one of its own. "Maybe they were sorry for Denver. Or for Sethe. Maybe they were sorry for the years of their own disdain" (249). Gifts of food begin to appear at the door, small conversations take place, and when the crisis comes, they are ready—this time—to stand with the residents of 124.

> Now [Sethe] is running into the faces of the people out there. . . . They make a hill. A hill of black people. . . . (262)

At this moment, in a bizarre scene of déjà vu, Sethe mistakes a sympathetic abolitionist for the evil Schoolteacher of eighteen years ago and rushes to attack him, inadvertently indicating how she would respond to a threat on her family's freedom if given a second chance. Shored up by community, Sethe can also begin to forgive herself and to learn that she need not fight the world alone. Sethe's validation of emotional expression forces Paul D to realize that he and the others had "been loving small and in secret," and that Sethe had been telling him all along that "to get to a place where you could love anything you chose—not to need permission for desire—well now, *that* was freedom" (221, 163).

The outlaw women in Morrison's texts exist outside the boundaries of community ethos for reasons that, for the most part, compromise the moral and cultural integrity of the collective. Pecola is ostracized simply because she is black and vulnerable; Sula is the quintessential nonconformist whose self-expression knows no boundaries; Sethe dares to love. Certainly, the issues are not so simple as this, and the outlaws are not merely saintly, one-dimensional figures. Their flaws, however, help to illuminate the power of cultural groundedness and the potential of mutual contributions between the individual and the collective to the other's positive growth and development. Morrison strikes at the very core of self-limiting practices and emphatically points to the nature of nurturing and of the environment to substantiate the notion that it *does* take an entire village, and a healthy one at that, to raise a child.

# References

1. Michael Awkward, *Inspiriting Influences: Tradition, Revision, and Afro-American Women's Novels.* (New York: Columbia University Press, 1989), 79.

2. W.E.B. DuBois, *The Souls of Black Folk.* (New York: Signet Books, 1969), 45.

3. Roberta Rubenstein, *Boundaries of the Self: Gender, Culture, Fiction.* (Urbana: University of Illinois Press, 1990), 126.

4. Toni Morrison, "Unspeakable Things Unspoken: The Afro-American Presence in American Literature," *Michigan Quarterly Review* 28, no. 1 (Winter 1989): 16.

5. See, for example, the version cited in *Crossing the Danger Water: Three Hundred Years of African-American Writing,* ed. Deirdre Mullane. (New York: Anchor Books, 1993).

# 6

# Bessie Head

## The Idealist

*Owen G. Mordaunt*

When one considers the circumstances of Bessie Head's birth and life (a life punctuated with bouts of deep depression), one cannot help but marvel at the genius of this self-made writer. Her determination to write against all odds (her alienation, her fragmented and somewhat neurotic personality, and her search for an identity as a mixed-race person in Africa) is intriguing. She lived in her own world of the intellect, and what went on in this world was given expression in her writing. Her social ecology, individuality (and alienation), exposure to religion (both Christianity and Hinduism), and determination to write helped shape her personality and philosophy of life and to propel her to produce novels, works of short fiction, and articles of literary value. Her works rank her quite highly on the scale of African writers. Bessie was also able to work in some capacity with the poor of this world, for whom she was concerned.

This paper highlights biographical information on Bessie Head from the standpoint of her social ecology and of the pivotal issues that nagged at her for the duration of her life. It seems appropriate to borrow Craig MacKenzie's notion of the three major periods of her life: "her early life in South Africa (1937–1964), her period of exile in Botswana (1979–1986, and . . . her life as a Botswana citizen (1979–1986)."[1] It is the first period of her life that I consider of utmost importance for getting at Head's roots and for understanding of her works. In the following pages, the latter two periods are sketched, followed by a survey of Head's works and a discussion of the sociopsychological issues that she had to contend with.

## Early Life in South Africa (1937–1964)

Background information relevant to Bessie Head is pertinent, particularly for the reader who is unfamiliar with her early life. She was born Bessie Amelia Emery in 1937 in Pietermaritzburg, Natal, South Africa, of mixed parentage. She was sent to foster care, where she lived until age thirteen. She considered her foster parents to be her parents, but 1950 she was moved from the foster home and placed in the custody of St. Monica's Home, an Anglican mission school for colored (mixed-race) girls located in Durban, Natal. Bessie had been raised a Catholic, so it must have been confusing to be torn away from her "mother" and the religion she had grown up with. She lived at the mission until she was eighteen years old. The missionaries at St. Monica's were strict but instilled discipline and character in the girls and also gave them the best education possible. Miss Cadmore, in particular, with her "off-beat sense of humour, her unconventionality, her earthiness and common sense" left a lasting impression on Bessie.[2] Bessie had craved books as a child growing up in the foster home, but here she had books at her disposal. She not only read everything in the school library, including Plato, but also began reading Margaret Cadmore's books and anything she requested from private libraries. And with Miss Cadmore's coaching, she was helped to understand the poet W.B. Yeats.[3]

While staying at the mission, Bessie Emery attended Umbilo Road High School where she completed tenth grade (junior certificate) and two years of teacher training as an elementary school teacher. From 1956 to 1959, she worked as a teacher. It was during her teaching stint that she began to realize how protected she had been and how her people were suffering from South Africa's racial discrimination. Several people from Bessie's circle of contacts distrusted the white man, and a small number "became active in the resistance movement," but Bessie was not an active participant, so she "could not really identify with this cause."[4]

For some reason or other, Bessie had begun to struggle with religion, especially when she learned from the indiscreet Miss Farmer something about her true origins: her foster mother was not her real mother and her real mother was a white woman. This revelation was a traumatic experience for Bessie, who had emotionally belonged to Nellie Heathcote, her foster mother. In fact "this event shaped and coloured the rest of Bessie Emery's life. Its emotional impact can only be imagined, never assessed."[5] Bessie rejected the religion represented by Miss Farmer but never renounced Catholicism even though she never again set her foot in a Christian church. Years later, she told her son that when she died, he should contact a Roman Catholic priest, something he did. When she died at the age of forty-nine in 1986, both an Anglican and Roman Catholic priest officiated at her funeral.[6]

After Bessie settled into her teaching job, she found she had no social life, and the time away from school was dull. To fill the void, she chose books. But she could not afford to buy them (at the mission, she had been able to borrow them). The Durban municipal library was accessible only to "whites." She had heard of the M. L. Sultan Library, a library donated to Indians by one of their wealthy merchants, which was open to anybody interested in reading. This library had large sections devoted to Hinduism. Her curiosity drew her to Hindu literature, and she became attracted to the all-encompassing philosophy that sets Hinduism apart from the somewhat narrow perspective of Christianity. Hinduism—its philosophy, rather than its ritual—appealed to her strong, individualistic nature because it was tolerant of other religions and did not compel adherents to adopt any particular rites and sacraments. She became particularly inspired by Mohandas K. Gandhi and what he stood for, nonviolent resistance to racial discrimination. (Gandhi had himself lived in South Africa from 1893 to 1915.) Eilersen reports that Bessie "assimilated especially Hinduism's pantheistic concepts and the idea of the sanctity of the common man, and in the years to come gradually gave them her own touch."[7] In the process of learning about this new religion, she befriended an ascetic follower of Ramakrishna, one of the leading Hindu teachers of the nineteenth century, whose main emphasis was on mysticism and a form of theocracy. Later she became a member of the Hindu sect.

Hinduism is an amorphous body of beliefs, philosophies, and values, and does not have a central authority, a single God, but rather acknowledges many gods. Samovar and Porter outline the central concepts of Hinduism's view of the world and of individual values and behavior:

> First intellect is subordinated to intuition. Truth does not come to the individual; it really resides within each of us. Second, dogma is subordinated to experience. One cannot be told about God; one must experience God. Third, outward expression is subordinated to inward realization. Communication with God cannot take place through outward expression; it must occur through internal realization of the nature of God. Fourth, the world is an illusion because nothing is permanent. All nature, including humankind, is in a constant cycle of birth, death, rebirth, and reincarnation and experience an internal state of bliss called *Nirvana*. One achieves Nirvana by leading a good life so one can achieve a higher spiritual status in the next life. The more advanced one's spiritual life, the closer one is to Nirvana. The path to a spiritual life, and therefore Nirvana, is meditation. The Hindu holds materialism in abeyance and instead practices introspection. *Karma* is the link that ties a person's acts in one life to the next life. Fatalism becomes important as past lives influence each new life.[8]

For Bessie, absorbing this complex religion was so rapid and overwhelming that she almost had a nervous breakdown. She abandoned Hinduism for a while.

In her disturbed mental state her teaching suffered; discipline became a problem, and going to school was no longer an enthusiastic experience but a burden. As a result, she resigned from teaching in June 1958 at the age of twenty-one. She left Durban in 1959 for Cape Town to work as a journalist for *Drum* magazine. There, she gained experience in freelance reporting and in writing articles, particularly about women and children, and short stories (which local newspapers and *The Readers' Digest* would not publish).

It was in Cape Town that Bessie became aware of the plight of the poor—those colored (mixed-race) people with which she, being herself destitute, identified. She observed a type of caste system among coloreds: the upper class, fair skinned and cultured; the middle class; the factory workers; and the poverty-stricken, who had degenerated morally. She felt she belonged to the lowest class. The upper class she considered snobs, but she considered herself "a mental snob" because she withdrew from the world of snobs into the "world of the intellect."[9] Her concern for the poor and downtrodden continued to be part of her life, even after she left South Africa and settled in Botswana.

In April 1959, Bessie moved to Johannesburg and worked as a columnist for *Home Post,* a tabloid supplement of the *Golden City Post* with a black readership. While in Johannesburg, Bessie got to know some reputable African journalists: Can Themba, Lewis Nkosi, and Dennis Brutus. More significantly, she became a supporter of the Pan-Africanist Congress with Robert Sobukwe as its leader. She was deeply impressed by Sobukwe and was a witness to his arrest in 1959. For the first time Bessie became involved in politics and this gave her a sense of belonging. As with Hinduism, it was the philosophy behind the Africanist concept that attracted her, particularly the ideas from George Padmore's writings. Padmore was an Africanist born in Trinidad and educated in the United States, who joined the Communist Party and was interested in the struggle for Africa. Bessie held so fiercely to her Africanist views that she made furious outbursts if these views were challenged.[10]

Bessie's departure from Johannesburg in 1960 was due to a unfortunate experience. Following a violent sexual encounter with an acquaintance, she took an overdose of sleeping tablets and ended up in the hospital. This experience and a subsequent similar experience when she moved to Botswana created a distrust of African men, and this feeling about men cropped up in her works. She did, however, prefer the company of men who were intellectually inclined. It was to Cape Town that she returned after being in the hospital—and to her job on the *Golden City Post.* She was, in a way, going back home—while in Johannesburg she had never forgotten Cape Town; she had even attempted to write a play based on District Six, the slum in which she had lived and for whose citizens she had a great concern. Her play, however, never went beyond the draft stage. The impact of stress and pressure that Bessie Head had suffered in Johannesburg had lasting effects on her health and work performance when she resided in Cape Town.

After recovering from the nervous breakdown, Bessie sought friends and became part of a circle of writers and political activists. Her ideas were still very strong pro-Africanist, and in 1961 at the age of twenty-four, she married Harold Head, a freelance journalist who shared her political views. At this time, she expressed her hatred for white people in a poem titled "Things I Don't Like," which was published in the *New African* in July 1962.[11] Her poem was about "victimization" and "oppression." Bessie and Harold lived in District Six where she found love and warmth, despite the conditions, and a sense of belonging. Residents were hospitable and welcomed strangers, but she observed that they were uncommitted to the struggle for freedom and were afraid of the oppressor because they were closer to him and really understood the "ruthless nature of his power." They accepted their fate passively. Their outlet for the "hidden rage and frustration" was to drink and to commit acts of violence on each other.[12] Notwithstanding the feelings she had for these people, Bessie was a veritable outsider and observer.

The fact that politically active acquaintances and friends were being arrested by the South African authorities made Bessie increasingly irate at whites. In a published letter to Dennis Brutus, her sentiment is clear: "Every white face that you see passing by churns you up till you just cry to be delivered from this unceasing torment of hate, hate, hate."[13] Added to this was her failing marriage to Harold Head. Not much is known about her marriage and the cause of the breakdown. By 1964 she was so unhappy that she was determined to leave the country for a free African country where she would find new inspiration writing. With the help of a friend, she was able to obtain an exit permit to Botswana (known as Bechuanaland at that time) to work as a teacher in village called Serowe. She and her two-year-old son "embarked on the most significant journey of Bessie's life."[14]

## Period of Exile in Botswana (1964–1979)

Bessie's departure from South Africa was a revolution in her life. In Botswana she could begin a new life, though as a refugee from South Africa, she was not officially welcome. Her troubles were not over. In 1969 she was stricken with a long and unnerving nervous breakdown. This incident is chronicled in her autobiographical third novel *A Question of Power*.[15] She was even committed to a psychiatric clinic. She did recover. Bessie's problem may have been a congenital one since her birth mother appears to have been afflicted by a progressive psychosis, and Bessie was herself always conscious of the tenuousness of her mental balance.

Moving from a city in South Africa to a remote African village was itself a tremendous adjustment: adapting to a teaching job; getting acclimatized to the living conditions and the climate of Serowe; and finding ways of relating to the inhabitants, both native and foreign. Tshekedi Memorial School was poorly equipped, and the students were starved. The people and Bessie were poor, which perhaps helped her identify with them. She was not on social terms with the tribal elite, who wielded control over the people, yet she was impressed by some of them. As she was not successful as a teacher, her inadequacy affected her relationship with the villagers. She was more of a journalist than an instructor. Botswana, however, did provide some stability for her, some sense of belonging. The country to a great extent provided a sanctuary for her and a resource for her writing. Some years later she wrote: "What have I said about the people of a free land, who borrowed their clothes, their goats, their successes and sunspots for my books?"[16]

## Life as a Botswana Citizen (1979–1986)

This period begins with Bessie Head being granted Botswanan citizenship. Her tenuous refugee status had lasted for fifteen years. She had applied in 1977 for citizenship and had been turned down, but she never reactivated her application. This rejection exacerbated the alienation she had felt as a stateless person. The granting of citizenship allowed her to travel on a Botswana passport to Germany in 1979 for the Africa Festival as a Botswana writer with international recognition. In 1982, she was a guest lecturer in Gaborone, Botswana's capital city, as well as a participant in a book-signing at an official display on "Writers of Botswana."

This phase of her life was the crowning point, when she became known both locally and abroad and could reflect on what she had accomplished with meaningful perspective. Craig MacKenzie—in the introduction to *A Woman Home*—writes:

> The publication of her eulogistic social history *Serowe: Village of Rain and Wind* in 1981 and her 'major obsession, the Khama novel' *A Bewitched Crossroad* in 1984 . . . was the culmination of a long hard battle for acceptance. Her death in 1986 was premature, a foreshortening of what could

otherwise have been a long and rewarding relationship as a citizen with her adoptive country Botswana.[17]

Commenting on her last novel, Bessie Head says:

> I am trying to gather several threads together to create a feeling of continuity in my work. . . to finally record some of the kind of welding I felt coming to a country like Botswana. It was like finding roots and these roots really go back, for me, to the old tribal way of life and its slow courtesies. . . . So this final work I am on will have the effect of rounding off my Southern African experience. I think I will then let it fall asleep in my mind.[18]

Did Bessie have a premonition of her impending demise?

## Bessie Head's Works

Bessie Head published six full-length works and about twenty-five short stories during her short life. Most of what she wrote relates to her years in Botswana. Her three excellent novels *When Rain Clouds Gather,*[19] *Maru,*[20] and *A Question of Power*[21] form "something like a trilogy."[22] *When Rain Clouds Gather* (1969), her first novel, is based on her stint as a refugee living at the Bamangwato Development Association Farm at Radisele, about eighty kilometers south of Serowe. This novel was well received by critics in the United States and England. Her second novel, *Maru,* was considered even better than her first. Her third novel, *A Question of Power,* considered her greatest work by critics today, was received with mixed reactions when it was first published. It is a very complex work, moving subtly from the theme of alienation to that of commitment. *A Question of Power* portrays the tormented protagonist, Elizabeth, who is facing Good and Evil, God and the Devil, and experiencing a nervous breakdown. These three novels are autobiographical on the surface, though this may not be obvious to most readers.

Bessie's short stories appeared as *The Collector of Treasures* in 1977.[23] In this anthology ordinary village women and their problems are the focus, and communal life, togetherness, and various customs and practices are touched upon. When this anthology was published, Bessie had already begun work on her novel of social history, *Serowe: Village of the Rain Wind,* which finally was published in 1981.[24] The novel is a reconstruction of the history of Serowe in an engaging way, and is based on interviews with people of different age groups and occupations relevant to oral tradition and recollections. *A Bewitched Crossroad*[25] is a historical novel that has connections with preceding ones. African history is viewed from a black perspective and focuses on the Bamangwato clan and its renowned leader, Khama III, who lived and died in Serowe and was buried with his descendants, including his grandson, Seretse Khama. *A Woman Alone,*[26] *Tales of Tenderness and Power,*[27] *A Gesture of Belonging: Letters from Bessie Head, 1965–1979,*[28] and *The Cardinals*[29] were published posthumously. *The Cardinals,* a novella, written South Africa during 1961–1962 is also autobiographical and dwells mainly on Bessie's state of mind at the time. Bessie is presenting a perspective of herself (portrayed as Mouse) and handles being illegitimate, the lack of a father figure, incest, and insanity. The most potent theme of the book is Mouse's fight to become literate and then to master the art of writing.

## Some Sociopsychological Considerations

The driving force behind a writer's success can be both internal and external. In Bessie Head's case, something internal seemed to compel her to write even under extremely difficult circumstances; even mental depression could not halt the indomitable Bessie Head. Writing for Bessie was connected with the world of the intellect. She stated:

> I view my own activity as a writer as a kind of participation in the thought of the whole world. No other occupation provided for such an international outlook as writing. I have my African side but I am also very much an international kind of person.[30]

When asked how one becomes a writer, Bessie responded by saying that "writing first begins with love of reading and a love of books, a feeling for all the magic and wonder that can be communicated through books."[31] Physical conditions for writing in Botswana were far from adequate: poor lighting (she used candles in Serowe), a rickety typewriter, physical (and certainly mental) discomfort, but she was committed to expressing her thoughts on paper.

It is clear from her writings that Bessie had a keen sense of observation. Her reconstruction of village life—its traditions and customs, the power of its traditional chiefs, the plight of its poor and downtrodden, its discrimination against women, and the village struggle to eke out a living in an arid part of the world—is remarkable. Her own struggles and alienation are also woven into this tapestry of her life. In his introduction to *A Woman Alone,* MacKenzie writes:

> For in the process of unraveling the strands of her anguished life story one encounters instances of immense suffering and privation, crippling alien-

ation, and perhaps most of all, personal confusion. It is this personal confusion (no doubt wrought by the bureaucratic callousness of a regime that legislates against people of colour) that is at the centre of Bessie Head's troubled life.[32]

One issue, then, at the root of Bessie's problems is South Africa's apartheid and all it entails. Her sensitivity to racial discrimination in South Africa affected her greatly in Botswana as well, for she felt prejudiced against because she was of mixed origins and classified as a *Masarwa,* or Bushman, a demeaning designation applied to the San people. In fact many aspects of Bessie's life are incorporated into her novel *Maru,* where she is represented by one of the main characters, Margaret.

As alluded to earlier, Bessie's awareness of oppression and the suffering of the poor makes such an impact on her on her arrival in Botswana that she cannot help but notice the situation and living condition of the downtrodden. In her three novels—*When Rain Clouds Gather, Maru,* and *A Question of Power*—the novelist condemns the misuse of power by any individual or group. The misuse of power by racists in South Africa or any other bigots elsewhere can be catastrophic.[33] In Botswana it is the powerful chiefs and those in collusion with them who exert power and authority over others. The novelist considers the psychological basis for power—the world is dominated by people hungry for political ascendancy—but also "looks ahead to the future to the ultimate survival of the oppressed"[34] To implement her philanthropic ideas, the writer worked at the Bamangwato Development Farm to help improve the lot of the destitute. Later she took a course in agriculture so that she could offer professional expertise. Her involvement with agriculture, even though fulfilling, was short-lived. An individualistic person like Bessie just could not work in cooperation with other people. Her expertise was more intellectual than practical; the product of this skill is her novel *When Rain Clouds Gather.* This work is a reflection on changes in traditional family patterns, crop production, how political status affects the lives of people, particularly women, and the traditional distribution of power.

Religion played a role in Bessie's life—as evidenced by her constant references to it. As a child she was steeped in Christianity, a religion she turned her back on quite early in her life, but its symbolism and ideas never left her thoughts. Her embracing of Hinduism added a new and perhaps meaningful dimension to her life. The practice of Hinduism was not her forte, but the philosophical pursuit of it appealed to her. Her belief in reincarnation helped her to somewhat focus on a purpose for her life—she felt she was created for something. Moreover, Hinduism was a religion that incorporated everybody and gave each person a status in this world. Hinduism broadened her perspective on who God is, "people who are holy to each other." Bessie believed that humankind would one day be "ruled by men who are God and not greedy, power-hungry politicians . . . not the effort of a single man but a collaboration of many great minds in order that integrity be established in the affairs of men [and] only then can the resources of the earth be cared for and shared in an equitable way among all mankind."[35] A parallel exists between some Hindu concepts and what apparently attracted her to Robert Sobukwe's Pan-Africanist Congress: Sobukwe affirmed her Blackness. But politics in a practical sense is something Bessie avoided both personally and in her work. She considered her world "a quiet backwater where ideas and inventions dominate and where people have time to love each other."[36]

Many more ideas on Bessie Head, her life, and her works can be explored, and I anticipate a growing interest in her as her life and works touch many people. She definitely will enhance Botswana's reputation and African literature generally. Much credit is due to all those people and publishers, some of whom were friends, acquaintances, and researchers who brought her works to light.

## References

1. Bessie Head, *A Woman Alone: Autobiographical Writings,* ed. Craig MacKenzie (Oxford: Heinemann, 1990) p. x.

2. Gillian Stead Eilersen, *Bessie Head—Thunder Behind Her Ears* (Portsmouth, NH: Heinemann, 1995) p. 30.

3. Ibid., 30.

4. Ibid., 32.

5. Ibid., 25.

6. Ibid., 293.

7. Ibid., 35.

8. Larry Samovar and Richard Porter, *Communication Between Cultures* (Belmont CA: Wadsworth, 1991) p. 123.

9. Eilersen, p. 40.

10. Bessie Head, *A Gesture of Belonging: Letters from Bessie Head, 1965–1979,* ed. Randolph Vigne (London: SA Writers; Portsmouth NH: Heinemann; Johannesburg: Witwatersrand UP, 1991) p. 2.

11. Bessie Head, "Things I Don't Like." *New African* 1, no. 7 (1962): 10.

12. Head, *A Woman Alone,* pp. 9–13.

13. Bessie Head, "Letter from South Africa: For a Friend,'D.B.'" *Transition* 3, no. 11 (1963): 40.

14. Eilersen, p. 62.

15. Bessie Head, *A Question of Power* (Oxford: Heinemann, 1974).

16. Head, *A Woman Alone,* p. 101.

17. Ibid., p. xii.

18. Linda Susan Beard, "Bessie Head, Cape Gooseberry and the question of power," *ALA Bulletin* 12, no. 2 (1986): 41.

19. Bessie Head, *When Rain Clouds Gather,* (Oxford: Heinemann, 1971).

20. Bessie Head, *Maru* (Oxford: Heinemann, 1971).

21. Head, *A Question of Power.*

22. Oladele Taiwo, *Female Novelists in Modern Africa,* (London: Macmillan, 1984) p. 185.

23. Bessie Head, *The Collector of Treasures and Other Botswana Village Tales* (Oxford: Heinemann, 1977).

24. Bessie Head, *Serowe: Village of the Rain Wind* (Oxford: Heinemann, 1981).

25. Bessie Head, *A Bewitched Crossroad: An African Saga* (Johannesburg: Donker, 1984).

26. Head, *A Woman Alone.*

27. Bessie Head, *Tales of Tenderness and Power,* ed. Gillian Stead Eilersen (Oxford: Heinemann, 1989).

28. Head, *A Gesture of Belonging.*

29. Bessie Head, *The Cardinals, With Meditations and Short Stories,* ed. M.J. Daymond. (Oxford: Heinemann, 1993).

30. Head, *A Woman Alone,* p. 95.

31. Ibid., 93–94.

32. Head, *A Woman Alone,* p. ix.

33. Emmanuel Obiechina, "Victimization as a Theme," in *Language and Theme* (Washington, DC: Howard University Press, 1990) pp. 150–81.

34. Taiwo, p. 193.

35. Head, *A Woman Alone,* pp. 99–100.

36. Ibid., 97–98.

# 7

# Working toward the Betterment of the Community

## Elizabeth Ross Haynes

### *LaVerne Gyant*

*[I]t may be woman's privilege from her peculiar coign of vantage as a quiet observer, to whisper just the needed suggestion or the almost forgotten truth. The colored woman, then, should not be ignored because her bark is resting in the silent waters of the sheltered cove. . . . Her voice, too, has always been heard in a clear, unfaltering tone, ringing the changes on those deeper interests which make for permanent good. She is always sound and orthodox on questions affecting the well-being of her race.*
*—Anna Julia Cooper*, A Voice from the South *(1969)*

These words from Anna Julia Cooper can describe the life and work of Elizabeth Ross Haynes. Little is known about the woman who wrote the first major study on black domestic workers; who was the first Black to serve on the National Board of the Young Women's Christian Association (YWCA); who has helped us to see why black women's activism focuses on the linkage between social, politics, and economics; or who was considered one of the outstanding woman in race relations. Elizabeth Ross Haynes is a member of the "talented tenth" (Bardolph 1959). She is one of those invisible black women whose leadership during the early twentieth century had a major impact on the issues affecting black women today.

In Mount Willing, Lowndes County, Alabama, Elizabeth Ross was born to Henry Ross and Mary Carnes Ross, both former slaves. At the outbreak of the Civil War, her father ran away to join the Union Army. When Henry left the service, he used his savings to purchase a small plot of land in Alabama, which he increased to 1,500 acres after a decade of hard work. Recognizing that their daughter was bright, her parents had high aspirations and provided Elizabeth with the best educational opportunities they could. Upon graduation, she attended Alabama State University (where she was class valedictorian), Fisk University, and Columbia University, where she received a Master of Arts in sociology. In the process of completing her education, she also taught school in Alabama and Tennessee.

Little is known of when and how George Edmund Haynes and Elizabeth Ross met, but it is known that their careers and commitment to the betterment of humanity was unparalleled. They both attended Fisk University and attended summer school at the University of Chicago. He worked for the Young Men's Christian Association (YMCA) with black college students; she held a similar position with the YWCA. They both were committed to the ideal of interracial cooperation. George Edmund Haynes was cofounder and executive director of the National Urban League. He was recognized as one of the nation's most highly qualified social scientists (Blackwell and Janowitz 1974). Haynes gained this recognition because he had studied sociology at the University of Chicago, was a fellow at the New York Bureau of Social Research, graduated from the New York School of Philanthropy (the New School of Social Work), and was the first Black to receive a Ph.D. in sociology from Columbia University. While a fellow at the Bureau of Social Research, he completed his studies on the Negro migration and the conditions they faced in the North. Out of these studies came *The Negro at Work in New York City* (Haynes 1912).

The year 1910 was significant for two reasons. First, it was the year George and Elizabeth were married. The Haynes had one son, George Edmund Haynes. Second, Fisk established the first officially recognized department of sociology at a Black institution that year (Blackwell and Janowitz 1974; Richardson 1980). Haynes was hired to organize and head the department. During his tenure at Fisk, he made it possible for Fisk to become a major library resource for materials on the study of Blacks in the United States and taught one of the first systematic courses in Black history. Around 1918, Haynes was asked to serve as special assistant to the secretary of labor. In this position he was director of Negro Economics Division. Elizabeth served as his assistant director.

When they were married, Elizabeth no longer sought paid employment. Instead she served as consultant to various organizations and agencies and undertook volunteer work in social service, politics, and temperance. The Haynes later moved to New York City, where George worked as executive director of the National Urban League and as secretary of the Commission on Race Relations with the Federated Council of the Churches of Christ in America (the National Council of Churches); Elizabeth also served as an intern to the council for several years. Her other activities included being elected coleader of the Twenty-First Assembly District of New York, being superintendent of the juniors' department at Abyssinian Baptist Church, where she was a member, being secretary for the board of managers at the Adam Clayton Powell retirement home, being a member of the National Association of Colored Women and of the Alpha Kappa Alpha Sorority. She was appointed to the New York City Planning Commission by the mayor, served on the National Advisory Committee on Women's Participation in the 1939 World's Fair in New York, and supported the Emergency Committee to Save the Jewish People. As coleader of the twenty-first assembly, her duties covered employment, assisting the elderly, administering the soldiers' and widows' pensions, delinquency, zoning, and legislating. She was also a member of the Colored Division of the National Democratic Speakers' Bureau. In this position, she encouraged women not to accept subordinate roles in the party structure and to "aspire for political plums" (Bogin 1980, 325). As a member of the Harlem Better School Committee, she worked to upgrade the schools and library services and to integrate the nursing and social work staff in city hospitals.

How many black women today are members of the YWCA? How many are involved in the leadership of the organization? How many know about the Black women who were instrumental in the YWCA movement? Eva del Vakia Bowles, Juliette Derricote, Addie Waites Hunton, Lugenia Burns Hope, and Elizabeth Ross Haynes are only a few of the women who were involved in the movement. These women spoke out against the YWCA's segregated and racist policies and were instrumental in assisting its transition to being interracial.

Since the early nineteenth century the YWCA has been an important avenue for black women (Giddings 1984). Black women were interested in the YWCA because of its mission to educate young black women and provide them both with tools for survival in the city and a sense of the organization's Christian ethics and standards (Salem 1990). The first segregated YWCA was chartered in Dayton, Ohio, in 1893 (Giddings 1984; Salem 1990). This was the beginning of the colored branch of the YWCA, many of these branches were located in cities. At the same time, student Christian associations were organized on black colleges and universities. It was not until 1906 that the national board was formed and brought both the colored YWCA branches and the student Christian associations under their jurisdiction. Until that time the colored branches were operating autono-mously from the YWCA (Giddings 1984; Salem 1990). Under the jurisdic-tion of the national board, the colored branches and the student Christian associations could not be recognized without the approval of the local white branch. Members of black clubs and the colored branches reported to the national board about the prejudices and discrimination they encountered in local YWCAs. For example, when the Colored Women's Christian Associ-ation (CWCA) in St. Louis sought advice from the national board to start a branch, they sent Elizabeth to speak with the Central Y and to assist the YWCA in stimulating interest and pledges for the black branch. The Central Y feared that a black branch would overburden prospective donors and drain their potential resources, and because of the possibility of conflict between blacks and whites, it feared attendance of both races at regional conferences. Haynes advised them to recognized the work accomplished by the CWCA by making them a branch. The Central Y agreed to organize the branch while "reserving . . . the right of supervision . . . [of] financial and general management—and that a legal contract be made to that effect" (Hunter 1940, 90–91). This procedure was common between the local and black branches of the YWCA.

Upon the recommendation of Addie Waites Hunton, first black secretary and first paid black worker with the YWCA, the national board appointed Elizabeth Ross Haynes as national student secretary for the YWCA (Bogin 1980). As secretary (1908–1910), she traveled to various black colleges and universities, observing students' life on campus, and had supervisory respon-sibilities for the colored branches. In observing young women on campuses, she noted they "are being turned inward to their own beliefs and ideals, and outward to the part they can play in helping to better . . . social conditions" (Bogin 1980, 324). As supervisor, she found irregularities in program offer-ings, lack of coordination with the national board, and distrust between black and white women. As supervisor, Haynes assisted colored branches fundrais-ing, program planning, and developing educational and training programs. During her tenure as secretary, she submitted plans for the development of work among black women, chartered thirty-eight student organizations, and emphasized the social service of black women in organizing art and reading clubs, lodges, hospitals, and orphanages (Salem 1990).

Elizabeth continued to work with the YWCA until her marriage. However, she and Addie Hunton returned to work at the YWCA in 1911 and began to investigate city associations and managed to find volunteer secretaries for some of the local and colored branches. With the assistance of W.E.B DuBois and Haynes's husband, Hunton and Haynes were able to locate "college young [women]—fitted physically, spiritually as well as intellectually to be College

Secretary for the National Board of the YWCA" (Salem 1990, 131). When Hunton and Haynes left the YWCA the following year, they felt very positive about the "increased volunteer service . . . by our best educated young women, and larger facilities in buildings and equipment" (Hunton 1911, 17). Despite the leadership of these two women, representation on the board was difficult—but "Black women continued to organize both city and student associations as groups self-help efforts" (Salem 1990, 48).

Despite the reports by black women of prejudice and discrimination, the YWCA and other white organizations continued to encourage black women's clubs to join them in providing services and programs to the black community. For several years the YWCA and the National League for the Protection of Colored Women sought support from the National Association of Colored Women (NACW) in providing services to black women. At the NACW conference in Louisville, Elizabeth had hoped to convince the club women that the YWCA was trying to overcome some of its segregated policies. She noted that many of the black women's clubs were doing similar work without YWCA affiliation and cautioned them against using the name YWCA without meeting the requirements and urged them to follow the general guidelines and utilize the leadership training offered. Many of the club women were in agreement, but they did not forget about the "white control and racial segregation/separation policies of the two bodies" (Salem 1990, 49) and were not convinced of white women's dedication to cooperation and support. They also remembered the "importance of working for racial issues through the NACW" (Hunton 1911, 17). Even though they were in agreement with Elizabeth's argument, they were aware of and experienced the racial insensitivity of the white YWCA. It was not until 1912 that the NACW endorsed the work of the YWCA, and three years later the NACW agreed to cooperate with YWCA. The decision was based on the work of Eva del Vakia Bowles, director of the Colored Work Committee, who had increased the number of programs available for black women.

Elizabeth returned to work with the YWCA in 1922 when the Colored Work Committee was organized. She was later elected to the national board (1924–1934), where she helped develop the Industrial Division and worked with Bowles, Hope, Brown, and other women in the movement to integrate the YWCA. It was at the 1946 convention that the "Interracial Charter" was adopted by the YWCA. The charter called for interracial experiences and reorganization of the system. Dorothy Height was one of the key figures in providing educational programs during the transitional period.

In 1918 the Commission on Interracial Cooperation (CIC) was formed by white professional men who had worked or were interested in the area of race relations. They sought to study the conditions of Blacks and to learn what they wanted. By 1920 thirty-one black men had been hired by the CIC to organize and develop county committees (Neverdon-Morton 1989). Recognizing the lack of women's participation in the CIC, three white women established a framework to organize women who were interested in interracial cooperation. These women—Estelle Haskin, Mary de Bardelehen, and Mrs. Luke C. Johnson—sought support from black women and spoke at the 1920 meeting of the NACW. Mrs. Johnson was impressed by the women, "I saw colored women, graduates of great institutions of learning. I saw lawyers, doctors, poets, sculptors, and painters. I saw women of education, culture and refinement. I had lived in the South all my life, but didn't know such as these lived in the land" (Neverdon-Morton 1989, 228).

After meeting with Haskin and Johnson, Charlotte Hawkins Brown, Mary McLeod Bethune, Lugenia Burns Hope, Janie Porter Barnett, and others agreed to explore the possibility of planning joint activities. They drafted a statement about "Southern Negro women and race cooperation," which noted that all black women suffered from racial bias, addressed the problem of children who did not have adult supervision while parents worked, and suggested ways to improve education (Neverdon-Morton 1989). This statement was presented at the Women's Inter-Racial Conference in Memphis, Tennessee, in October 1920. Elizabeth Ross Haynes was one of four black women—the others being Jennie Moton, Charlotte Hawkins Brown, and Margaret Murray Washington—who spoke at the conference. Her speech was described as low keyed, analytical, and dramatic (Giddings 1984; Salem 1990). She focused on "Sojourner Truth and the humiliating experiences of living in a segregated society" (Giddings 1984, 174). Washington spoke of the achievements of rural Blacks, the values of organized family life, and the debt that Blacks living in the South owed to southern white women. In response to Washington's speech, Brown stated that "everything that happens to the members of her race [can be laid] at the door of the Southern white women" (Giddings 1984, 174). She highlighted racial unrest, charges of black immorality, and the failure to address black women as "Mrs.," and challenged white women to reject the stereotypes and myths about black men and women (Giddings 1984; Salem 1990). White women in attendance finally saw "the aspirations and the determination and the longs of the Negro woman's hear as they had not seen it before" (Salem 1990, 249).

Even though the conference was a model for interracial meetings in the future, problems of trust, double standards, and communication between Blacks and Whites were still evident, especially in the area of employment.

In working to build interracial cooperation, Elizabeth Ross Haynes was also concerned about the employment and working conditions of black women.

Since their arrival in the United States, black women have always worked. They have been field workers, domestic and house servants, laborers, cooks, laundresses, as well as professional women. They have started working at an early age and many have continued to work up until their death. They worked long hours and experienced sexual and racial harassment; their work environment was poor and physically challenged, and their wages were minimal. As the migration of Blacks to the North continued to increase and as World War I came to a close, attention was finally given to women in the work force. Most of the attention was given to white women, but it was the black women's club movement who made sure the problems and concerns of their black sisters were included in the dialogue. Thus, Elizabeth Ross Haynes and members of the NACW, the National Association of Colored Wage Earners, and other clubs supported and joined with Mary Church Terrell to have the Women's Bureau of the Department of Labor establish a Colored Women's Division. Their request was denied. So when the First International Congress of Working Women met in 1919, Haynes was with Terrell and other black women when they asked the conveners to include black women's issues on the program. They were excluded. The congress focused on equal pay for equal work, inclusion in areas reserved for men, the forty-four hour work week, social insurance, and maternity benefits. The same issues the women's movement would focus on in the sixties and seventies. In response to the exclusion of black women, the "Representative Negro Women of the United States in behalf of Negro women laborers of the United States" sent a message to the congress stating their position. Elizabeth Ross Haynes, joined Terrell, Nannies Helen Burroughs, Elizabeth C. Carter, and other black women in signing the message. The message made note that black women were

> very little organized in unions or other organizations, . . . [had] very limited means of making their wishes known, and of having their interests advanced through their own representatives. . . . We, a group of Negro women, representing those two million of Negro wage-earners, respectfully ask for your active cooperation in organizing the Negro women workers of the United States into union, that they may have a share in bringing about industrial democracy and social order in the world (1980, 131; Giddings 1984, 155).

Again, the request of black women was denied and excluded, from discussion. And Haynes was more determined to make sure that black women laborers voices were heard.

In her position as a "dollar a year" worker for the Department of Women in Industry Service, Haynes collected data on the wages, health, employment agencies, and hours of Black women in the areas of domestic and personal service, agriculture, and manufacturing. The collection of data continued when she was appointed domestic secretary for the U.S. Employment Service. Both of these positions allowed her to visit various employment agencies throughout the country and talk to women in the areas of domestic and personal service, agriculture, and manufacturing. At the Women Industry Service, Haynes and Helen Irving participated in a study on Black women laborers. The study recognized the conflict between labor and management; noted that when training was provided for women, production and quality increased; and recommended improving working conditions. In response to the study, an article entitled "Colored Women Represent Their Race in State and Nation," suggested how black professional women were to respond to critical issues affecting all black people (Neverdon-Morton 1989, 75).

As domestic secretary and examiner for the employment service, Haynes reported that a majority of black women workers were mainly in service, agriculture, and manufacturing, as previously noted. She also noted that they were being displaced as World War I ended and labor needs declined, and that employers were requested to hire white women first. Along with their displacement, companies no longer paid black women minimum wage, but even expanded employees' duties. Wages were also decreased in domestic and personal services.

Based on the data that Haynes collected while working with the Women's Industry Service and as domestic secretary and examiner for the U.S. Employment Service, she wrote the first major study on domestic workers in the United States. The results of this study, "Negroes in Domestic Service in the United States" (Haynes 1923), was the bases of her master's thesis; was later printed in the *Journal of Negro History,* and was the basis for an article, "Two Million Negro Women at Work" (Haynes 1922). She received her master's degree in sociology from Columbia University in 1923. "Negroes in Domestic Service in the United States" was an in-depth study that looked at every aspect of domestic work—age, marital status, turnover, training, occupation, hours and wages, health, living environment, and social organization. Haynes defined domestic service as the performance of household duties for pay, including the work of chamber maids, coachmen, butlers, janitors, waiters, and bellboys. She also noted that the term *domestic* implies "little or no discretionary power and responsibility in the mode of performing duty" (Haynes 1923, 384). That was exactly the condition of black domestic and personal workers—they had no power. They were hired to answer the door bell, to serve as confidant to the mistress and her children (if she had any), to mend, wash, iron, and fold the clothes, and to perform any other job the mistress or master or child requested. The duties shouldered by Blacks as domestic and personal workers in the United States had not change much from what Blacks did in the early 1800s.

Haynes found that between 1900 and 1920 the average domestic worker was aged between 16 and 24 years for women and 25 to 44 years for men, with women working longer hours than men. Many women did not give their age to prospective employers for fear they would not be hired. When asked they would hesitate and say "settled woman" (Haynes 1923, 391). Some mistresses felt that older women were settled in their ways, were cranky, and were unable to handle general housework. On the other hand they found young women inexperienced, unwilling to sleep in, saucy, and neglectful due to their interest in men. She also found that once black women married they continued to work, while white women remained home after they married. Many mistresses hesitated to hire married women because they took food home for their families, had a number of responsibilities and problems at home, and were not able to live in.

One of the major problems for married women and women who had children was how to provide proper care and protection for their children—the same problem many of us have today. Day care was available, but like today, it was expensive. Many of the black women's clubs tried to provide day-care service at a reasonable cost for domestic and personal servants. This was especially a problem for women who were live-ins. To support this point further, Haynes notes that these women saw their children maybe only once a week, or if the children came to the house when the mistress was not home, or if mothers and children accidentally met in the park.

The opportunities for training domestic workers was limited. The National Training School for Women and Girls, which was founded by Nannies Helen Burroughs, was one of the few schools that trained black women how to be efficient and skilled domestic and personal servants. Tuskegee, along with various other educational programs and organizations, also offered training in domestic service. Haynes found that Blacks who completed high school or normal school were less likely to enter domestic service. When she looked at high school graduates from several cities, Haynes found only 5 were housekeepers, 32 were in miscellaneous occupations, and none were domestic servants (Katzman 1978). What she found was that a majority of domestic workers had at less than an eighth grade education. The lack of training and education prevented them from calculating their salary and being efficient.

> An elderly cook who had been at the business for 50 years wished cooking and cooking only. Her price was $75 per month. That's what she "ingenally" got. When she was asked if she could read or write she said she could not. She had never been to school a day in her life, but she realized that cooking is a tedious work. "Everythin I does, I does by my head; its all brain work, you see I has a good 'eal to remember," said she. However, she felt confident that she could cook anything that was put before her to cook (Haynes 1923, 411).

> A . . . laundress . . . not knowing how to cut off the current and unscrew the wringer on an electric washing machine, when a garment wrapped around the cogs, ruined the cogs by trying to cut the garment from between them (410).

Despite their lack of training and their inefficiency, domestic workers were generally honest.

Domestic servants' wages varied widely by activity, despite the passage of the minimum wage law for women and minors. Between 1889 and 1897, the average wage for cooks and laundress was $4.00 a week, $3.00 for chambermaids and waitresses, and $7.50 for coachmen and gardeners. By 1906, there was less than a $1.00 increase for the same positions (Haynes 1912; as cited in Haynes 1923). Yet, many employers refused, for example, to pay a black bellboy $16.50 a week, but would pay the same salary to a white bellboy. "The more things change, the more they stay the same."

Haynes in her 1923 study referred to living conditions as they relate to the employer's premises. Women who were live-in workers generally lived on the first or third floors, very few lived in the basement or in separate quarters—in an attic or over a garage. Some rooms had private baths. Some of the women told her that the tension which occurred between them and the mistress was due to a lack of separation between job and residence and the monotony and loneliness of restricted areas. One young woman stated that "she lives a life of loneliness, 'in' a family but not of it" (Haynes 1923, 434). This is one reason why days off were important and why some live-ins shared rooms with other domestic and personal workers so they could have some privacy and a concept of home (Katzman 1978; Clark-Lewis 1994).

Social life for older and married domestic and personal workers centered around their family, secret societies and organizations, and the church. Many of these women accepted lower paying jobs so they could be with their family and attend church. Young black men and women could attend the movies, theaters, pool halls, cabarets, and dance halls—not to mention the church. Some also attended night classes or other educational and training programs.

As mentioned earlier, Haynes along with other black women supported the ideal of unions to meet the problems and concerns of black women laborers. Many domestic workers attempted to improve their working conditions by organizing unions and clubs. The Progressive Household Club in California provided "a cheerful and welcome home for a domestic worker taking a rest or not employed for a time" (Haynes 1923, 435). Under the auspices of the American Federation of Labor, the Domestic Workers' Alliance was granted a charter. This was one of ten domestic unions affiliated with the American Federation of Labor (Haynes 1923, 423; Katzman 1978; Foner 1980; Giddings 1984). The National Association of Colored Wage Earners and the National Colored Labor Union are the two of the oldest unions that assisted black laborers in negotiating contracts, placing grievances about working conditions, and fighting for fair wages and hours.

Haynes also noted in her 1923 study the increase of Blacks entering the trade, transportation, and manufacturing and mechanical industries. But for those who are still in domestic and personal services, she recommends that the opportunities for training increase, that working conditions improve, and that standards be set for private household work. She also noted that the health of domestic and personal workers should be taken into consideration. The most prevalent illnesses were consumption, sore throat, rheumatism, neuralgia, quinsy, chills and fevers, and dyspepsia (Haynes 1923). These illness were not only common among domestic and personal workers but also among those who worked in various other industries. If the health of these workers continued to be ignored, Haynes warned, it could have dangerous effects on the nation. In other words, there was an opportunity for infections to spread from workers to families or customers, thus causing an epidemic.

In "Two Million Women at Work" (1922), Haynes wrote,

> The thought realm in which two million Negro women in the United States, gainfully employed, live and work, vibrates with pathos and humor, determination and true heroism, belief and expectation that with the coming years, they too, as a group, with training and larger opportunities, will come into their own as real women. (64)

In the area of domestic and personal service, she noted,

> To-day they are found in domestic service, nearly a million strong, with all their shortcomings—their lack of training in efficiency, in cleanliness of person, in honesty and truthfulness, and with all of the shortcomings of ordinary domestic service; namely basement living quarters, poor working conditions, too long hours, no Sundays off, no standard of efficiency, and the servant brand. (64)

She also found a decrease in the hiring of black women as domestic and personal servants, an increase in the hiring of white women for the same positions, and a decrease in wages. For example, in Washington, D.C., during the 1920s, 90 percent of the laundry workers were black women. But a decade later, laundries began to fear that they would have to pay minim wages, they began to hire white women. Thus, they did not have to pay minimum wage to black women, some who had worked as laundresses for almost twenty years. Domestic wages went from $10.00 a week without laundry work to $8.00 with laundry work. Less money for more work.

Another area Haynes discussed in her 1922 article was the relationship between the mistress and the maid. What she found were many of the same old customs and conventions that had occurred during slavery. Mistresses had little interest in learning the maid's surname or place of residence; mistress and maid had a lack of personal interest in each other, feelings of dislike for each other, and a lack of confidence in each other. Domestic and personal servants spoke of their pathos, restlessness, ignorance, and inefficiency; the need to standardize domestic service as an occupation or industry, and the need for domestic training. Haynes explored this more in her 1923 master's thesis, "Negroes in Domestic Service in the United States."

Black women who worked in agriculture spoke of how they left home early in the morning to go to fields that were close to home or five miles away, not returning home until twelve hours later. Some women even worked late because it was better working "in the cool of the evening" (Haynes 1922, 68).

> Farm conditions are as bad as we have ever seen them. The cotton crop is very poor. Women can pick on an average from 85 to 110 pounds of cotton per day, for which they get 40 cents a hundred. The peanut farms also furnish some work for women at 50 cents a day ... Down here women do almost any kind of work on the farm from handling a two horse plow, and hoeing and pulling fodder, to cleaning new ground. Women in domestic service here get from $7 to $8 per month. (67)

Not only did these women work long hours for low wages, but the only recreation and social activities they enjoyed were monthly church meetings, funerals, weddings, or the annual trip to town at planting or harvesting time. Organizations such as the Slater and Rosenwald Funds, the Jeanes supervisors, and the General Education Board were working with the various black colleges in educating ministers, teachers, welfare workers, and nurses interested in making life for these women endurable.

In the manufacturing and mechanical industry, thousands of black women were working in cigar and tobacco factories. They were paid $6 to

$10 a week, while working in poor and unhealthy factories; some women almost suffocated from the dust and fumes, and lunch and bathroom facilities were lacking. "Yes, ma'am, the floors gen'ally fills you full o' rheumatism. Some mo'nin's I kin hardly get out o' bed, I'se so stiff and painful" is how one woman describe the working conditions (Haynes 1923, 72).

Prior to and during World War I, black women worked in the clothing, food, and metal industries, slaughtering and meat-packing houses, furniture and shoe factories, printing and publishing establishments, and in skilled industries such tailoring, coppersmithing, and upholstering. After the war, many of these women lost their jobs. Some manufacturers informed Haynes that "We use Negro women only occasionally now for odd jobs" (Haynes 1923, 70). Women who lost their jobs or whose husbands had lost their jobs, tried to obtain jobs via employment agencies or through friends. They were willing to clean, wash, sew, do hair or manicures, sell goods, assist undertakers— anything whereby they could earn a living.

> Struggling against the lack of training and against inefficiency, restricted in opportunities to get and hold jobs, more than two million Negro women and girls are to-day laboring in domestic service, in agriculture, and in manufacturing pursuits with the hope of an economic independence that will some day enable them to take their place in the ranks with other working women. (Haynes 1923, 72)

Along with her civic and social activism, Elizabeth Ross Haynes wrote several articles, gave lecturers, and published two books—*Unsung Heroes* (1921) and *The Black Boy of Atlanta* (1952). *Unsung Heroes* was a collection of biographies of black leaders. Wilson notes that it was Haynes first-published book and was among the first to provide black children with historical biographies (1977, xxx). She joined DuBois and others who sought to provide positive reading material for black children. *Unsung Heroes,* like DuBois's *Brownies' Book* (1920–1922), was published by Du Bois and Dill Publications. In *Unsung Heroes,* seventeen black leaders were highlighted. Four of the Blacks lived in the African diaspora—African Russian poet Alexander Pushkin, Haitian French author Alexandre Dumas, African Haitian composer Samuel Coleridge-Taylor, and Haitian leader Toussaint L'Overture. In her review of the book, Wilson argues that many of the personalities had been recognized by whites and that she did not include the work these leaders had done in the struggle for black rights. Despite these omissions, Haynes's message to young people was to "work hard, endure slights, and remain faithful to God and justice would prevail" (Wilson 1997, xxiv).

*The Black Boy of Atlanta* was a biography of Richard Robert Wright Sr., an ex-slave who became president of the Georgia State Industrial College for Colored Youth and the founder of Citizens and Southern Bank and Trust in Philadelphia, Pennsylvania. Like *Unsung Heroes,* this biography was designed for children, but is one of only two works that has been written about Wright. (The other is an autobiography by Wright's son, *Eighty-Seven Years behind the Black Curtain* [1965]). Haynes chose to write about Wright because she was "in a quiet search for an unsung American Negro whose life and solid achievements would be an inspiration to folks irrespective of race" (7). His life has been used as a symbol of the freedman's faith in education and collective uplift and as a staple of black inspiration (Rowe 1920; Ebony 1945; Bacote 1969). "We are rising," was Wright's motto.

Richard Robert Wright Sr., was a strong supporter of black businesses and black history. He started was a co-owner in a coffee business in Haiti, tried to encourage Blacks to travel via the airplane, led the campaign for a postage stamp to honor Booker T. Washington, and participated in the conference establishing the United Nations. In her critique of *The Black Boy,* Wilson (1997) states that Haynes is "repetitive and leaps back and forth . . . [and] [says] little . . . about the lives and accomplishments of Wrights' eight children and his wife . . . often ignores or understates those aspects of Wright's life that contradict a portrait of a determined person moving from strength to strength" (xxx). Nevertheless, Wright continues by saying that this "was a fitting last work of a woman whose own life had been dedicated to the principles she celebrated in Wright's: hard work, race pride, and economic self help" (xxxii).

In looking at Elizabeth Ross Haynes, we see a woman who is devoted to the uplifting of her race, but who also believed in interracial cooperation. In reading about her contributions and activism, one could compare her to Booker T. Washington or Nannies Helen Burroughs, or, on the other hand, she could be compared to W.E.B. DuBois or Charlotte Hawkins Brown. In reality, she was a very low-key, analytical woman who, like so many other black women of her time, did what they had to do for the betterment of the community and humanity. She had faith in her people and encouraged them to improve their lives and to obtain an education and have faith in God.

## References

Bacote, C.A. 1969. *The Story of Atlanta University, A Century of Service, 1865–1965.* Atlanta, GA: Atlanta University.
Bardolph, R. 1959. *The Negro Vanguard.* Vintage Books: New York.
Blackwell, James E., and Morris Janowitz, eds. 1974. *Black Sociologists: Historical and Contemporary Perspectives.* Chicago: University of Chicago Press.

Blackwell, J.E. 1974. "Sociology Teaching in Black Colleges." In *Black Sociologist, Historical and Contemporary Perspectives,* ed. J.E. Blackwell and M. Janowitz, pp. 135–63. Chicago: University of Chicago Press.

Bogin, R. 1980. "Elizabeth R. Haynes." In *Notable American Women, the Modern Period,* ed. B. Sickerman, C.H. Green, I. Kantor, and H. Walker, pp. 324–25. Cambridge, MA: Belknap Press.

Clark-Lewis, E. 1994. *Living In, Living Out: African American Domestics in Washington, D.C., 1910–1940.* Washington, DC: Smithsonian Institute Press.

Cooper, A.J. 1969. *A Voice from the South.* New York: Negro Universities Press.

DuBois, W.E.B., ed. 1920–1922. *The Brownies' Book.* New York: DuBois and Dill.

*Ebony.* 1945. "From Slave to Banker: Major Wright, 91, Most Amazing Living Negro in America Today" (November): 43–47.

Foner, P.S. 1980. *Women and the American Labor Movement: From World War I to the Present.* New York: Free Press.

Giddings, P. 1984. *When and Where I Enter: The Impact of Black Women on Race and Sex in America.* New York: Bantam Books.

Haynes, E.R. 1921. *Unsung Heroes.* New York: Du Bois and Dill.

_____. 1922. "Twelve Million Negro Women at Work." *The Southern Workman* (February): 64–72.

_____. 1923. "Negroes in Domestic Service in the United States." *Journal of Negro History* 8, no. 4 (October): 384–442.

_____. 1952. *The Black Boy of Atlanta.* Boston: House of Edinboro.

Haynes, G.E. 1912. *The Negro at Work in New York City: A Study in Economic Progress.* New York: Columbia University, Longmans, Green and Company.

Hunter, J. 1940. *A Nickel and a Prayer.* Cleveland: Elli Kane.

Hunton, A.W. 1911. "Women's Clubs." *The Crisis* (July): 17–18.

Katzman, D. 1978. *Seven Days a Week: Women and Domestic Service in Industrialized America.* New York: Oxford University Press.

Neverdon-Morton, C. 1989. *Afro-American Women of the South and the Advancement of the Race, 1895–1925.* Knoxville: University of Tennessee Press.

Richardson, J.M. 1980. *A History of Fisk University.* Tuscaloosa: University of Alabama Press.

Rowe, G.C. 1920. "We Are Rising." In *Progress of a Race or the Remarkable Advancement of the American Negro,* ed. J.L. Nichols and W.H. Crogman, p. 12. Naperville, IL: Nichols.

Salem, D. 1990. *Black Women in Organized Reform, 1890–1920.* New York: Carlson.

Wilson, F.R. 1997. Introduction to *African American Women Writers, 1910–1940,* ed. H.L. Gates Jr., pp. xv–xxxvii. New York: G.K. Hall.

Wright Jr., R.R. 1965. *Eighty-Seven Years behind the Black Curtain.* Philadelphia: A.M.E. Book Concern.

# 8

# A Black Composer Speaks

## William Levi Dawson

## *Ralph Anthony Russell*

The first three decades of the twentieth century saw the emergence of a generation of African American composers who found inspiration for their vocal and instrumental works in the music and culture of black America. These composers used Negro folk music, quotes from Negro folk songs, and poems of black poets in their compositions to instill racial pride, espouse the African heritage, and describe the black experience in America. William Levi Dawson, one of the leading composers of this period, composed a collection of choral and instrumental works that uses the melodies and rhythms from the rich reservoir of African American folk music. Like his contemporaries—for instance, William Grant Still and Florence Price—within the Harlem Renaissance, Dawson spoke of slavery, the African heritage, spirituality, black pride, and the future of black America through his numerous choral and instrumental works. The purpose of this paper is to present an overview of Dawson's life and give a brief descriptive analysis of his symphonic work, the *Negro Folk Symphony.*

William Levi Dawson, the eldest of seven siblings, was born on September 26, in 1899 to Eliza and George Dawson in Anniston, Alabama (Malone 1981). His parents came from different socioeconomic backgrounds. Eliza grew up in a family of property owners who stressed the importance of self-sufficiency, religious faith, and education (Malone 1981). His father had a strong work ethic and believed that learning a trade was the practical way to earn a living and to support a family. Consequently, the value systems of both parents would leave an indelible mark on Dawson's emotional, intellectual, and spiritual development.

Education was of the utmost importance to William, and was a virtue that was in part instilled in him by his mother. Dawson's ambitious educational goals were furthered inspired after he met students and graduates of the Tuskegee Institute (Malone 1981). The kinds of students and graduates that the institute produced had a profound effect on the young Dawson. Because there were no schools in Anniston that catered to the educational needs of Blacks, "Dawson resolved that he would go to Tuskegee, pursue an education, and play in the band" (McMillian 1991, 68).

In 1913, at the age of fourteen and with approximately six dollars in his pocket, Dawson left home and boarded a train for Tuskegee. Founded in 1881 by Booker T. Washington, the institute began as an elementary and secondary school that offered instruction in grammar, mathematics, music, and industrial arts. After the turn of the century, the school's enrollment grew to nearly one thousand, with a student body made up of students from over twenty states and Puerto Rico and from foreign countries such as Cuba, Jamaica, and parts of Africa (McMillian 1991). For a young man from small-town Alabama, being a part of this culturally diverse student body must have been a truly rewarding educational experience.

Before Dawson was permitted to take classes, the institute administered diagnostic tests and, as a result, Dawson was placed in basic courses (McMillian 1991). Now that he was officially a student, he had to secure funds for his education. He paid his way through school by working on the school's farm during the day and attending school at night. For several years he worked two days a week and attended classes three times a week.

Dawson's interest in music began when he was a child. Prior to his arrival to Tuskegee, his musical training was purely informal. He recalled listening to his mother sing Negro sacred songs, hearing local church choirs, and attending a performance of the famous Fisk Jubilee Singers (Malone 1981).

However, it was at Tuskegee that Dawson's studies in music began in earnest. There he took courses in sight singing and ear training, and he studied harmony and piano with Alice Carter Simmons (Malone 1981). His ensemble studies included performances both with the institute's choir, under the direction of Jennie Cheatham, and with the institute's band, in which he played trombone under the leadership of Frank Drye (McMillian 1991). He also sang second tenor in the Male Quartett, a group that traveled north during the summer to publicize Tuskegee (Malone 1981). Dawson graduated from Tuskegee in 1921, having received a firm grounding in basic courses and a well-rounded musical education that included classroom instruction and concert performance.

After graduation, in the fall of 1921, he accepted a position as bandmaster at Kansas Vocational College (KVC) in Topeka (McMillian 1991). Although the school emphasized industrial education, music was, nonetheless, also an important part of the curriculum. Dawson, who became the school's first band director, also formed the school's first band and gave instructions on band and orchestral instruments. While at KVC, he continued his musical studies at nearby Washburn College, where he took courses in composition and orchestration, and received private lessons in double bass. His instructor, Dean Stearns, was so impressed with Dawson's skills on double bass that he urged him to study with Adolph Weidig at the American Conservatory of Music in Chicago. Dawson, on the other hand, had aspirations not to travel to Chicago but to Ithaca, New York, to study trombone with Pat Conway at the Ithaca Conservatory of Music.

After a year at Kansas Vocational College, he resigned and moved to Kansas City, Missouri, in 1922. There he went door to door trying to sell his first composition, *Forever Thine,* a piece for voice and piano, hoping to raise enough money to study at the Ithaca Conservatory. In 1922, he accepted a position at Lincoln High School in Kansas City. Dawson's tenure at Lincoln High was productive for him, the school, and the city. His administrative and educational duties involved directing Lincoln High's band, orchestra, and chorus, and developing and maintaining instrumental programs at over ten elementary schools. As a composer, Dawson continued his compositional output and benefited tremendously from the city's musical life during his four-year stay. First, he was able to have his compositions performed by the Lincoln High School Choir. For instance, the choir performed two of Dawson's arrangements, *King Jesus Is A-Listening* and *My Lord What a Mornin'* at a music convention in Kansas City (Malone 1981). Second, his music was attracting the attention of publishers. The music publisher H.T. Fitzsimmons of Chicago was so impressed with *King Jesus Is A-Listening* that the company published the work in 1925 (McMillian 1991).

Dawson continued his musical studies at the Horner Institute of Fine Arts in Kansas City, Missouri. Although the institute did not accept Blacks, Dawson was able to study privately with two of the school's best instructors, Dr. Carl Busch and Regina Hall (Malone 1981). During his three years at Horner, he studied musical theory, trombone, piano, composition, and eighteenth-century counterpoint, and he subsequently received a bachelor's degree in music with high honors in 1926. In spite of his academic achievement, segregation and racism forced him to sit in the balcony with other Negroes and not on the main floor with his white classmates during commencement. Dawson also received an important honor when his composition *Trio in A for Violin, Cello, and Piano* was performed by members of the Kansas City Symphony Orchestra at commencement. The piece was well received by the audience, but "despite the apparent enthusiastic appreciation by the audience, Dawson was not permitted to acknowledge the thunderous applause" (Malone 1981, 50).

In spite of the blatant racism that Dawson encountered during his years at Horner, he was undeterred by these small setbacks and diligently devoted his time to intense compositional studies. In 1926, Dawson resigned his post at Lincoln High School and moved to Chicago to study composition with composer, violinist, and German immigrant Adolph Weidig at the American Conservatory of Music (Malone 1981). Under Weidig's tutelage, Dawson—now a graduate student in his mid-twenties—studied composition, counterpoint, and orchestration, and discovered various methods of thematic development.

After Dawson received a master's degree in music in 1927, he stayed in Chicago and continued his compositional studies with Dr. Thorvald Otterstrom. Dawson's studies with Dr. Otterstrom marked the next stage of his development. During this period, Dawson was continuing to incorporate Negro folk melodies and rhythms in his choral and instrumental pieces. Otterstrom, who had composed the *American Negro Suite*—a work based on Negro folk melodies—encouraged his ambitious student to continue his experiments with black American folk music (McMillian 1991).

His time in Chicago was a very productive period for Dawson. He was finding plenty of work performing, winning awards, and, of course, composing. In 1930, he won first prize for two compositions, *Jump Back, Honey Jump Back* and *Scherzo,* from the Redman Wanamaker Music Contest, and he accepted both awards at the National Association of Negro Musicians where the contest was held (Malone 1981). His reputation as composer and performer was capturing the attention of many professionals in his field. However, he was also recognized as a fine educator—a reputation he had earned from his years in Kansas City. His adroitness as an educator caught the attention of one administrator at Tuskegee, Robert Moton, who had taken over the leadership role at Tuskegee University after Booker T. Washington's death in 1915. Moton was determined to build the university's school of music. Moton believed that Dawson was the right person to head the project and made numerous attempts to bring the composer and educator to the campus (McMillian 1991). Dawson, enjoying his stay in Chicago, promptly declined the offer. Of his meeting with Moton, Dawson reflects:

> Finally Moton himself came to Chicago to see me. He wanted a School of Music at Tuskegee. I told Moton, "I don't know: I am playing in an orchestra

and everything is going my way." Then Moton said, "Bill, what do you have against a homecoming?" I accepted that, so I told him I would come to Tuskegee around Thanksgiving just to talk. Moton was a great lover of music and he told me over and over how much he wanted a School of Music. The night I arrived on campus Moton showed me the chapel and introduced me to the soloists. The next day he convinced me of his seriousness in creating a School of Music at Tuskegee. He said, "You can get rid of anybody you want to. Do whatever you want to the program."(McMillian 1991)

After Moton's convincing presentation, Dawson accepted the position, and in 1931, became the director of the school of music.

One of Dawson's most lasting impacts on Tuskegee was the development of the university's choir. The Tuskegee Choir "had been an important part of the university's life for many years." The choir performed regularly in concerts and in the chapel on Sundays. Under Dawson's leadership, the choir eventually achieved national acclaim. During its national tour in 1932–33, the choir performed at the grand opening of Radio City Music Hall, Carnegie Hall, and the White House.

In the midst of the choir's success, Dawson continued his compositional output. The choral works *Soon Ah Will Be Done* and *Oh What a Beautiful City* were published in 1931 as part of his Tuskegee Choir Series. This period also saw Dawson complete his first work for large orchestra, the *Negro Folk Symphony*. He began composing the work while in Chicago during the late twenties but delayed completing the piece after accepting the directorship at Tuskegee. The *Negro Folk Symphony* is one of the earliest orchestral works composed by a black composer that evokes images of black America, celebrates the African heritage, and reaffirms racial pride. He found his inspiration in the music and culture of his people. Negro folk music, which had left an indelible impact on his life, now permeated his instrumental and choral works. Dawson had for quite some time wanted to composed a symphony based on black American folk music. His goal was to "write a symphony in the Negro folk idiom, based on authentic folk music but in the same symphonic form used by the composers of the [European] romantic-nationalist tradition" (McMillian 1991).

This symphonic work is in three movements and is subtitled "Missing Link." Dawson commented that "a link has been taken out of the human chain when the first African was taken from the shores of his native land and sent into slavery" (Brown et al. 1990). Dawson also subtitled each movement of this work. In the first movement, "The Bond of Africa," the "missing link" concept is embodied in the opening melody as played by the French horn. This "missing link" theme recurs throughout the work and becomes the unifying element. Dawson complements this theme with a second countermelody that is based on a Negro spiritual titled "Oh M' Lit'l Soul Gwine-A-Shine." The second movement, "Hope in the Night," has alternating sections and begins mournfully with three strokes of the gong. This opening section, marked *andante,* depicts the harsh reality of slavery through the use of dark instrumental timbres and poignant lyricism. An *allegretto* section follows that is replete with melodic and rhythmic imitation and is a musical illustration of the "hope in the night" that the slave envisions. Finally, the piece ends with the fast, lively, and rhythmic third movement. With the tempo *allegro* and subtitled "O Le' Me Shine, Shine Like a Morning Star," this movement uses two Negro folk melodies, "O Le' Me Shine" and "Hallelujah, Lord, I Been down into the Sea," bringing the work to an uplifting climax.

The *Negro Folk Symphony* was premiered on November 14, 1934, by the Philadelphia Symphony Orchestra under the direction of Leopold Stokowski. The performance was such a tremendous success that the audience erupted into a thunderous applause after the dramatically powerful second movement. Dawson's monumental work also received praise from several metropolitan newspapers. Critic Robert Simon of the *New Yorker* magazine described Dawson's work as "music in which well-defined themes are developed skillfully" (McMillian 1991). The *Washington Daily News* felt that the piece was "fresh and imaginative," while the *Philadelphia Inquirer* thought the orchestral scoring was "artfully and tastefully done." Dawson's hometown paper, the *Anniston Star,* wrote "Dawson's triumph seems to verify a statement that repeatedly has been made by the *Anniston Star*—that the first great American music would be written by a Negro" (McMillian 1991).

In 1952, believing that his work was incomplete, Dawson went on sabbatical from Tuskegee to travel to West Africa. Equipped with a portable reel-to-reel tape recorder, he traveled from village to village, listening and recording the melodies and rhythms of the inhabitants. As a result of his musical awakening, Dawson rewrote sections of the *Negro Folk Symphony* and added West African–inspired melodies and rhythms to the musical fabric and also added two African percussion instruments, the clave and adawura, to the orchestra. The revised symphony was performed and recorded in 1962–63 by the American Symphony Orchestra under the direction of Leopold Stokowski. Conductor Stokowski was so affected by the work that he commented: "He has voiced the spirit of his people struggling in a new land; the ancient voice of Africa transferred to America and here expressed through the medium of the white man's highly developed instrument, the symphony orchestra" (McMillian 1991).

After Dawson's retirement from Tuskegee in 1955, he remained active as a composer into the late seventies. He published such choral works as

"Zion's Wall" (1961), "I Want to Be Ready" (1967), and "Feed-a-My Sheep" (1971). Awards and honors were also bestowed upon him because of his many accomplishments in musical composition and education. He was honored by the Tuskegee-Philadelphia Alumni (1971), inducted into the Alabama Arts Hall of Fame, and received two honorary doctorate degrees from Ithaca College and Lincoln University in Pennsylvania. The climax of Dawson's extraordinary career was in March 1990, when, after receiving a plaque from the American Choral Directors Association at its Southern Division Convention, he conducted the entire convention in an emotional rendition of "Every Time I Feel the Spirit" (McMillian 1991).

On May 20, 1990, at the age of ninety, William Levi Dawson died of pneumonia in a Montgomery, Alabama, hospital. The university that had been so much a part of his life held a memorial service. He was interred on the campus of Tuskegee University.

In conclusion, Dawson spoke with sincere honesty of the black experience in America. Because of his familial roots, his encounters with racism, and his undying pride in his identity, he empathized with the various periods of the black American experience. In *Soon Ah Will Be Done,* the *Negro Folk Symphony,* and nearly seventy other choral and instrumental works, Dawson's music illustrates dramatic and picturesque images of the weary soul of the slave, the rejected spirit of the oppressed, and the optimistic vision of the liberated. With his many accomplishments, Dawson truly holds a place within the pantheon of black music and culture and American classical music.

## References

Brown, Rae L. 1990. "William Grant Still, Florence Price, and William Levi Dawson. Echoes of the Harlem Renaissance." In *Black Music in the Harlem Renaissance,* ed. Samuel Floyd, pp. 71–85. Knoxville: University of Tennessee Press.

Malone, M. 1981. *William Levi Dawson: American Music Educator.* Tallahassee: Florida State University School of Music.

McMillian, R. 1991. *The Choral Music of William Dawson.* Greeley: University of Northern Colorado.

## Discography

Dawson, William Levi. 1993. *Negro Folk Symphony,* Detroit Symphony Orchestra, Neeme Jarvi, conductor. Chandos Records 9154.

Still, William Grant. Symphony no. 2. Colchester, Essex, England. Chandos, 1992–1993, Chandos 9226.

# 9

# Keeping Truth on My Side

## Maria Stewart

### *Ida Young*

One autumn evening in 1832, Maria W. Stewart, like no other woman before her, revolutionized prolific speaking by presenting a public lecture sponsored by the African American Female Literary Society at Franklin Hall in Boston, Massachusetts. In a bold rhetorical style Stewart delivered her message by asking her audience that night, "Who shall go forward, and take off the reproach that is cast upon the people of color? Shall it be a woman?" Stewart went on to reply to her own inquiry by stating, "If it is thy will, be it even so, Lord Jesus!" (Quarles 1969).

Apparently, Stewart's message and the fact that a woman would speak with such fiery zeal was enough to make some in her audience's blood boil. And, if there was some outrage, it was most likely among the men in attendance whose agitated murmurs ran through the hall. Among those who disagreed with Stewart's message were some influential members of the African American community. The attitude then was to denounce a woman who dared to step forth to engage publicly in social engineering—shaping the social climate of a community created by male dominance. And, although Stewart's audience's reactions were initially divided between males and females that evening, within a year murmurs from both genders rose to a unanimous call upon her to relinquish her public lecturing career.

As the first African American female political writer and lecturer, Stewart presented her Afrocentric convictions to a European, male-dominated authority. Her values had African origins, which she embraced while stepping into the realm of the public lecture circuit. This gesture is one that the notable scholar Molefi Asante assesses as "seizing the territory" (1987). It is within this realm that Stewart attacked male supremacy and posed many questions in defense of women and African liberation.

Thus, when Stewart emerged to prominence by publicly lecturing for African liberation and the reform of community activism, she became America's first woman—black or white—to deliver a public political lecture before an audience composed of both men and women. This historical first established Stewart as a predecessor of such notable African American historical figures as Frederick Douglass and Sojourner Truth. Stewart enacted theories of collective solidarity when her victorious voice rallied crowds to the abolitionist cause. Her message forged a path for others to follow by dispelling the prevailing opinions of the black woman's role in America.

The foundation for Stewart's public activism was established through her first essay, published in *The Liberator* in October 1831. This essay, entitled "Religion and the Pure Principles of Morality, the Sure Foundation on Which We Must Build," gave Stewart the opportunity to summarize the transformational phases of her life by revealing:

> I was born in Hartford, Connecticut, 1803; was left an orphan at five years of age; was bound out in a clergyman's family; had the seeds of piety and virtue early sown in my mind, but was deprived of the advantages of education, though my soul thirsted for knowledge . . . in 1826 was married to James W. Stewart; was left a widow in 1829 . . . bought to the knowledge of the truth, as it is in Jesus in 1830; in 1831 made a public profession of my faith in Christ. (Richardson 1987, 56).

Stewart's activism evolved at a time in American society when it was eminently improper for a woman to be too outspoken. Axiological questions are raised on the validity of these dictated standards of feminine character. In Afrocentric thinking, character encompasses that which triumphs over one's sacrifices for the good of the entire community. Of this notion, Molefi Asante argues that "right conduct" represents a category of the axiological issues in Afrocentricity. He further maintains that "it isolated conduct rather than physical attributes of a person in . . . social analysis." If the true motivation for one's behavior is to advance the humanity of one's people, then Maria Stewart's pioneering efforts to uplift all humanity can never be defined as "improper" (Asante 1990, 10).

As an African American, Stewart's triumphs and achievements stand out in the history of the nineteenth century. This was a period of great turmoil in American society and equally a time of great discord between Americans concerning the anti-colonization efforts, the Fugitive Slave Act, and the David Walker appeal. Yet Stewart's voice clamored over the walls of injustice to rally African Americans in the battle to liberate their enslaved brethren, saying, "African rights and liberty is a subject that ought to fire the breast of every free man of color in these United States, and excite in his bosom a lively, deep decided and heart-felt interest" (Loewenberg and Bogin 1976, 282).

Since African Americans first arrived in America, there has always been a challenge presented to black men and women to advance the social, political, and economic status of the black community. In keeping with this notion, it's clear that Stewart's political activism was not necessarily foreign to the general ideals of her people. By soliciting the efforts of females to complement the efforts of males working toward political, economic, and social progress, Stewart raised awareness of African tradition in her audience, saying that "in ancient times women were sages . . ." (Richardson 1987, 29).

With the celebration of this African woman's victory and her repeated call for equality came the bittersweet dialectic of discourse. Stewart's public lectures had caused great concern in Boston because in her plea for African liberation there sparked the appeal for a critical review of women's roles. In her plea for human equality, Stewart fueled a critical consciousness of feminist discourse that was unwavering. Her assertiveness encouraged women to establish their own political voice by providing strategic measures for them to forge ahead, beyond the dictates of a male-dominated society. Through tireless revolutionary struggles, Stewart threw off the shroud of race, class, and gender distinctions and communicated her rage in a frank and direct manner. She primarily addressed woman's role in the fight for African liberation, and once proclaimed her concerns for these issues by saying:

> What if I am a woman: is not the god of ancient times the God of these modern days? . . . What if such women . . . should rise among our sable race? . . . for it is not the color of the skin that makes the man or woman, but the principle formed in the soul. (Richardson 1987, 58)

Public lecturing initially transformed Stewart's public image and sense of militancy, but her final lectures remained particularly true to her African ancestry. In these, we find that she grounded herself in an African cultural expression by categorizing African American women as instinctive nurturers, leaders, reformers, and healers. With her distinct rhetorical style, Stewart symbolically wove the ancestral fabric of the African foremother at a time when many looked away from Africa. Her lectures evoked an African past of pride and great achievement. She reaffirmed an ancient African collective identity by saying:

History informs us that we sprung from one of the most learned nations of the whole earth; from the seat, if not the parent, of science. Yes, poor despised Africa was once the resort of sages and legislators of other nations, was esteemed the school for learning, and most illustrious men in Greece flocked thither for instruction. (Richardson 1987, 55)

Nineteenth-century America was structured around the notion that women should seek to advance their husbands' and fathers' philosophies. In light of these standards, Stewart faced great opposition. She shattered the myth of women's roles by heralding a message that later became a synthesis of diverse concerns of gender, race, and class distinction. The essence of her teachings offered women of the future a vehicle for activism, but her message appealed to African American women of the day—her revolutionary overtones echo in the following statement:

O woman, woman! Upon you I call; for upon your exertions almost entirely depends whether the raising generation shall be anything more than we have been or not. O woman, woman! Your example is powerful, your influence great; it extends over your husbands and your children, and throughout the circle of your acquaintance. (Richardson 1987, 54)

Again and again, Stewart accessed the status of free blacks, whom she urged to challenge the consciences of white America to liberate enslaved Africans. The thematic glue of her message attempted to bond the commitments of the Boston African American community when she once asked, "Did every gentleman in America realize, that if they got to become bondsmen, and their wives . . . sons . . . and daughters, servants forever, to Great Britain their brethren would be filled with horror, every nerve and muscle would be forced into action? . . . Then why have not Africa's sons a right to feel the same?" (Porter 1936, 569)

One would think that the achievements of such a woman would be well chronicled in the annuls of nineteenth-century history, but nothing could be less true. Stewart was neglected by historians and bibliographers, and it was not until 1936 that historians first chronicled her contributions to the abolitionist movement. This came about when the notable historian Dorothy Porter wrote a ground-breaking investigation. Porter's work was published just one year after the 1935 second edition reprint of Maria Stewart's 1879 autobiography, entitled *Meditations from the Pen of Mrs. Maria W. Stewart.* At that time, Porter's analysis appeared in an essay entitled "The Organized Educational Activities of Literary Societies, 1828–1846." In that study, Porter described Maria Stewart as "probably the earliest Negro woman lecturer and writer in America." Porter goes on to reveal that Stewart was "the first

American woman, African or European to defy the social mores of the nineteenth century by presenting a public lecture of a political nature" (Richardson 1987, 20–21).

It was not until five decades later that Marilyn Richardson produced an edited compilation of Stewart's antislavery essays, speeches, and lectures. Richardson espoused the view that Stewart made "the earliest recorded call to black women to take up what would become one of the great traditions in their social and political history." Moreover, Richardson argues that Stewart's pioneering work inspired teachers, founders of schools, and innovators in many areas of black education. Richardson is accurate in assuming that Stewart augmented the intellectual history and culture of black female activism. For not only did Stewart's activism rank as an important morale victory, but she also posed as an historical example of human tenacity in the struggle for liberation (Richardson 1987, xiv).

As a pioneering activist, Richardson says, "in both the formulation and the articulation of the ideas central to the emerging struggle for black freedom and human rights, Stewart was a clear forerunner to generations of the best known and most influential champions of black activism" (1987, 30). Today, the contemporary chronicling of Stewart's contributions addresses the inequality of women and African Americans. But many scholars argue that much of her discourse fits squarely among women's rights issues. In feminist literature, many scholars maintain, her philosophy stands among those who circumvented nineteenth-century patriarchal tradition. Some feminists suggest that Stewart focused her efforts more on gender issues than on race. However, the themes of race and gender are equally pertinent to her argument, specifically because she challenged women of "sable hue" to fight against inequities. Stewart states her paramount concerns through the following appeal: "O, yea daughters of Africa, awake! Awake! No longer sleep nor slumber, but distinguish yourselves. Show forth to the world that ye are endowed with noble and exalted faculties" (Richardson 1987, 30).

In the quest to liberate the African, we find that the abolitionist movement was itself not devoid of discrimination. During Stewart's activism in the 1830s, relations between black and white activists were strained— and the charge of discrimination was the most common source of conflict within the movement. Clearly, the influences of racism played a definite role in shaping different realities for both Blacks and Whites working together, so much so that Stewart felt that white female activists were "nursed in the lap of . . . ease" (Stewart 1835, 63–70). Stewart goes on to expose those disparities between the respective treatment of black and white women:

O ye fairer sisters whose hands are never soiled, whose nerves and muscles are never strained, go learn by experience! Had we the opportunity that you have had, to improve our moral and mental faculties, what would have hindered our intellects . . . Had it been our lot to have been nursed in the lap of affluence . . . and fortune, should we not have naturally supposed that we were never made to toil? (Gates 1988, xxxi–xxxiv)

Black women had rallied together for the abolitionist cause long before any major alliances were established between black and white female activists. In fact, the first female abolitionists organization is credited to African American women of Salem, Massachusetts. In 1832, these pioneering women established the Female Anti-Slavery Society of Salem, motivated by the ideals expressed in the following excerpt of their constitution:

We, the undersigned, females of color . . . being duly convinced of the importance of union and morality, have associated ourselves together for our mutual improvement, and to promote the welfare of our color. . . . (Loewenberg and Bogin 1976, 194)

Less than two years after the black women of the Female Anti-Slavery Society of Salem drafted their historical inaugural constitution, white women joined their ranks. Within a short time, the Blacks of this reorganized, integrated group relented to pressures of discrimination. The white members took full control, renaming themselves the Salem Female Anti-Slavery Society. In the end, black members in leadership positions who chose to remain active were rarely acknowledged in the decision-making process of the organization.

The black women of the Female Anti-Slavery Society of Salem are important historically for three reasons. First, they preceded white females in organizing for the abolitionist cause. It was not until one year after the Salem women organized that Lucretia Mott modeled their actions by establishing the Philadelphia Female Anti-Slavery Society in 1833. Second, with Mott serving as their president, Philadelphia women became known as the first female integrated antislavery society to form in America. Third, once the Philadelphia women organized for the abolitionist cause, they, like the Salem women, experienced problems with discrimination. Sarah Mapp Douglass, one notable black member of the Philadelphia group, wrote to her a white counterpart, Angelina Grimke, about discrimination saying:

I have heard it frequently remarked and have observed it myself, that in proportion as we become intellectual and respectable, so in proportion does their disgust and prejudice increase. (Richardson 1987, xiv)

Maria Stewart was cognizant of the psychological effects of discrimination. It was she who advanced the idea that, in many ways, slavery in the South was but a fraction worse than the sanctioned inferior status of some free blacks in northern communities. Stewart analyzed the effects of enslaving the minds of free Blacks, commenting on the lack of self-esteem and the crippling aspects of fear:

> Most of our color have been taught to stand in fear of the white man from their earliest infancy, to work as soon as they could walk, and call "master" before they could scarce lisp the name of mother. Continual fear and laborious servitude have in some degree lessened in us that natural force and energy which belong to man; or else, in defiance of opposition, our men, before this, would have nobly and boldly contended for their rights. (Richardson 1987, 59)

Assimilation in nineteenth-century America seemed to make the conditions of life more endurable for free African Americans. Many had feared risking the loss of whatever gains they'd already made in society and so had readily embraced patriarchal attitudes. In doing so, they hoped to acquire acceptance from their white counterparts.

In retrospect, when we consider the conditions of the times, it's understandable why assimilation remained a popular mode of conduct for some free African Americans in Boston. This equally allows us to understand why Maria Stewart's more nationalist approach to protest was ultimately rejected. Being far ahead of her times, Stewart defined the role for women of the future by validating their goals and aspirations. As a "bold and militant orator," she called on black women "to develop their highest intellectual capacities, to enter into all spheres of the life of the mind, and to participate in all activities within their community, from religion and education to politics and business, without apology to notions of female subservience" (Richardson 1987, 29).

The drive to assimilate greatly influenced those who rejected Stewart's call for more militancy in abolitionist reform. Her tactics were antipathetic to the modes of behavior many African Americans in Boston adhered to. These African Americans were equipped with social values handed to them by white society, and they viewed Stewart as a woman who defied the role of the subservient or docile female in society. Within their own boundaries of race, class, and gender distinctions, the more educated class of African Americans impressed standard behavior upon their community as a whole. In their view, Stewart acted improperly by choosing her public career, and it was up to these advocates of assimilation to set the trend for rejecting her message.

This massive movement toward accepting European values was most effectively impressed upon the African American community by the press.

The most notable influential publications responsible for the drive to assimilate included *Freedom's Journal,* the *Colored American,* and the *Weekly Advocate.* These black-owned-and-operated publications circulated codes of behavior for the black community. The *Freedom's Journal,* in particular, printed editorials that suggested how a woman should publicly conduct herself for acceptance in American society. These same editorials also cautioned that outspoken women violated the presumed standards of female behavior. Moreover, such a woman was one who "could not keep her mouth shut" (Horton and Horton 1986, 672).

The African American press provided one of the more substantive measures for female aspirations to higher ideals. And, in some respect, the press reinforced the feminine perspective through the interpretation of ideals to their community. These ideals were often diverse views embraced by influential leaders of the African American community. Many of these same leaders dictated that Stewart's militancy hindered the free black community as a whole. Moreover, these publicized views rigorously aspired for acceptance in society by sharing the thoughts of the masses. All of these factors affected the social attitudes of the masses who attended Stewart's lectures. They echoed much of the same sentiments projected in the press, and they placed many constraints upon Stewart's role.

During the period of the 1830s, hostile reactions fell upon women who mustered the courage to emulate Stewart's words and deeds. Although more social and political energy was spent sanctioning this type of activism, it still helped Stewart rise to historical prominence. Her activism came several years after the publication of David Walker's appeal and his mysterious death in 1829. If Walker's philosophies countered advocates of assimilation by calling for more militancy, so too did Stewart, who promoted that same philosophy. Perhaps her agitational tone of discourse urged some African Americans to appeal for moderation in her revolutionary posture. Just months before her first essay was published in 1832 in William Lloyd Garrison's *Liberator,* the Nat Turner Rebellion in South Hampton, Virginia, nearly crippled the country with fear of widespread black uprisings. These conditions of the time are referred to in Angela Davis's study *Women, Race, and Class,* which asserts that:

> The turbulent 1830s were years of intense resistance. Nat Turner's revolt, toward the beginning of the decade, inequitably announced that Black men and women were profoundly dissatisfied with their lot as slaves and were determined, more than ever, to resist. In 1831, the year of Nat Turner's revolt, the organized abolitionist movement was born. (1983, 32)

Davis's description of the conditions under which Stewart had to operate and function illustrates just how great the risk Stewart faced—and at one point, Stewart challenged the American system of slavery on the basis of the American constitution. Stewart argued that the legal enslavement of Africans was unjust and unconstitutional:

> According to the Constitution of these United Sates, he hath made all men free and equal. Then why should one worm say to another, "Keep you down there, while I sit up yonder; for I am better than thou." It is not the color of the skin that makes the man, but it is the principles formed within the soul. (Richardson 1987, 30)

If Stewart fueled more hostilities toward her discourse, it was coupled with the notion that she emulated the activism popularized by the militancy of David Walker. Once she proudly heralded Walker as one who "shall be had in everlasting remembrance" and who risked the livelihood and status of freedom to emancipated African Americans. These multiple transformations of her experience, projected a tone of discourse that characterizes the preacher, reformer, and agitator—all of which were then male roles, but which proved to enhance Stewart's strong sense of independence and self-realization.

Ultimately, Stewart's greatest desire was to motivate and enlist more African warriors like Walker to challenge oppression. And with courageous zeal, she challenged those fearful ones to come forth to take Walker's place in the battle for human rights. But Stewart's promotion of Walker's legacy prompted some to scorn her for categorizing black men as "lethargic" in their approach to abolitionist reform. Although she was quick to react to such criticisms with outspoken determination, her message brought more outrage when she responded to their pious appraisals, "It is of no use for us to wait any longer for a generation of well educated men to arise" (Richardson 1987, 62).

With tenacious drive and stamina Stewart had all the qualities to succeed in her chosen profession as public lecturer. But given the times, she had pursued one route of public activism that no other American woman had dared to venture upon. Unfortunately, a little after her emergence on the public lecture circuit, she was ostracized by those who strenuously opposed her discourse. Clearly, they were not amenable to her message, and their denouncement gave Stewart few options but to abandon her public political lecturing career—after delivering just four speeches between 1832–1833.

Stewart's victorious voice was silenced in the public arena because her chosen rhetorical discourse infuriated some with words like: "We have slumbered and slept too long . . . let every man of color . . . who possesses the spirit and principles of a man, sign a petition . . . to abolish slavery."

Since such inspirational words were mouthed by a woman, daring to give directives to men from a public podium, the message was denounced. Finally, Stewart responded to her audience in her fiery farewell address. In this last speech, Stewart said:

> I am about to leave you perhaps never more to return. For I find it is no use for me as an individual to make myself useful among my color in this city. It was for my moral and religious opinions in private that drove me thus before a public. Had experience more plainly shown me that it was the nature of man to crush his fellow, I should not have thought it so hard. Therefore, my respected friends, let us no longer talk of prejudice, till prejudice becomes extinct at home. Let us no longer talk of opposition till we cease to oppose our own. (Lowenberg and Bogin 1976, 200)

Soon after the public denouncement of Stewart's appeal to those who "should rise among our sable race," she left Boston, torn by strife and abandoned. By 1834, one year after her farewell speech and departure from Boston, Stewart compiled a collection of writings originally published under the title *Productions of Mrs. Maria W. Stewart, Presented to the First African Baptist Church & Society, of the City of Boston*. Historically this publication is the first example of an African American female autobiographer writing from her own perspective.

Throughout the remaining years of her life, Maria W. Stewart continued to be active in many social, political, educational, and religious organizations. From Boston, she settled in New York City where she spent several years teaching in public schools. But life in New York was not devoid of difficulties, and her philosophy again clashed with the established norms of feminine conduct. In 1879, decades after her initial activism began, Alexander Crummel met Stewart, living in New York:

> I remember very distinctly the great surprise . . . at finding in New York a young woman of my own people full of literary aspiration and ambition authorship. In those days, that is at the commencement of the anti-slavery enterprise, the desire for learning was almost exclusively confined to colored young men. (Richardson 1987, 93–94)

During those years in New York, not only did Stewart chronicle those experiences of her lecturing career in Boston, but she also found ways to established positive alliances for future achievements. According to Marilyn Richardson, those New York years were emphasized by continued political activities, in which Stewart

> joined women's organizations, attended Women's Anti-Slavery Conventions of 1837, and was an active participant in black women's literary society.

While it appears that she did not pursue a public speaking career there, according to the advertisements for the 1879 edition of her work, she did lecture in New York. (1987)

After almost twenty years of political activism, while simultaneously teaching in both Brooklyn and Manhattan, Stewart left for Baltimore, Maryland. In subsequent years, she taught school in Baltimore under the debilitating constraints of poverty. Stewart reveals of this experience, "an order was passed that none of the poor people need pay their rent; so the money I had saved to pay my rent I took and paid my way to Washington." (Richardson 1987, 98)

Stewart's move to Washington, D.C., in 1859, enabled her to elevate her status by securing a position as the Matron of the Freedmen's Hospital (presently Howard University Hospital). In 1864, she was listed in Washington as residing at 441 West 14th Street; from the years 1866 to 1870, she is listed as a teacher residing at 53 Ridge Street, N.W. It is probable that Stewart also spent her last years as an employee and resident at the Freedmen's Hospital, where she later died in 1879. One can find in the February 28, 1880 issue of the *People's Advocate,* a Washington, D.C. area African American newspaper, an announcement of the death of Maria Stewart.

Maria W. Stewart's discourse of truth offered the African American community a glimpse of possibilities that they were on the verge of claiming. The political transitions of her activism flow from the recognition of her victorious emergence into a male-dominated lecture circuit. There, Stewart's acquisition of power resonates in a bold militant stance that countered those preconceived myths of the African American woman.

This study of Stewart's activism reconstructs her role as a viable historical figure among nineteenth-century women. She was among to first to articulate the ideologies later popularized by activist Marcus Garvey and Malcolm X—both of whom heralded the idea that America depended on the blood, sweat, and tears of the African American. As a forerunner of these contemporary activists, Stewart alluded to the bitter truth of America's woes by saying:

> Cast your eyes about, look as far as you can see—all, all is owned by the lordly white, except here and there a lowly dwelling which the man of color, midst deprivation, fraud and opposition has been scarce able to procure . . . We have pursued the shadow, they have obtained the substance, we have planted the vines, they have eaten the fruits of them. (*Liberator,* April 27, 1833, 6; see also Golden and Ricke 1971, 196)

Through the multiplicity of her activism, Stewart exhibits an Afrocentric approach in divulging her powerful inspirational message. She used biblical passages woven into secular themes—a style of discourse that Molefi Asante asserts is not uncommon to traditional black audiences, who often demanded to hear such expressions. Asante further argues that "the sermons of the black preacher—oral tradition and call—response—relate to African origins of cultural behavior . . . communication styles are reflective of the internal mythic clock, the epic memory, the psychic stain of African in our spirits" (Asante 1987, 41).

The revelation that Maria W. Stewart's experience gives significance to the African American woman's role in nineteenth-century America and places her life story into historical context. Whatever else historians may view of her, none can deny that she made the most of whatever opportunities that were available to her in a time when the struggle for African liberation was of paramount concern.

## References

Aptheker, Herbert, ed. 1989. *The Literary Legacy of W.E.B. DuBois.* New York: Kraus International.

Asante, Molefi. 1987. *The Afrocentric Idea.* Philadelphia: Temple University Press.

———. 1990. *Kemet, Afrocentricity and Knowledge.* Trenton: Africa World Press.

Asante, Molefi, and Kariamu Welsh-Asante, eds. 1990. *African Culture: The Rhythms of Unity.* Trenton: Africa World Press.

Bergman, Peter M., ed. 1969. *The Chronological History of the Negro in America.* New York: New American Library.

Davis, Angela. 1983. *Women, Race, and Class.* New York: Random House.

Gates, Henry Louis, ed. 1984. *Black Literature and Literary Theory.* New York: Methuen.

———. 1988. *Spiritual Narratives.* New York: Oxford University Press.

Giddings, Paula. 1985. *When and Where I Enter: The Impact of Black Women on Race and Sex in America.* New York: Bantam Books.

Golden, James, and Richard Rieke. 1971. *The Rhetoric of Black Americans.* Columbus: Charles Merrill.

Horton, James Oliver, and Lois E. Horton. 1979. *Black Bostonians: Family Life and Community in the Antebellum North.* New York: Holmes and Meier.

———. 1986. "Freedom's Yoke: Gender Conventions Among Antebellum Free Blacks." *Feminist Studies* 12, no. 1 (Spring).

Loewenberg, Bert James, and Ruth Bogin, eds. 1976. *Black Women in Nineteenth Century American Life: Their Words, Their Thoughts, Their Feelings.* University Park: Pennsylvania State University Press.

Porter, Dorothy. 1936. "Activities of Literary Societies, 1846." *The Journal of Negro Education* 5, no. 4 (October).

Quarles, Benjamin. 1969. *Black Abolitionist.* London: Oxford University Press.

Richardson, Marilyn, ed. 1987. *Maria W. Stewart, America's First Black Political Writer.* Bloomington: Indiana University Press.

Stewart, Maria W. 1835. *Productions of Mrs. Maria W. Stewart, Presented to the First African Baptist Church Society of Boston.* Boston: Friends of Freedom and Virtue.

# Part III

# Oral History and Biography as Teaching Tools

# 10

# Through Trinbagonian Eyes

## Self-Portrait of a Caribbean Country

*Clement London*

## Introduction

"Through Trinbagonian Eyes" draws its sustenance from a previous work, *On Wings of Change: Self-Portrait of a Developing Caribbean Country* (London 1991), which was based on the eminent study of the husband-and-wife team, Melville J. and Frances Herskovits: *Trinidad Village* (1947). This study elevated them on the academic scene, with their work being defined as one of the most scholarly ethnographies in contemporary times.

Using the Herskovitses' work as a point of departure, this paper treats the product-outcomes in the form of a trilogy and retraces the dynamic watersheds as a continuing work in progress. First, there is an identification of these watersheds, which begin with background awareness, leading finally to the choice of Toco, a village on the Northeast corner of Trinidad, as the area under study. This locality is discussed in cogent detail in order to give a concept of formation in examining African diaspora history and culture. This paper then shifts to a discussion of initial reaction to misconceptions reflected in the volume and the feeling of a need to deal with refutations to the resultant decision to mount a proactive project that sought to provide involvement and instruction of persons, young and old, from Toco in 1976.

Plans to follow through failed to materialize because of reasons identified as being beyond the control of the research team. Nonetheless, another related project using similar research facilities and processes was launched.

It incorporated a widening of the population under study to include participants drawn from across the Caribbean and elsewhere who had settled permanently or were temporarily in Toco residing or were in transit to other places. Out of this project came the volume, *Through Caribbean Eyes: Self Portrait of a Developing Country* (1989). This was the second phase of the trilogy.

The third phase of the trilogy came with the research project that sought to assess the people's perception of the Nation of Trinbago's stewardship after twenty-five years of independence. The outcome of this study was the publication *On Wings of Change: Self-Portrait of a Developing Caribbean Country* (1991).

What does all of this mean in the context of the Herskovitses' study? This is essentially what this paper attempts to address. It points out the critical significance of preparation, goals, commitment, and other relevant factors associated with the conduct of this kind of research; it calls into question the emergent impediments to progress and the need to stay focused—so that priorities may find pragmatic response, but not be allowed to squelch other ambitions or accomplishments.

Finally, a model of basic procedures is submitted, addressing the uninformed or unsophisticated reader who may thereby be saved the embarrassment of obvious pitfalls associated with the undertaking and demystifying while the process of basic research. Participants themselves may benefit in several ways, which they may then utilize, in community outreach towards the improvement of the human condition or for their own personal or educational edification.

From these phases of the trilogy, one may learn that in the translation of the theoretical into the practical, the encounter of the dynamic essences of people, including representatives of all segments of society, should heighten awareness of human conditions. Bases for establishing biographical statement are supported by interviews, comments, impressions, observations, and official documents.

## Through Trinbagonian Eyes:
## Self-Portrait of a Caribbean Country

There is a sense in which the research leading to and providing the underpinnings for *Through Caribbean Eyes* has assumed the character of a trilogy. According to Funk and Wagnalls' *Standard College Dictionary*, a trilogy is defined as a group of three literary or dramatic compositions, each complete in itself, but continuing the same general subject. In light of this definition, the central focus of this essay becomes the task of chronicling the dynamic linkages identified in the context of their growth and development in a unique research undertaking that continues to be a work in progress. We begin by taking a retrospective view of cogent factors that identify and contextualize watersheds relative to the developmental processes.

As a point of departure, there is the issue of initial reactions to perceived inaccuracies of the Herskovitses' book, *Trinidad Village* (1947), which was followed by renewed urge to act in a proactive way to attempt to secure, through structured interviews and gathered data, a sense of the lived experiences of senior citizens of selected villages throughout Toco Ward, County St. David's, Trinidad, the Republic of Trinidad and Tobago. Even more important, it is to be considered here as the first aspect of the trilogy, because it is the outcome of the initial effort, using proaction rather than refutation.

Second, there is the issue of interviewing, not only native Trinbagonians,* but persons who for various reasons came from throughout the Caribbean region to Trinbago as settlers or were in transit to other countries such as the United States, Canada, England, or elsewhere in Africa, Asia, Europe, or Latin America. Based on their life spaces and styles, largely the experience of the Caribbean island societies, these selected interviewees reflected a remarkable sense of life in the Caribbean, hence the name of the product-outcome, the book *Through Caribbean Eyes*.

Third comes the issue of attempting to derive a sense of the people's perception of the status of the nation of Trinbago, after the first twenty five years of independence from British colonial rule. At this juncture, it should be noted that there was a major concern of having the people themselves speak their minds, to have them narrate their lived experiences, rather than to provide many abstract analyses as they evaluated, making comparisons of sorts between the dichotomous encounter of dependence and independence, versus life under a statutory, independent period of existence.

The outcome of this third dimension of the trilogy is the aforementioned volume, *On Wings of Change: Self Portrait of a Developing Caribbean Country, Trinidad-Tobago,* which provides the theme of this paper, "Through Trinbagonian Eyes." It should be restated and clarified that the research that informed this trilogy derived its genesis from a work of exceptional scholarship, the Herskovitses' remarkable *Trinidad Village*.

---

*Trinbago is the current popular name by which the twin island-state of Trinidad and Tobago has been called since independence; hence, the name Trinbagonians for the inhabitants. The union of the twin island-stae was established in 1884 by the British as a significant part of their colonial policy in the British Empire.

## The Herskovitses, Their Research,
*Trinidad Village*

Sometime, about 1929, the Herskovitses were returning from an anthropological study of the so-called Bush Negroes* of Dutch Guiana, one of the places they had made the focus of ethnographic study. They spent several days at Port-of-Spain, the capital of Trinidad, the Republic of Trinidad and Tobago, waiting for a ship to take them back to the United States. While waiting, they read in the *Trinidad Guardian,* a local newspaper, a letter from an aroused citizen expressing indignation at certain practices then being carried out on the outskirts of the city by local people who were worshipers of Shango, a religion derived from the Yorubas of Nigeria.

These African cultural retentions, diffused through the incidence of slavery, attracted the Herskovitses, who decided there and then that they would return to Trinidad to study events, issues, and occurrences. Many years passed before they returned, pursuing their promise to themselves. They believed then that, based on their anthropological expertise and that letter to the *Trinidad Guardian,* they would likely encounter the Shango religious practices and retentions of African ways of life in greatest purity in largely rural districts, remote from Port-of-Spain's center of European contact. In addition, they preferred to work with a small, ideal anthropological community, away from much urban influence and manageable enough so that they could come to know it well. They chose the village, Toco.

It should be of interest to know that, contrary to expectations, their chosen locality—although a remote community—was devoid of Shango worship and had only the attenuated African antecedents that any rural Negro community elsewhere in Trinidad or the southern United States. What the Herskovitses found was a community reflecting a transition from African customs to ways of life preponderantly European, a fact that was thought to be clearly indicative of the powerful colonial cultural dominance.

The African legacy had been diluted, but the Herskovitses found the Baptist Shouters sect at Toco. It revealed to them the influence of African worship that is reflected also in the Shango religion found elsewhere in Trinidad. Included also at Toco were kinship-plural marriages, as well as the transformation of Sankey and Moody hymns into "shouts," parallel points of transition in musical styles, found throughout the African diaspora. Altogether, the concepts of cultural focus, cultural retentions, and

---

*"Bush Negroes" are people whom some historians speak of as descendants of proud, defiant, runaway slaves. They took their own freedom from slavery.

mechanisms of adaptation, readaptation, and reinterpretation of customs, helped the people retain the inner meanings of traditionally sanctioned modes of behavior, while adopting new outer institutional forms. In essence the Herskovitses were quick to recognize elements of African customs— that is, learned traditions that spring from African sources and are driven by the subject's desire to acquire the benefits that arise from their ability to manipulate European culture to their advantage.

The Herskovitses' study was conducted around the beginning of the post–World War II period, a period that was characterized by a local Trinidad-Tobago economy of cash-crop agriculture, which was responsive to the prices of mona and cobra coffee set in London and New York; by large estates, absentee-owned, but organized for profit-making; by the introduction of universal adult suffrage; and, also by a public works department of the colonial government, paying wages that were determined in the colonial capital through a monetary system that reflected the combined influences of English sterling and United States–Canadian currency.

The comprehensive anthropological work produced an impressive ethnography that focused largely on the social and religious aspects of Toco Village, capital of Toco Ward, against a backdrop of the then predominantly African cultural antecedents.

*Trinidad Village* (1947) grew out of the research project and became a classic work. It has since been rated as one of the finest ethnographies ever written. The study stands unique and constitutes a systematic, rounded view of all the phases of life of any Negro community in the English-speaking Caribbean at the time of its publication. Until then, while many studies on the Caribbean understandably focused their efforts on immediate political and economic issues, on facilitating interracial harmony, or on ameliorating the plight of the underprivileged. This volume appealed to the need to take into account traditional sanctions no less than overt institutions.

## Toco and Trinidad in the Caribbean Universe

Although the Caribbean region is essentially multiethnic in character, there is yet a very special sense in which it may be perceived as an African space providing an awakening aspiration that emerges from a rugged sleep of yesteryear. However, in truth and in fact, the Caribbean is multicultural, multilingual, and multipolitical. At the most southern end of the Caribbean archipelago sits the island-state Trinidad-Tobago. Geologically, Trinidad is an ait of the Orinoco delta and has more of American continental characteristics than its sister islands.

The Republic of Trinidad-Tobago consists of the two most southerly islands of the Lesser Antilles chain within the Caribbean. Trinidad, lying only seven miles from the closest point north of Venezuela, has an area of 1,864 square miles—about the size of Rhode Island or Delaware in the United States. Tobago, lying twenty-two miles northeast of Trinidad, is 116 square miles in area. An independent state and developing country, the twin islands—both former British colonies—were united by political fiat in 1884 and, following Ghana, Nigeria, and Jamaica, became independent in August 31, 1962, a unitary state and member of the Caribbean Commonwealth Community (CARICOM).

Since independence, the nation-state has referred to itself as "Trinbago" and the people as "Trinbagonians." Despite prolonged periods of slavery and its bastard issue, colonialism, like many English-speaking Caribbean island-states like Trinbago have emerged within recent times as independent nations, their small size notwithstanding. By incorporating modified versions of the British system of parliamentary government, as well as other vestiges of traditional British socioeconomic, political, and educational models, these island-states have begun the awesome journey of independent development, despite the vagaries of regional and international challenges. In the main, these nations, in spite of their relatively small size, have replaced much, if not most, of their foreign, colonial personnel with essentially nonwhite leadership that is largely African and Asian.

In the 1980s I undertook research in many places throughout the English-speaking Caribbean. One such place was Trinbago, where an attempt was made to get a sense of the nation's stewardship after its first twenty-five years of independence. The reportage, derived from Trinbagonians themselves, was based on extensive interviews, comments, observations, and impressions. These were the views of active cultural beings who were suffused with the promises and defects of their society, biographical vignettes that were not the product of detached sociological participants or interviewees as neutral dispensers of information, but were, indeed, the thoughts of persons who, in extended tape-recorded interviews, answered specifically fielded questions as well as shared anecdotes about their lived experiences, activities, and perceptions.

The product-outcome of this research became the volume *On Wings of Change: Self Portrait of a Developing Country*. The research has been also about Trinbagonians' thinking, aspirations, successes and failures; about their bruised egos, battered pride and prejudices; their passions and pleasures within the context of their day-to-day encounters with their own reality. The book is about a people's view of themselves: how they perceived their own stewardship during the unique era of independence.

This work provides the theme of this paper, *"Through Trinbagonian*

*Eyes: Self Portrait of a Caribbean Country."* It is the third dimension, to date, of the trilogy of investigative research efforts planned and executed against telling challenges. The import of this paper is the chronicling of the process of biographical, oral history research experienced during a work in progress.

Toco Village, with a population of about five hundred, is located on the northeastern corner of Trinidad; it is bounded on the north by the Caribbean Sea and on the east by the Atlantic Ocean. The population of Toco is almost entirely of African descent, with sprinklings of East Indians, Chinese, Whites, Koreans, and Hispanics. The African elements are a mixture of islanders from Barbados, Jamaica, Haiti, and many from the eastern Caribbean area with a preponderance from Grenada. In point of fact, there are more Grenadians in Trinidad than on the island of Grenada itself.

Life of residents of Toco (Tocans) parallels that of Africans in many other Caribbean islands and rural sections of the United States, the legacy of the vicissitudes of slavery and its attendant historical, political, and economic problems. At the time of the Herskovitses' attempt to describe the customs of Toco, their derivation and effect on the life of the people, and the compensation for them which has given Tocans continuity and a measure of adjustment, many factors emerged as skewed or misrepresented. To the unaided eye of the outsider, the information presented appears rational, but to a sophisticated inhabitant such misrepresentations leap out of the printed page at the reader.

Whether one wishes to ascribe such research discrepancies to oversight or to the short sojourn of researchers, the fact is that many interviewees said what they thought the investigators wished to hear. There is the need to authenticate further by repeating questions among several persons in several places within a population. There are perhaps also matters that require further investigation. At any rate, for this author, these issues were obvious enough to have critical attention. I was born in that part of the country and grew up there. I saw the researchers when they visited and investigated. I was a child then, but remember the occurrence. Later when I read the volume, *Trinidad Village,* I was able to detect some discrepancies.

A mundane example should suffice to explain my point. The Herskovitses, in describing the local use of ground, parched corn (called by the villagers *samsam* or *chilli-bibbi*), spoke of its being eaten as a full meal. This was not so then nor is it true now. While it is true that *samsam* is eaten, this is not eaten as a meal. Children generally savor it as a snack during recess at school. Possibly, a case can be made that since the village is in a rural area—in a historical and cultural context, rural areas can be interpreted as aesthetic and ideological reflections of the dominance of colonial regimes—abject poverty may have led to the use of this snack as a meal among inhabitants who lived at subsistence levels.

Trinidad offers a striking exception to the rest of the Americas regarding the late introduction of African slaves. In light of this factor, readers are likely to assume that Trinidad, as a consequence, was kept a poverty-stricken backwater island of the flourishing Caribbean. To readers who support the theory that slavery was a "blessing," the reference to eating *samsam* or *chilli-bibbi* will find credence as a justification for slavery. Understandably there are many such persons today who share and espouse such heinous views—even though, by the turn of the twentieth century, the discovery of oil was already attracting many people from elsewhere in the Caribbean, as well as the United States, Canada, England, and other European countries as they sought employment in the growing oil industry. Whereas blacks were not considered humans, but rather as a commodity, there were similar patterns of exchange for oil products and enslaved Africans. That there are, today, more Grenadians for example, living in Trinidad than in Grenada itself, constitutes part of the Caribbean, American, Asian, and European exodus to Trinidad-Tobago, giving it its uniquely plural demographic character.

Moreover, as an agricultural district, the village of Toco and its littoral abound with food crops, fruits, vegetables, and a bountiful sea of fresh fish, lobsters, crabs, shrimps, and whelks, as well as numerous wild animals from neighboring forests. The Herskovitses make little or no mention of these factors. To the contrary, they turn some things around. Thus, while crucial and very significant anthropological mirage was otherwise accomplished, there were these issues that would repel the Tocan reader.

Needless to say, one of my strong initial reactions to perusing *Trinidad Village* several years ago was the desire to nationally refute such incongruous statements. Such sentiments however, gave way to more reasoned thoughts. And, instead, there originated the innovative, proactive idea of an oral history-ethnographic project that, following the appropriate methodological strategy of using a structured, balanced interview schedule, could ferret out some valuable empirical information about the area by and on behalf of the people themselves—who, speaking on crucial aspects of their life to young residents of Toco could heighten the foreign ethnologist's vision of what is seen rather than unseen, close rather than far, personal rather than impersonal.

I reasoned that the methodology of investigation should involve multiple strategies, including the use of the interview schedule. Students, for example, if they wished to pursue a single, total life history, might interview and record relatives or nonrelatives about their lives and then transcribe these recordings. Such kinds of exercises would also serve local children, giving them an opportunity to explore their community and environment.

Young people in general sometimes seem to think that life has always been the way they know it, with its current modern conveniences. So too, they tend to see the elderly as citizens of yesteryear—those same individuals who, by dint of their fortitude, determination, and industry delivered to the young generation, the very facilities that they now take for granted and enjoy. Awareness teaches them that they too have the responsibility as part of their citizenship—an obligation to improve on past efforts. In essence, many senior citizens argue that the younger generation of citizens seems to be caught in a syndrome of disappearing cultural traditions, which if it continues unabated may cause a sense of rootlessness that may limit young people's self-understanding and jeopardize a source of their sustenance—a sense of where they have come from, where they are in time and space, and where they may be heading towards the future. Meeting these needs became a goal.

Hence, involving the young in basic research would expose them to senior citizens, repositories of living history, through whom they would derive a sense of the past of their community, which is always undergoing change. By speaking with senior citizens, they would be exposed to the dynamics of translating basic research theory into practice. Such involvement allows them the opportunity for relevant participation and let them discover within the parameters of their own immediate environment information that would provide the basis for viable history, science, and social studies education and, appreciation for their own community—and be as well an opportunity to bridge the generation gap by sharpening their awareness of the importance of the industry and responsibility of senior citizens in delivering a proud heritage.

Thus, far from a willingness to write off senior citizens as being of little use now, the experience of bringing the young into closer contact with them through research engagement and genuine human interaction with a reality that is linked with their very presence and beyond this, would so charge the young with the dynamic responsibility to both replicate the selected qualities of their seniors and improve on their efforts.

In the process of extrapolating information from the various resource systems that abound in the immediate environment and using this information to organize relevant history and social studies curricula, I hoped that the research team members would derive educational and community satisfaction from their own experience, that they would have an opportunity to "peep" into the past and salvage those valued components which have been hidden by time. Perhaps the younger generation could use them with modification to further societal progress and to chant of the human condition.

But, in addition to doing these particular things, I had an overriding concern of teaching and learning. More specifically, the question as to how I could transcend the immediate and go beyond the rhetoric of chalk and talk. I felt that one should do something rather substantive. This should become part of the academic outreach as well as my act of returning thanks to my birth community. Indeed, service should be the rent paid for one's sojourn as a citizen. Therefore, the involvement of young people in the research project at Toco should essentially provide the opportunity for doing something substantive on behalf of the people of Toco, Trinidad, and the Republic of Trinidad amd Tobago. In the end, analysis should deem it quite prudent to link the work done in association with Toco to the larger constituency of Trinidad itself.

A decision to have young people and others from the Toco community participate in the project was factored into the plans. Also included was the idea of a set of procedures—a handbook if you will—that would explain the processes for conducting oral history. This handbook was to be based on oral history theory as well as on research practices derived from the field-work at Toco. Here, within the context of their varied experiences, it was reasoned that as the young nation of Trinbago struggled with the dynamics of independence, the young people would be required to grow and develop as citizens within the atmosphere of agony and ecstasy and experience the growing pains of independence. The fieldwork would give a better under-standing of some of the crucial socioeconomic as well as political circum-stances of the nation's new status, independence.

Implicit in the concept of independence is the assumption that, among other responsibilities, a nation must look within itself at its own available resources for facilities and opportunities that may be used for fostering its own growth and development. And as opportunities, resources, and facili-ties are identified, needs arise for the creation of agencies, expertise, and institutions that may assist in the nurturance of the culture. In the pantheon of the replication of values, the prime movers of the legacy of civilization—schools—have been developed as instruments for the grand function of translating the social heritage.

Foresightful planning is essential in carrying through the simplest or grandest design. The availability of funding for setting the mechanism of research underway is always a problem for most researchers. It became a harbinger of bad news that dogged us all the way throughout these phases. It interfered with the follow-up on the initial effort. Despite genuine efforts to secure a grant, financial support came from the author's modest salary, plus a few hundred dollars of "seed" money as a mini-grant from the home institution's faculty research fund; altogether modest sums indeed, which were partly absorbed by international travel to the field. Thus, in large measure, this initial effort was conducted in the context of a "dry run," with the hope of a follow-up during ensuing years. The data from this project remain intact, but are still unpublished.

But an overriding factor is the issue that despite impediments, there must be a compelling sense of commitment to the task ahead. It was assumed that the direct involvement of students in helping to write or reconstruct their own local history should be paramount among decisions—that participating would give them a sense of satisfaction, accomplishment, and appreciation for their own history, their own nation, and themselves. Moreover, materials and skills utilized in their pursuit of innovative educational experiences could become the catalytic, motivational underpinnings for meaningful social science or social studies as well as for other related disciplines and programs that may facilitate the teaching-learning transaction, especially for students living in far-flung rural areas.

Thus, armed with a typewriter, a structured interview schedule, tape recorders, blank tapes, prepared forms, stationery, and good intentions, the research expedition began with the departure of the project director and his preteen son, Sherwyn, from New York City in July 1967, for Toco, Trinidad, the Republic of Trinidad and Tobago.

Of course, advanced arrangements were made through letters, telephone calls, and by word-of-mouth messages. The way was cleared for foreign intervention—the Toco English Catholic (E.C.) Elementary School was involved as the center of operation; the cooperation and participation was secured of the principal, Mr. Marcus Joseph, and one of his young, bright male teachers, Mr. Peter Thomas; the involvement was obtained of two high schoolers (studying in Port-of-Spain) and of several post-primary and upper-elementary students. There was work to be done: interviewing, transcribing, visiting, talking with people from all walks of life in the community (civil servants, postal personnel, fishermen, policemen and women, landed proprietors, laborers, gardeners, the registrar of births and deaths, as well as estate and farm overseers and religious leaders).

With the fine cooperation and support of Mr. Joseph, the Toco E.C. Elementary School was used as the research center during the entire life of the program in the summer of 1976.

## Fieldwork at Toco, Summer 1976

Seminars were offered for orientation concerning the nature, purpose, and function of the project. Methods and techniques were taught—the use of the tape recorder and interviewing, recording, translating, transcribing, and editing for the best effect, including trial-runs with two-person interview teams; the importance of checks and balances during interviewing and taping; and the sharing of duties and responsibilities; the required courtesy and professionalism in actualizing the project. Participants were oriented to strategies for dealing with the intended and unintended, the serendipitous, and to the care and vigilance needed for establishing authentic, professional products-outcome and good conduct.

After the seminars, which lasted days, the membership fanned out in pairs, with clear assignments, a tape recorder and related literature and equipment. They went about their task with diligence and enthusiasm. At the end of every day, they returned to the center for conversations, discussions, and sharing of experiences. At those times, too, some recordings were transcribed and a few edited.

One major highlight of the research experience was the group's visitations to village institutions that they ordinarily overlooked of even bypassed. They visited the registrar of births and deaths, the police station, the post office, the warden's office, and other places of interest. At those places, they were accorded the privilege of scrutinizing valuable records that the public seldom see; they perused books of data, including valuable information of happenings in decades past. They were awed by this discovery and by the fact that such information exists at all. They felt special and promised to return with others to share. We became a family unit of probers into our own village, our own space with all of its essences.

The participants were indeed proud to be designated as "researchers"— that they were able to talk with the elderly, whom, they found, were full of knowledge and were happy to share their wisdom. They all came away realizing that it was not "cool" nor good sense to write off old people; instead, they felt a closeness with most of them and, in some instances, established pal-relationships here and there along the way. As a gesture, each research participant wrote and submitted a short autobiography with the promise to follow through the next year, 1977.

Altogether, our research team members expressed the vision that the history of one's own people is something that most ideally should start at home even before a child enters formal schooling. To all, the experience came to more than just learning history; it had to do with, if you will, a sense of their "roots" in Toco and beyond. In a sense, it is probably the most genuine, helpful area of knowledge for them, young citizens, growing up into adulthood with security of self, a sense of independence and of being self-possessed persons.

However, project-participants also learned that the study about one's own people should be extended to include studying about other people, their history, and culture. Indeed, a great need of humanity today is that all people within their nations, including the Caribbean region and all the world, need to know about others of different races, religions, and nationalities as being all human beings in the global village. This is extremely important, if only because it is they who will inherit the world, and, therefore, it will become their responsibility in time to make a difference in the improvement of the human condition.

**Conclusion**

"Through Trinbagonian Eyes: Self-Portrait of a Caribbean Country" seeks its figure and ground from a previous work, *On Wings of Change: Self-Portrait of a Developing Caribbean Country*. But, such works share parallels with similar investigations. Indeed, this theme derived its impetus from the scholarly work of the Herskovitses, whose *Trinidad Village* emerged on the academic scene as one of the finest ethnographies in many years.

The personal research stimulated by this volume remains a work in progress. In fact, it is fair to assume that this effort may never really see closure. Since there is always something else to be done, it is therefore, quite possible that the context of a trilogy may change with factors of progress and time. As one keeps trying other things, the vistas keep opening up and expanding. A general sensibility is sometimes sufficient to create end-products out of research efforts. Often, it is beyond a researcher or author to seek a perfect ending; he/she may prefer to approximate; and this allows for creativity. Stumbling on new things is essential for creativity for taking along works in progress.

Speaking about the trilogy should, it is hoped, provide some sense of linkage, sequence, and follow-through as development expands. The chronicling of events is not meant to assume the proffering of the self as a "research maverick" with supposedly all of the "expert" answers. Instead, the purpose here was primarily that of sharing experiences as they have occurred in the dynamic thrust at seriously engaging a worthy academic undertaking. Regardless of what one may or not choose to accord the effort, it remains in the context, a simple and honest effort to retrace the process utilized in the conduct of this particular research. It is meant to be shared.

Financial support and other critical elements are crucial for carrying through such work—as with most other undertakings that enter into the equation of perceiving life as a balance. As such, true success comes with the investment of many factors, not the least of which is commitment to the research task, be it ever so humble or exasperating if it is to be accomplished at all. This position brings to the fore the reminder that the efficaciousness of the exercise lies primarily in the rigor of the effort.

Neither the beginning nor the destination is really as important as the journey of *getting there*. It is not simply a matter of arriving at the end, for example, that defines the recognition of the human condition; but, instead, it is the journey of arriving there. Give a man a fish and he may feed his family a meal, but teach that man how to fish and he may feed his family for life. Implicit here is the moral implication as to how we behave as shapers of cultures—educators—and assume our responsibility amid the challenges of attempting to demystify the process.

Indeed, Alex Haley captured the implicit significance of this kind of commitment and persuasion when he discussed the journey he traveled while preparing his now famous epic. He opined that

> The idea was that I had gotten myself into this and was trying to make it. That was the attitude I kept. . . . It was a pact I made with myself . . . ! had chosen the direction I was in, and so it was up to me . . . as a human being, was going to cope with the challenge of this path that I had chosen for myself.

The "Process Guidelines" in the appendix should help those who plan to travel the oral history highway.

## References

Allen, B. 1978. "Personal Experience Narratives: Use and Meaning in Interaction." *Folklore and Mythology Studies* 2: 5–7.
Allen, B., and W.L. Montell. 1981. "From Memory to History: Using Oral Sources in Local Historical Research." Newsletter. Nashville: The American Association for State and Local History.
———. 1982. *From Memory to History.* Nashville: The American Association for State and Local History.
Alvarez, R.A.F., and S.C. Kline. 1977. *Self-Discovery through the Humanities 1: Exploring Local History.* Washington: The National Council on the Aging.
Andrews, M. 1991. *Lifetimes of Commitment: Aging, Politics, Psychology.* Cambridge, England: Cambridge University Press.
Baum, W.K. 1971. *Oral History for the Local Historical Society.* 2d ed. Nashville: American Association for State and Local History.
Berman, M. 1971. *The Politics of Authenticity.* New York: Atheneum.
Davis, C., K. Bock, and K. McLean. 1977. *Oral History: From Tape to Tape.* Chicago: American Library Association.
Frisch, M. 1990. *A Shared Authority: Essays on the Craft and Meaning of Oral and Public History.* Albany: State University of New York Press.
Goldstein, K.S.A. 1964. *A Guide for Field Workers in Folklore.* Hatboro, PA: Folklore Associates.

Gould, P., and R. White. 1986. *Mental Maps*. 2d ed. Boston: Allen and Unwin.

Griswold, W. 1982. "Education as Transformation: Commentary and Replies." *Harvard Educational Review* 52, no. 1: 45–60.

Gwaltney, J.L. 1981. *Drylongso: A Self Portrait of Black America*. New York: Vintage Books.

Havlice, P.P. 1985. *Oral History: A Reference Guide and Annotated Bibliography*. Jefferson, NC: McFarland.

Hensen, P.M., and T.A. Schorazman. 1991. "Videohistory: Focusing on the American Past." *Journal of American History* 78: 618–627.

Herskovits, Melville J., and Frances Herskovits. 1947. *Trinidad Village*. New York: Knopf.

Horowitz, M., ed. 1971. *Peoples and Cultures of the Caribbean*. New York: Natural History Press.

Ines, E.D. 1981. *The Tape-Recorded Interview: A Manual for Fieldworkers in Folklore and Oral History*. Knoxville: University of Tennessee Press.

Ken-Faxworth, M. 1985. "Beyond Roots: An Exclusive Interview with Alex Haley." *The Black Collegian* 16, no. 1 (September/October: 116–124; 186–188.

Krippendorf, K. 1988. *Content Analysis*. Beverly Hills: Sage.

London, C.B.G. 1979. "Carnival: A Religious Right of Passage." *Negro History Bulletin*, 42: 4–6.

———. 1984. "Caribbean Turning Point through Education." *NOMMO, The African Studies and Research Center Newsletter* (February–March: 1–2.

———. 1989. *Through Caribbean Eyes: Self-Portrait of a Developing Country*. Chesapeake, VA: ECA Associates.

———. 1991. *On Wings of Change: Self-Portrait of a Developing Caribbean Country*. Wellesley, MA: Calalous.

Madhubati, H.R. 1994. *Claiming Earth: Race, Rage, Redemption: Blacks Seeking a Culture of Enlightened Empowerment*. Chicago, IL: Third World Press.

McFeely, W.S. 1994. *Sapelo's People: A Long Walk to Freedom*. New York: W.W. Norton.

McMahan, E.M. 1989. *Elite Oral History Discourse*. Tuscaloosa, University of Alabama Press.

Montell, W.L. 1970. *The Saga of Coe Ridge: A Study in Oral History*. Knoxville: University of Tennessee Press.

Moss, W.W. 1970. *Oral History Program Manual*. New York: Praeger.

Nettleford, R. 1979. *Caribbean Cultural Identity*. Los Angeles: University of California Press.

Ong, W.J. 1982. *Orality and Literacy*. London: Methuen.

Bellandro, R. 1993. Interview by Julia Ardery, Berea College, KY, 13 April. University of Kentucky Oral History Collection, Lexington.

Rosenstone, R.A. 1990. "Revisiting History: Contemporary Filmmakers and the Construction of the Past." *Comparative Studies in Society and History* 32: 837.

Shumway, G.L., and W.G. Hartley. 1973. *An Oral History Primer*. New York: Praeger.

Smith, M.G. 1965. *The Plural Societies of the British West Indies*. Berkeley: University of California Press.

Stave, B.M. 1977. *The Making of Urban History: Historiography Through Oral History*. Beverly Hills: Sage Publications.

Sutton, J. 1981. *Praise the Bridge That Carries You Over*. Cambridge: Harvard University Press.

Thelen, D. 1989. "Memory and American History." *Journal of American History* 75: 117–129.

Thompson, P. 1978. *The Voice of the Past: Oral History.* Oxford: Oxford University Press.

Vasina, J. 1973. *Oral Tradition: A Study in Historical Methodology.* Trans. H.M. Wright. Chicago: Aldine.

Waserman, M.J. 1975. *Bibliography on Oral History,* rev. ed. New York: Oral History Association.

White, H. 1987. *The Content of the Form.* Baltimore: Johns Hopkins University Press.

———. 1973. *Metahistory.* Baltimore: Johns Hopkins University Press.

# Appendix

## Suggested Guidelines for Travel Along Oral History Interviews

### *The Process*

Important curricula of the research process leading to the product-outcome, *Through Caribbean Eyes,* may include:

- Exposing young people to the dynamics of basic research theory and practice;
- Providing opportunities for relevant participation;
- Having students discover meaning making within the parameters of their own immediate environment;
- Developing opportunities for the appreciation of one's own surroundings;
- Providing opportunities for enabling students to bridge the generation gap and to participate in community outreach for the improvement of the human condition; and
- Heightening awareness of the importance of responsibility of and toward senior citizens in delivering a proud heritage, their legacy of civilization.

## Preparing for the Research Operation

- Secure funding, through proposal(s) if possible;
- Schedule appropriate time (sabbatical, if eligible);
- Establish contacts before arrival and start of project;

- Obtain permission for local/foreign protocols;
- Have relevant forms ready (e.g., legal documents);
- Provide appropriate equipment such as recorder(s), tapes, stationery, and batteries; and
- Identify your subjects beforehand and make clear your purpose.

To some degree, this research with its numerous points of development and its constructs of a trilogy may be defined essentially as work in progress.

## Ethical/Legal Guidelines

Some special issues of oral history/biographical vignettes include ethical and legal guidelines. In effectuating oral history procedures, for example, there are some overlap between and among guidelines. In particular, while such overlaps become obvious in the areas of primary and secondary education, there are sufficient differences to warrant specific guidelines that educators may turn to. Some specific areas of concerns involve responsibilities and obligations as they affect teachers, students, and interviewees.

Procedures to be followed so that interviewers honor their responsibilities to the interviewees take into consideration the relationship between the two. However, most of the issues involving those two essential groups are in the areas of ethics and legality.

### *Educator and Student Guidelines*

*The Educator*

- Become familiar with the established guidelines;
- Become knowledgeable of the literature, techniques, and processes (of oral history), so that the best possible instruction can be presented to the student;
- Ensure that each student is properly prepared before going into the community to conduct interviews;
- Work with other professionals and organizations to provide the best research experience for the student;
- Consider that the project may merit preservation and the need to work with other professionals and repositories in order to preserve and disseminate these collected materials; and
- Show willingness to share one's expertise with other educators, associations, and organizations.

*The Student*

- Become thoroughly familiar with the techniques and processes of interviewing and the development of basic research principles involving interviewing. Structured seminars can facilitate this process;
- Explain to the interviewee the purpose of the interview and how it will be used;
- Treat the interviewee with respect;
- Sign a receipt for and return any materials borrowed from the interviewee;
- Obtain a signed legal release for the interview;
- Keep your word about oral or written promises made to interviewees; and
- Give proper credit (verbal or written) when using testimony or other material in context.

## *Interviewees*

- The interviewees must be made fully aware of the goals and objectives of the project;
- The interviewees must be made fully aware of the various stages of the program/project and the nature of their participation at each stage;
- The interviewees must be given the opportunity to respond to questions as freely as possible and not be subjected to stereotyped assumptions based on ethnicity, race, gender, class, or any social or cultural characteristics;
- The interviewees must understand their right to refuse to discuss certain subjects, to seal portions of interviews or, in extremely sensitive circumstances, even to choose to remain anonymous;
- Interviewees must be fully informed about the potential uses to which the material may be put, including deposit of the interviews in a repository, publication in books, articles, newspapers, or magazines, as well as all forms of public programming;
- Interviewees should be provided with full and easily understood explanation of their legal rights before being asked to sign a contract, deed, or gift, and/or visual or audio tapes and transcripts to an administering authority or individual; and, whenever possible, the interviewees should be consulted about all subsequent use of material;
- All prior agreements made with interviewees should be honored;
- Interviewees should be fully informed about the potential for and disposition of royalties that might accrue from the use of their interviews, including all forms of public programming;

- Interviews and other related materials must remain confidential until there is agreement to release them for use; and
- Care must be taken when making public all materials relating to the interviews.

### Recognizing and Honoring the Responsibilities of Interviewers/Programs to the Profession

Procedures should include assurances that:

- Interviewers considered the potential for public endeavor and research use of the interviews, and have endeavored to prevent any exploitation of or harm to interviewees;
- Interviewers are well trained and conduct their interviews in a professional manner;
- Interviewers are well grounded in the background of the subject(s) to be interviewed;
- Interviews will be conducted in a spirit of critical inquiry and efforts will be made to provide as complete a record as possible;
- Interviewees should be selected on the basis of the cogency of their experience to the subject at hand;
- Interview equipment should include tapes, transcripts, agreements, tape-recorders, and documentation of the interview process. The products will be placed in a repository after a reasonable period of time. This decision is subject to the agreements made with the interviewees; and that depository will administer their use in accordance with those agreements.

### Mutual Responsibilities and Obligations of Interviewers and Programs

- Interviewers should be made aware of the program goals and be fully informed of ethical and legal considerations;
- Interviewers should be fully informed of all the tasks they are expected to complete in a project;
- Interviewers should be made fully aware of their obligations to the project, program, or sponsoring institution, regardless of their own personal interest in a program/project; and
- Interviewers should be fully informed of their legal rights and of their responsibilities to both the interviewees and the sponsoring institution.

## Procedures Followed to Assure That Interviewers and Programs Recognize and Honor Their Responsibilities to the Community/Public

- The research materials and all works created from them are made available and accessible to the community that participated in the project;
- Sources of external funding and sponsorship should be clearly noted for each interview and project;
- Interviewers and projects should endeavor not to impose their own values on the community being studied;
- The tapes and transcripts should not be used in an unethical manner; and
- While there are still many issues that emerge during fieldwork, and that, indeed, require additional attention, the above instructions are sufficient at least for the beginner, and they are presented in this spirit.

# 11

# Life Ain't Been No Crystal Stair

## The Rhetoric of Autobiography in Black Female Slave Narratives

### Olga Idriss Davis

Employing the metaphor of the crystal stair from Langston Hughes's poem "Mother to Son" this essay examines the rhetorical nature of autobiography and its significance in black female slave narratives. This essay contends that black female slave narratives both explore the genre of autobiography as a vehicle for shaping black women's identity and serve as a foundation for establishing black women's intellectual, rhetorical, epistemological, and ontological tradition in American autobiography.

## Introduction

The role of black women in African American cultural life reveals the tenacity and ironclad resilience of a people denied common humanity and yet relentless in their search for self-definition. Poised at the intersection between race and gender, class and nationalism, black women learned to transform their identity through symbolic means of change. The relationship between language, culture, and autobiography reveals the legacy of black women as survivors in their attempt to maintain ancestral traditions and negotiate the demands of the New World in the face of brutality and degradation. The symbolic ways in which enslaved black women responded to domination, power, and control provides a lens for exploring the rhetorical brilliance of black women's resistance to oppressive realities.

The symbolic nature of resistance points to the liberating power of the slave narrative. This genre of literary expression informs the ways in which black women created language to build coalitions of sisterhood, to invent strategies of defiance, and ultimately to change the course of history with their autobiographical accounts of inhumanity. The resilience of spirit evident in the oral tradition of narrative discourse defines the place of autobiography in the social construction of black women's reality. This essay explores how black female slave narratives illuminate the role of autobiography in explicating black women's culture. The rhetorical distinction of black female slave narratives points to language as an act of reshaping social reality and offers a new way of exploring language as a symbolic means of liberation. Langston Hughes's poem "Mother to Son" offers a metaphor of the crystal stair to illuminate the symbolic liberation of black women and their struggle to bring forth a race of achievers by redefining, transforming, and transcending the crystal stair of exclusion and oppression.

## Redefining the Crystal Stair

Langston Hughes's "Mother to Son" captures the dimensions of black womanhood in ways that advance our understanding of the contradictions and paradoxes black women confront in a racist and sexist society. That the crystal stair is juxtaposed to life suggests black women's experience is defined by the negative—or, rather, by what life is not, in order to redefine what life is through an understanding of the obstacles they face. The stair in its crystal-like construction offers life as brilliant, clear, and upwardly mobile in its clarity of direction and opportunity. Its stair-like characteristic suggests an invitation to climb it as a means of achieving glory, fame, fortune, or simply inclusion in the American Dream. The contradiction of the aesthetic stair is grounded within DuBois' concept of the veil and blackness and Braxton's conceptual framework of blackness and gender equity (Braxton 1986, 386). Life is not a crystal stair, notes the mother, for it has "tacks in it, and splinters, and boards all torn up, and places with no carpet on the floor—bare." But what she does to redefine and transcend the stair points to the concept of reflectivity and redefining oneself through rhetorical discourse and black women's autobiography.

The experience of black womanhood in America is a paradox between living within a veil of blackness and femaleness (Braxton 1986, 379). Black women have been invisible to the dominant culture; their unique ways of knowing and understanding the world have not been known. Moreover, they articulate their meaning of structuralism in the way of critically examining literature in the field of communication studies from an interdisciplinary perspective. What little history that has included Blacks has disregarded the black woman and opted to frame her experiences and those of the race in general, through the life of the black man. Catherine Clinton, a feminist historian, reveals the paucity of scholarship on black slave women:

> Unfortunately, the literature on slave women is even more impoverished than the scholarship on plantation mistresses. The study of slave women has been hampered by both racist and sexist attitudes. In the limited historical work on slave rebellions, for example, many scholars have promoted an unsubstantiated image of slave women as "collaborationists." In addition, historians have, in passing, claimed that the sex roles of slaves were blurred by the system: that the gender differential was inadvertently reduced for blacks by the "equalizing" slavery brought about. (1982, 200)

The experience of black women in slavery is traditionally devalued, and the image of black women tainted by unsupported claims. Loewenberg and Bogin comment on the scarcity of black women in recorded history and how the black woman's voice has been silenced in society's attempt to generalize her unique political concerns:

> Not only do black women seldom appear in treatments of black history, but historians have been content to permit the male to represent the female in almost every significant category. Thus it is the male who is the representative abolitionist, fugitive slave, or political activist. Women are conspicuous by their silence. (1976, 4)

Throughout our textbooks, America has told and retold the history of this country through the eyes of the white European male. The stories and life experiences of black women and men, Native Americans, and other minorities who compose the marginal voices in this country have been discarded, passed over, and negated under the guise of historical authenticity. Unfortunately, what conventional historians failed to write about was the tapestry of culture, language, and human worth in America—rich with the potential of being weaved into a fine fabric of social and political harmony in American society.

The experience of living the intersection (Sanders 1995, 11) between race and gender points to black women's desire for inclusion and acceptance without inferior status and, more specifically, to their quest for survival, wholeness, and liberation. The world of African American autobiography reveals how black women negotiate, inform, and redefine the crystal stair of exclusion in a world bent on denying them equal status. The liberating quality of discourse illuminates the way in which language affords the declaration of self through various rhetorical acts while recreating and redefining one's place in the scheme of American society. Thus, a redefinition of the crystal stair challenges historical and contemporary views of history, American public address, and theoretical paradigms and methodologies that have excluded black women at the expense of providing a broader understanding of the nature of human communication and rhetoric.

The black female slave narrative genre redefines autobiographical accounts of slavery from a black woman's experience. The genre is typically male-represented with issues of primacy, authorship, criteria of unity, and coherence dominating the scholarly questions of efficacy (Braxton 1986, 382). Authors such as Frederick Douglass, Moses Roper, and William Wells Brown introduced white people to the feelings and sufferings of slaves—generally speaking—but the male narratives did not capture the female salve and her suffering—her unique experience as a mother separated from her children and of the sexual exploitation confronting her at every turn. The experiences of black women slaves such as Harriet Jacobs, Mary Prince, and Old Elizabeth, however, cannot be confined to questions of unity, coherence, length, primacy, and authorship, for in describing and evaluating these texts, alternative query of discourse is raised to define the experience of enslaved Africans across gender lines. Their autobiographical writings revealed slave life never before told from their vantage point. In redefining the crystal stair, black female slave narrators presented their lives as living proof of their identity and self-worth—and in so doing provided a catalyst for liberation.

Hortense Spillers speaks of the tradition of black female autobiography and its pioneering journey as a symbol-making task to confront the suppression of the enslaved woman's existence and of her realities (1988, xi). The narrative genre afforded black women, for the first time in American history, a chance to declare their presence by rhetorically stating, "I am here." This symbolic expression of claiming self and, more specifically of claiming existence, begins the momentum for creating an oppositional discourse that identified black women as thinkers, creators, and namers of themselves in attempts to confront dominant discourses that mythologized their existence as breeding sows. Kimberly Benston supports this notion of naming in the slave community:

> The narrator, like all Afro-American writers, finds it necessary to name herself and her existence. The act of naming allows the narrator to identify and define herself on her own terms and simultaneously unname all descriptions and definitions which would relegate her to a position of weakness and helplessness. The simultaneous naming and unnaming affirms at once autonomy and identification in relation to the past. For the Afro-American, then, self-creation and reformation of a fragmented familial past (historical and immediate) are endlessly interwoven: naming is inevitably genealogical revisionism. . . . All of Afro-American literature may be seen as one vast genea-

logical poem that attempts to restore continuity to the ruptures or dis-
continuities imposed by the history of Black presence in America. (1982,
152–53)

Female slave narratives situate enslaved women as subjects rather than as
objects. The subject-object split in black women's autobiography encour-
ages the rhetorical act of writing as a way to claim their space in life.

The value of autobiography is its argument for justifying that a narrator's
life is worth being written down (Olney 1993, 212). The slave narrative
provided black women and men a way to declare a chronological place
among the human race and to claim a central tenet of identity—to redefine
the stairway of exclusion by creating a space of existence. Narrative affords
a social process of sharing accounts of experience. It is a mode of expression that enables a person to retell, recreate, and revitalize experiences of
the past and share those experiences with others. As stories are lived from
generation to generation through discourse, the narrative genre provides a
format for a person to understand who they are to become and what social
role they are to play in society. By relaying their experiences in narrative
form, black women redefined their roles, their virtues, and their purposes.
The narrative genre provided the development of black women's persona.
Nobel Laureate Toni Morrison states that "she had nothing to fall back on;
not maleness, not whiteness, not anything. And out of the profound desola-
tion of her reality the Black female may well have invented herself" (quoted
in Giddings 1984, 15). Thus, the symbolic act of writing autobiography
liberates the narrator and provides a socially shared experience between
audience and narrator through the creation of persona.

The genre of autobiography not only claimed black women's existence
but let them to find their voice. The voice of the narrative was a rhetorical
act of response to physical, emotional, and psychological abuse. Revealing
slave life from their vantage point, autobiography became a rhetorical expression of social and political value. That black enslaved women learned to
confront the crystal stair of exclusion despite the forces against their literacy underscores the significance of autobiography as a vehicle for change.
Black women built coalitions through midwifery, quiltmaking, cooking,
cleaning, and plotting escapes in the kitchens of their oppressors, and their
stories reveal their struggle for change. The voice of enslaved women is a
continuum linking the ancestors of Africa, the living ones in slavery, and
those who are not yet born. Locating voice provides a way to create identity, which leads to resistance and liberation.

The rhetorical act of creating a functioning world out of a chaotic one
situates language at the very essence of experience. In short, an engagement

in the rhetoric of autobiography of female slave narratives informs an understanding of the crystal stair turned on its head through the experiences of black women and their ability to transform adversity.

## Transforming the Crystal Stair

Rhetorical discourse provides language strategies for transforming social reality. Douglas Ehninger notes that rhetoric arises out of a need to express the complexities of time within a specific intellectual and social context (Ehninger, "On Systems," 1968, 142). Rhetoric presents us with choices and requires us to respond with appropriate discourse and actions.

Transforming the crystal stair implies the way in which black women employed rhetoric to shape their experience of oppression into a public discourse and redefine the prevailing ideologies of the period. Rhetoric is inventional, so argues Aristotle, and as such female slave narrators challenged the moral considerations and ideological networks of the period by transforming their audiences into readers with convictions against slavery. They employed rhetoric to invent audiences with moral judgment. Inventing the audience meant that commonly agreed upon views of society would be shaped into a public language of inclusiveness as a distinct vision of society.

Slave narratives were written as a response to multiple public-political impulses. First, the female slave narrative was written to define and create black identities. Out of their experiences emerged a response to a particular historical period in which female slaves examined, interpreted, and created the importance of their lives. Second, the slave narrative was written as protest literature in response to the nature of the slave system and as a means for moral instruction. Sidonie Smith points out that the narrative afforded slaves the avenue to make statements about the system as well as to relate events that occurred in their lives (1974, 10). This unique position of analyzing the institution of American slavery allowed the female slave to understand herself as a product of the forces against her. Third, but most importantly, the slave narrative was written as an attempt to alter and later abolish the institution of slavery. Smith contends that because the slave narrative appealed to the religious and moral structure of its white readership, it was politically useful for converting people to the abolitionist cause (1974, 7). Rhetoric offers human beings an opportunity to find their personal and political identities by inventing and engaging in persuasive discourse. Female slave narrators understood the dynamics of rhetorical discourse and constructed images that would both appeal to the virtues esteemed by the white culture and that would create self-identity to serve as a means of survival, control, and power.

The characteristics of the black autobiographical tradition are rooted in a rhetoric that evokes the self. Stephen Butterfield notes that, traditionally, the slave narrative has examined the importance of a life "in response to a particular historical period," and that through that examination, the autobiographer reveals a pride in race, an awareness of the political chains which enslave the physical, psychological, and spiritual self, and a sense of self "as a member of an oppressed social group, with ties and responsibilities to the other members" (1974, 1–3). This sense of self, or the personal voice of the narrative-rhetorical artifact, unites with the collective voice in a major effort to expose white oppression (1974, 2–3). For enslaved black women, language modified the dysfunctional relationship between mistress and slave. Female slave narrators applied rhetoric to evoke an image of self consonant with the rhetoric of virtuous womanhood and motherhood. Creating a liberating image of self in response to a historical situation transcended their inferior position in society and provided new ways of defining blackness and femaleness with a spirit of strength, tenacity, and defiance.

**Transcending the Crystal Stair**

Robert Stepto in his study of African American narrative states that autobiography serves as a catalyst for the slave to transcend the contradictions of life (1979, 3) and bringing them into a collective effort, rather than an individual one. The female slave narrative genre and the rhetorical value of autobiography permitted both white and black people to explore the contradictions of race, gender, and class in America. Taking Stepto's notion further, I contend that the rhetoric of black women's autobiography transcends the crystal stair of exclusion and oppression by creating a space for response that invites readers of contemporary times to make meaning of black women's experiences in a dialectical relationship between self and Other.

Narrative documents become liberating artifacts for students engaged in the critical evaluation of language and culture. The classroom study of female slave narratives uncovers the interior of discourse and invites them to discover the forms and channels power takes and the discourses it permeates in society (Gordon and Foucault 1980, 11). Students create a response to the narratives as rhetorical artifacts by interrogating the systems of power existing both then and now.

The value of teaching female slave narratives is the transcendence of the classroom as a site for dialogical communication. Place is redefined, transformed, and transcended by allowing students to discover how we are symbolically constructed and conditioned by dominant ideologies. As students critically assess female slave narratives they become transformed by rhetoric. The late educational theorist Paulo Freire suggests that transformation is possible because "we can learn how to become free through a political struggle in society. We can struggle to become free precisely because we can know we are not free! That is why we can think of transformation" (1985, 13).

Black women's rhetoric of autobiography challenges educators to make the political more pedagogical—that is, to make critical reflection and action a fundamental part of education that not only engages forms of oppression but also develops a deep and abiding faith in the struggle to humanize life (Freire 1985, xv). Critical education suggests to the student not to simply learn how to read words, but rather to learn how to read the world. The Negro spiritual "My Soul Looks Back in Wonder How I Got Over" illuminates the tradition of struggle by the matrilineage and illustrates how critical education liberates and transcends with tools of critical thinking and response.

> So, boy, don't you turn back.
> Don't you set down on the steps
> 'Cause you find it's kinda hard,
> Don't you fall now,
> For I'se still goin' honey,
> I'se still climbin' on,
> And life for me ain't been no crystal stair.

# References

Braxton, Joanne M. 1986. "Harriet Jacobs' *Incidents in the Life of a Slave Girl:* The Redefinition of the Slave Narrative Genre." *The Massachusetts Review,* 27: 379–87.

Benston, Kimberly W. 1982. " 'I yam what I am': The Topos of Un(naming) in Afro-American Literature." *Black American Literature Forum* 16.

Butterfield, Stephen. 1974. *Black Autobiography in America.* Amherst: University of Massachusetts.

Clinton, Catherine. 1982. *The Plantation Mistress.* New York: Pantheon.

Ehninger, Douglas. 1968. "On Systems of Rhetoric," in *Philosophy and Rhetoric* 1: 131–44.

———. 1975. "A Synoptic View of Systems of Western Rhetoric." *Quarterly Journal of Speech* 61: 448–53.

Freire, Paulo. 1985. *The Politics of Education.* South Hadley, MA: Bergin and Garvey.

Giddings, Paula. 1984. *When and Where I Enter: The Impact of Black Women on Race and Sex in America.* New York: Bantam.

Gordon, Colin, and Michel Foucault, eds. 1980. *Power/Knowledge: Selected Interviews and Other Writings 1972–1977.* Brighton, Sussex, U.K.: Harvester Press.

Hughes, Langston. 1926. *Selected Poems.* New York: Knopf. Reprinted in *The Harlem Renaissance Reader,* ed. David Levering Lewis. 1994. New York: Viking, 261–62.

Loewenberg, Bert J., and Ruth Bogin. 1976. *Black Women in Nineteenth-Century American Life.* University Park: Pennsylvania State University Press.

McGuire, Michael. 1982. "The Structural Study of Speech." In *Explorations in Rhetoric: Studies in Honor of Douglas Ehninger,* ed. Ray E. McKerrow. Glenview, IL: Scott, Foresman.

Olney, James. 1993. "The Value of Autobiography for Comparative Studies: African vs. Western Autobiography." In *African American Autobiography: A Collection of Critical Essays,* ed. William L. Andrews. Englewood Cliffs, NJ: Prentice Hall.

Sanders, Cheryl J. 1995. *Living the Intersection,* Minneapolis: Fortress.

Smith, Sidonie. 1974. *Where I'm Bound.* Westport, CT: Greenwood.

Spillers, Hortense. 1988. Foreword to *Six Women's Slave Narratives,* ed. Henry Louis Gates Jr. New York: Oxford University Press.

Stepto, Robert. 1979. *From Behind the Veil: A Study of Afro-American Narrative.* Urbana: University of Illinois Press.

# 12

# Literary Biographical Profiles as Teaching Tools in a University Black History Course

*Robin Balthrope*

Teaching a course in African American history over the last four years has been by turns frustrating, hair-raising, and rewarding. Part of the frustration comes from trying to find readings that will interest the students enough to participate in class discussions—through either my questioning or involvement between students. While anthologies of academic articles or even primary-source materials have generally proved unappealing in the past, biographical and literary profiles brought my fall 1996 black history class to life.

I have limited this paper to the most recent class completed, since this quarter's black history class has yet to discuss one of the literary/biographical works assigned, Robert Allison's *The Interesting Narrative of the Life of Olaudah Equiano, Written by Himself* (1995). My class this quarter has already read and discussed Chinua Achebe's *Things Fall Apart* (1987) in the context of Africans' way of life prior to the international slave trade. A few years ago, I assigned *Three Negro Classics* (1965)—Washington's *Up From Slavery* (1901, DuBois's *Souls of Black Folks* (1903), and Johnson's *Autobiography of an Ex-Colored Man* (1927). The last work in particular generated animated discussions in class.

After reading *Uncle Tom's Cabin* (Stowe, 1852) and *All God's Dangers: The Life of Nate Shaw* (Rosengarten 1974), the students were given a paper assignment comparing the (fictional) experiences of Tom with the (real life) journey of Nate Shaw. The class also had to view a local museum exhibit that represented the history of an Inland Empire black community (Riverside Municipal Museum 1996).

Both *Uncle Tom's Cabin* and *All God's Dangers* are lengthy works, which led a few students to complain about the onerousness of the reading, given their other classes. This is one of the difficulties of teaching on a quarter system, that there are serious time constraints to giving some types of assignments. However, most students managed to complete the readings on time (due in weeks three and seven of a ten-week quarter) and once the students began the books, they became sufficiently stimulated to finish the stories. The books brought to mind my minister Rev. Charles Brooks's definition of good literature, which "pulls you in, gets you to relate to the story and identify with the people." The students were quite vocal about their love for and intense dislike of *Uncle Tom's Cabin,* while the almost universal sentiment about *All God's Dangers* was approbation.

The lecture immediately preceding the in-class analysis of *Uncle Tom's Cabin* concentrated on slavery, and the lecture the day of the initial discussion focused on free blacks, abolitionism, and Blacks (Bérard 1983). In choosing *Uncle Tom's Cabin* to serve as background, it appears that I am following a tradition of using Stowe to "supplement lectures on slavery and abolition" (Otto 1992, 57). Though the book was published during a decade of rising tensions, ultimately erupting in war, it was nevertheless purely accidental that similar though less explosive tensions developed in the class discussion of *Uncle Tom's Cabin.* The black history class last fall, as is generally the case at my institution, was mixed in composition. I assumed, correctly as it turned out, that this fact could dictate the students' reaction to the classic. More of the white students felt positively about Stowe's novel than the more numerous nonwhite students (defined here as non-American blacks, African Americans, and Latinos). The discussion revealed that more of the white students were swept up in the emotional power of the novel than their classmates, while many of the nonwhite students were angered by Tom's passivity (among other things). In the context of the 1850s, the novel was intended to invoke sympathy for the antislavery cause, and the class was informed that it had such an impact in 1852 that it spawned several proslavery novels in response (Gossett 1985).

Stowe painstakingly paints a portrait of an honest, pious, loving slave, Tom (Fields 1897), who lived much of his life with the Shelbys—until his owner's debts "forced" him to sell Tom and Eliza's young son Harry. Tom was such a faithful servant to Mr. Shelby that many of the minority students felt he was more attentive to the Shelbys than to his wife Aunt Chloe and their three children. The minority students were particularly upset that Tom accepted his fate so stoically; but as I pointed out in class that was one of the crucial points of the novel—that Tom's Christianity did not bring forth any anger on his part, even though he was frustrated at having to leave his family behind.

Stowe intentionally focused on the most brutal aspect of slavery—the breakup of black families—in part because she was a woman who took her home and family responsibilities as her *primary* duties even while she balanced a developing literary career in the 1830s and 1840s (Hedrick 1994). In this respect, Stowe was a product of her society, influenced by the prevalent domestic ideology known as the "cult of true womanhood" (Welter 1966). As a woman writer, she "adhered to many of the rules of feminine fiction [by] present[ing] an endless array of domestic scenes, and featured an innocent, virtuous, dying child-heroine" (Woloch 1994). But her novel also became a weapon in the ongoing struggle against slavery, and it has been often considered a model of activism to be emulated (Donovan 1991).

The students recognized some of Tom's good qualities, such as his devotion to his family (as when he dictated a letter to them from his new home in Louisiana). However, many of the minority students, particularly the African American students, merely thought of him as the proverbial "Uncle Tom." The class then embarked on a discussion of the stereotype to which Tom's name has become linked, in order to determine if the fictional Tom actually fit the stereotype. The *American Heritage Dictionary* defines an "Uncle Tom" as a "Negro who is held to be humiliatingly subservient or deferential to whites"—a definition which, after discussion, most students concluded did not really apply to Tom. At first, many of the African American students viewed Tom as simple, childlike, and obsequious; this reaction was in contrast to that of the white students, who viewed him as a slave who still had dignity.

Even though Tom was not a "militant" black, just about all of the students acknowledged that he did stand up to Simon Legree, who offered him a position as a slave driver on his Red River plantation if Tom would beat the quadroon Cassy. Tom refused, suffering Legree's wrath at asserting his Christian stand of nonviolence. Far from being humiliatingly subservient, Tom was a proud man whose fearless defense of his beliefs ultimately cost him his life.

Tom, the Christ-like figure, who suffered and died for his fellow slaves, was useful in exploring the "tangled consciences" of antislavery advocates during the 1850s (see Mugleston 1974). While the class could agree on Tom's "mission" in the novel, there was lively conversation about the remainder of the black characters in *Uncle Tom's Cabin,* particularly the mulattoes George and Eliza Harris. While many of the white students pointed to George and Eliza as positive black characters, many of the nonwhite students asserted in turn that George and Eliza were practically white. The two were variously described as handsome/beautiful, intelligent, refined, industrious, and other positive characteristics, but the darker slaves (with the exception of Tom and perhaps Aunt Chloe) were portrayed as irresponsible, lazy, untrustworthy, and less physically attractive—among other negative qualities.

In pointing out to the class that mid-nineteenth-century men and women, including antislavery advocates such as Stowe, held "racist" views about black inferiority relative to the white majority, Stowe's use of stereotypes in *Uncle Tom's Cabin* only reflected and reinforced her contemporaries' views about the impossibility of Blacks and Whites living in the United States as equals; Stowe herself saw colonization as the only real solution to slavery (Ammons 1994; Lieber 1978; American Colonization Society 1972; Fredrickson 1971). Her depictions of the African race as exotic yet gentle (hence natural Christians) offended many of the nonwhite students, whose classmates did not initially understand their reaction. The subsequent discussion on Stowe's racial views clarified the non white students' feelings and influenced some of their classmates to revise their first interpretation of some of the slave characters and of the book in general.

The class moved from the volatile antebellum period to the creativity and energy of the 1920s. The lecture preceding the discussion on *All God's Dangers* centered on the Harlem Renaissance with its emphasis on black writers' and on Marcus Garvey's calls for racial pride. This historical background served to promote profound respect and admiration for Nate Shaw's many efforts to improve his life in the midst of a racist southern environment. The book spanned several decades, from the 1880s to the 1960s, which provided example after example of his struggles on behalf of his family and of his successes despite a limited education.

That Shaw "wrote" his autobiography with the help of author Theodore Rosengarten impressed most of the class, although some of them complained that the reading itself was tedious due to Shaw's constant repetitions and recitals of so many names. Rosengarten in his preface explains why Nate's story unfolded as it did, in that "Shaw belong[ed] to the traditional farmer-storytellers" (Rosengarten 1974), which illustrates the degree of detail common to autobiographical writings (see Allison 1995). The class overcame its general annoyance at all the details to appreciate Shaw's enduring lessons of one man's ability to triumph over adversity. As Robert Bérard aptly stated, "The purpose of . . . literary work in the history classroom should be to generate images and concepts related to the politics, thought, and social life of the world in which it deals" (Bérard 1983).

The book was very informative about the restrictions Whites placed on Blacks' lives after the end of slavery and revealed the fact that many Blacks acted like slaves long after the institution ended. Nate Shaw was exceptional in that he stood up for himself, which gratified the class. His imprisonment for union activism on behalf of his fellow farmers did not discourage him from his goal of bettering his life despite any obstacle, and he never regretted his stand afterwards. Nate Shaw was an ordinary person, whose life the class might not otherwise have read about, which was one of the reasons it was included in the class (Otto 1992).

The paper assigned last fall required a comparison between Tom and Nate Shaw in terms of their commitment to their families, their religious beliefs, and their views on work. In addition, the students had to critique the characters' views about Blacks' place in the world, particularly whether that place was subject to improve over time. It should be noted that while the assignment did not explicitly refer to Tom as a fictional character—in contrast to Nate Shaw's real life experiences—many of the students used the distinction to address questions of whether literature adequately reflects a historical event or institution such as slavery. The assignment thus assumed the legitimacy of this use of novels, even though one of the major problems with fiction is the literary license authors have (Macune 1989). Since the novel came under close scrutiny in class for its various biases and exaggerations in order to make its point against slavery, I felt the students could use Tom's depiction as the basis for comparison with Nate Shaw.

Both men were considered positive role models for their devotion to their families, especially during antebellum America when slavery meant regularly separated families due to factors like marriage, bankruptcy, or death of the owners. Tom's nonaggressive response to his initial (as well as subsequent) sale was simultaneously interpreted as spineless and courageous, but both men were hardworking individuals, although it may be unfair to compare someone compelled to work like Tom with a man like Nate, whose sense of industry came out of his need to distinguish himself from and do better than his father. For the students, Nate was more admirable because he was a self-made man, whose achievements came from a great sense of determination as he faced white neighbors who did not want him to become independent.

The students drew some parallels between the religious beliefs of both characters, since Christianity sustained them both during adversity. Tom's values were constant throughout the novel, reflecting Stowe's thinking about the nature of Blacks—emotional, spiritual, loving—whereas Nate was not baptized until late in life, although he'd always believed in God. While many students saw Tom's reliance on religion as a crutch of sorts, because it soothed away the agonies of slavery, Nate's religious views were never viewed in the same way because he was a man of action. In this sense the religious beliefs of the two are related to their notions of Blacks' place in the world—Nate more than Tom is seen as a positive force for change. I had to point out to the class that Tom did *not* defend slavery, and in fact informed St. Clare that he would rather be free and poor than slave and well taken care of when St. Clare started the process of emancipating Tom. Tom would not take freedom into his own hands, however, while Nate did not submit to overbearing people once he was an adult. The minority students particularly found Nate Shaw inspirational, but all of them found his life story moving and educational. So much so that some former students still tell me how much they enjoyed reading about Nate Shaw, and the lessons they learned from him.

While the two readings and the paper assignment generated very lively, thoughtful examination of the aforementioned thematic approaches, the museum exercise provoked a strong response from only a few students. For most it seemed a perfunctory activity—which could be attributed to the low percentage of the final grade it presented (10 percent) as opposed to the paper (25 percent). The museum exercise was incorporated into the course to take advantage of a local museum's year-long exhibition on Blacks who migrated to Riverside from Georgia in the late nineteenth century. I viewed "Westward to Canaan: African-American Heritage in Riverside, 1890–1950" as a worthwhile representation of the past, one that students could both enjoy as well as "active[ly] participat[e] . . . with history as a process of inquiry and exploration" (Franco 1995). Indeed, a few students were able to do exactly that, because they met the relatives of some of the men and women featured in the exhibit. They found out firsthand about discrimination in a community similar to the ones where they grew up, which proved to be a revelation.

The historical exhibit's artifacts—furniture, clothes, books and other writings (e.g., sermons), and music—could be analyzed, which a few students complained about when they called the exhibit "informal"; perhaps they were also referring to the manner in which the assignment could be carried out: on their own, using either the day set aside on the syllabus for individual visits or some other day prior to the end of the quarter. It seems that only a few students made the visit together, which I would more strenuously encourage the next time I can incorporate a museum exhibit in this or another small (upper-division) class.

While I considered making the museum assignment optional, I decided that it should be a required part of the course because it carried out the course objectives for the class: to gain a basic factual knowledge of this historical period with specific emphasis on African Americans; to develop the ability to critique historical issues and interpretations of those issues; and to develop some competence in analyzing historical data and presenting informed conclusions about these data. The question they had to answer in a two-page essay asked about the restrictions Blacks faced in Riverside between 1890 and 1950 and the ways in which they overcame those restrictions—an objective that I believed from my preview of the exhibit would be specific and yet allow for a bit of choice in selecting relevant facts.

All of the teaching tools under discussion here—novels, autobiographies, and museum exhibits—have limitations that must be considered before deciding to use them in a college course. Historians are naturally wary of using novels in their classes, making such statements as "How can a writer of fiction tell us about the world of fact? . . . How good a witness to fact can a person be whose craft is the telling of fictions?" (Payne 1978). It is these kind of judgments that went into the decision to use *Uncle Tom's Cabin.* By focusing on the more negative aspects of slavery (families being separated, forced miscegenation, etc.) as well as on the abolitionists' views about slavery, the students can become better acquainted with a social and economic system that is now foreign, but which once caused the nation to go to war.

In using autobiography, the students became quickly aware of some of the drawbacks—for example, the author and subject may recite events that do not particularly interest readers but which nevertheless formed a part of their daily activities. Also, the peculiar words, grammar, and spelling that Nate Shaw employs is a minor impediment to reading his autobiography, one which a few students mentioned but which made his story more personal (see Brown 1962; Allison 1995). One last consideration with autobiographies is the matter of age—here, Nate Shaw was eighty-six when he dictated his life story to Rosengarten. One must be aware that an older person's memory may fade, or a person may not want to recall painful episodes in their past. Shaw's memory seemed unimpaired, and he supplied a barrage of details about relatives, other people, and events that indicated a firm grip on the past (Allison 1995).

In terms of museum exhibitions, several have raised controversial questions within the last decade or two, particularly when the public has disagreed with the curators' revisionist view of an event—such as the unleashing of atomic weapons to end World War II. The Enola Gay exhibit in the National Air and Space Museum thus spawned considerable dialogue among historians about the intended message and its unintended consequences (see Thelen 1995; Kohn 1995; Harwit 1995; Sherwin 1995; Linenthal 1995; Harris 1995; Woods 1995; Sodei 1995; Dower 1995). While this particular exhibit angered members of the public because, as veterans, they believed that their "collective memory" of World War II was being trashed, the Riverside Municipal Museum's exhibit last year received nothing but positive popular acclaim in the local press and from the public. Blacks' arrival into and adjustment to California, compared to the bombings of Hiroshima and Nagasaki, is a less controversial topic—although with multiculturalism engendering a backlash today, the Riverside exhibit may have provoked tensions about race among some people. The curator's acknowledgments in the exhibit program, in appreciation of the input from the local black community to the success of the project, only highlighted the role of museums—to transmit cultural values. Here, the exhibit considered the strength of the black community in fighting racism while seeking normal, happy lives in California relevant to today's visitors, which is critical as more museums "are increasingly the loci of multicultural negotiation, rather than Olympian pronouncement, as to what our shared history is" (Blatti 1990).

The teaching tools thus outlined above proved to be fairly successful in getting students to care about the past and to critically think about the individual and collective experiences of African Americans in American society. Novels, autobiographies, and museum exhibits give a voice to the hopes and aspirations of people whose very survival under constant threat of attack attests to the strength and support they receive from God, family, and friends.

## References

Achebe, Chinua. 1987. *Things Fall Apart.* London: Heinemann Educational Books.

Allison, Robert J. 1995. *The Interesting Narrative of the Life of Olaudah Equiano, as Written by Himself.* Boston and New York: St. Martin's Press, Bedford Books.

American Colonization Society. 1972. "Amalgamation of Races." In *The Poisoned Tongue: A Documentary History of American Racism and Prejudice,* ed. Stanley Feldstein. New York: William Morrow.

Bérard, Robert Nicholas. 1983. "Integrating Literature and History: Cultural History in Uiversities and Secondary Schools." *History Teacher* 16 (August): 505–18.

Blatti, Jo. 1990. "Public History and Oral History." *Journal of American History* 77 (September): 615–25.

Brown, Richard C., ed. 1962. *They Were There: A Guide to Firsthand Literature for Use in Teaching American History.* Washington, DC: Service Center for Teachers of History.

Donovan, Josephine. 1991. *Uncle Tom's Cabin: Evil, Affliction, and Redemptive Love.* Boston: Twayne.

Dower, John W. 1995. "Triumphal and Tragic Narratives of the War in Asia." *Journal of American History 82* (December): 1124–1135.

DuBois, W.E.B. 1903. *The Souls of Black Folk.* Chicago: McClurg.

Fields, Annie, ed. 1897. *Life and Letters of Harriet Beecher Stowe.* Boston and New York: Houghton Mifflin.

Franco, Barbara. 1995. "Doing History in Public: Balancing Historical Fact with Public Meaning." *Perspectives* (May/June): 5–8.

Fredrickson, George M. 1971. *The Black Image in the White Mind: The Debate on Afro-American Character and Destiny, 1817–1914.* New York: Harper and Row.

Johnson, James Weldon. 1927. *The Autobiography of an Ex-Colored Man.* New York: Hill and Wang.

Gossett, Thomas F. 1985. *Uncle Tom's Cabin and American Culture.* Dallas: Southern Methodist University Press.

Harris, Neil. 1995. "Museum and Controversy: Some Introductory Reflections." *Journal of American History* 82 (December): 1102–1110.

Harwit, Martin. 1995. "Academic Freedom in 'The Last Act.' " *Journal of American History* 82 (December): 1064–1082.

Hedrick, Joan D. 1994. *Harriet Beecher Stowe: A Life.* New York: Oxford University Press.

Kohn, Richard H. 1995. "History and the Culture Wars: The Case of the Smithsonian Institution's Enola Gay Exhibition." *Journal of American History* 82 (December): 1036–1063.

Lieber, Francis. 1978. "The Stranger in America: Comprising Sketches of the Manner, Society and National Peculiarities of the United States, in a Series of Letters to a Friend in Europe." In *Black Image: European Eyewitness Accounts of Afro-American Life,* ed. Lenworth Gunther. Port Washington, NY: Kennikat Press.

Linenthal, Edward T. 1995. "Struggling with History and Memory." *Journal of American History* 82 (December): 1094–1101.

Macune, Charles W. Jr. 1989. "Latin American Literature as a Source of History: Why It Flies in the Classroom." *History Teacher* 22 (August): 497–509.

Mugleston, William F. 1974. "Southern Literature as History: Slavery in the Antebellum Novel." *History Teacher* 8 (November): 17–30.

Otto, Paul. 1992. "History as Humanity: Reading Literacy in the History Classroom." *History Teacher* 26 (November): 51–60.

Payne, Harry C. 1978. "The Novel as Social History." *History Teacher* 11 (May): 341–49.

Riverside Municipal Museum. 1996. *"Westward to Canaan," African American Heritage in Riverside, 1890–1950.* Riverside, CA: Riverside Museum Associates.

Rosengarten, Theodore. 1974. *All God's Dangers: The Life of Nate Shaw.* New York: Avon Books.

Sherwin, Martin J. 1995. "Hiroshima as Politics and History." *Journal of American History* 82 (December): 1085–1093.

Sodei, Rinjirō. 1995. "Hiroshima/Nagasaki as History and Politics." *Journal of American History* 82 (December): 1118–1123.

Stowe, Harriet Beecher. 1854. *A Key to Uncle Tom's Cabin; Presenting the Original Facts and Documents Upon Which the Story is Founded.* Boston: John P. Jewett; Cleveland, OH: Jewett, Proctor, and Worthington.

———. 1994. *Uncle Tom's Cabin,* ed. Elizabeth Ammons. New York: Norton.

Thelen, David. 1995. "History after the Enola Gay Controversy: An Introduction." *Journal of American History* 82 (December): 1029–1035.

*Three Negro Classics.* 1965. New York: Avon Books.

Washington, Booker T. 1901. *Up from Slavery.* New York: Doubleday, Page.

Welter, Barbara. 1966. "The Cult of True Womanhood, 1820–1860." *American Quarterly* 18 (Summer): 151–75.

Woloch, Nancy. 1994. *Women and the American Experience.* 2d ed. New York: McGraw-Hill.

Woods, Thomas A. 1995. "Museums and the Public: Doing History Together." *Journal of American History* 82 (December): 1111–1115.

# 13

# An Intellectual Aesthetic for Black Adult Education

## Malcolm X

## *Andrew Smallwood*

When examining the history of the United States it is important to recognize the legacy of racism in society. The impact of cultural hegemony has led to a failure to recognize the rights and privileges of certain U.S. citizens based on their ancestry. Social stratification has resulted in an inequality of opportunity for minority groups to participate in society.

This has been an especially difficult problem for the African American population, given their original status as involuntary migrants under the system of slavery that existed circa 1619–1865. Advocating the rights of African Americans has traditionally fallen on prominent black figures such as Frederick Douglass, Booker T. Washington, W.E.B. DuBois, and others during the late nineteenth and early twentieth centuries. These men articulated the problems facing their people and suggested solutions for the various problems faced by black people in the United States.

One solution for assisting the successful adjustment of African Americans in society was through the development and participation of educational programs. During the late nineteenth and early twentieth centuries a number of leading black figures advocated black participation in adult education, so that they would have the skills necessary to integrate successfully into American life. Reconstruction in the United States (approximately 1865 to 1877) witnessed a widespread focus by the U.S. government on education for African Americans.[1] Because of their commitment for improving the overall conditions of black people, black leaders served as cultural advocates for black self-improvement. This relationship between black leadership and the black masses via cultural identification is one that deserves serious exploration. A further legacy of racism in society has led to the contributions of these African American leaders being ignored. As a result there exists a lack of research examining the full impact of leading African American historical figures to various aspects of black life from a cultural standpoint.

The field of adult education is no different than other academic areas in higher education by failing to include the contributions of significant African American figures of the nineteenth and twentieth centuries. In order to address the omission in research, this study will examine the contributions of Malcolm X to the field and function of adult education for African Americans. Malcolm X is a significant figure to African American culture in the late twentieth century. A national figure in the 1960s, his impact on the African American community is still being examined from a wide range of areas. When examining research on Malcolm X, there are several perspectives from which he has been frequently viewed: as a cultural hero, a political activist, a historical figure, and a religious leader.

## Cultural Hero

According to Michael Dyson, a "hero" for African Americans is a person that has exemplified the social concerns of this group of people denied equality in society.[2] As a cultural hero Malcolm urged African Americans to take pride in their African heritage and rid themselves of the effects of the negative self-images evident in society. In his autobiography Malcolm X points out that his parents were followers of Marcus Garvey in the 1920s.[3] Garvey's philosophy of Black Nationalism, expressed in his organization the Universal Negro Improvement Association and emphasizing cultural pride, social separation, and economic empowerment, had a significant influence on Malcolm's family. This early exposure was important in laying a foundation that would lead to the later development of his political ideology in early 1964.[4] Another important influence of Black Nationalism for Malcolm X occurred after his religious conversion to Islam, which led to his joining the Nation of Islam while in prison during the late 1940s. During his involvement in the Nation, Malcolm adopted the philosophy of the organization's leader, the Honorable Elijah Muhammad, whose adaptation of Islam had elements of Garvey's Black Nationalism. Emphasis on African American cultural celebration through social separation is a common element of Black Nationalism shared by both organizations.[5] Upon his break from the Nation, Malcolm went further and openly declared an acceptance of Black Nationalism for his political organization, advancing a return of African Americans to a collective consciousness rooted in common cultural concerns.[6] Several authors take a closer examination of Malcolm, showing that he adopted a philosophy of Black Nationalism and thus laid the groundwork for the Black Power and Cultural Nationalist Movement of the late 1960s.[7] Malcolm X's cultural legacy for African Americans is still being debated with social critics and intellectuals, struggling to offer definitive perspectives.

**Political Activist**

Another debate related to Malcolm finds writers attempting to define his political views. As a political activist Malcolm X offered a critique of federal, state, and local governments' role in formulating and implementing policy that had a negative impact on black life. By using his public rhetoric to organize Black community residents around common issues, Malcolm X put public pressure on the political establishment to address societal conditions adversely affecting African American life. Surveillance of Malcolm by the Federal Bureau of Investigation demonstrates the perceived national threat that agencies within the federal government attributed to Malcolm's statements.[8] As a member of the Nation of Islam, Malcolm X adhered to the organization's adaptation of Garvey's sociopolitical philosophy of Black Nationalism, emphasizing group empowerment through cultural pride, economic development, and social separation.[9] During this period (1953–1964) Malcolm was restricted to a position of nonengagement on civil rights and other social issues affecting African Americans. As leader of the Nation, Elijah Muhammad expressly forbade all members from participation in civil rights organizations, marches, or any political activity in general.[10] It was the Nation's emphasis on political nonengagement that contributed to differences resulting in Malcolm X's eventual departure from the organization. Malcolm himself experienced an ideological shift just prior to his leaving the Nation and changed his public rhetoric, aligning himself more with Black Nationalist philosophy. It was this change that would lead him to seek more involvement in the political activism of the Civil Rights Movement.[11]

To what extent he changed his political ideology in the last year of his life is the subject of debate and discussion. Malcolm X's position on politics and the African American community, at the very least, indicates an attempt to internationalize the struggle against oppression, linking black oppression in the United States to colonial oppression of Blacks on the African continent. This ultimately led to Malcolm to take two trips to Africa in 1964 in an effort to solicit the support of African leaders.[12]

To broaden the struggle against black oppression, Malcolm X solicited considerable public attention. Lending a national and then international voice to black suffering, the commonality among different commentators on Malcolm X's life is that he remain as a significant twentieth century African American historical figure.

## Historical Figure

Malcolm's use of rhetoric examining African American history and politics to explore social problems demonstrates an attempt to enlist political action for black community empowerment. By taking Black community issues to an international forum, he attempts to use his position as a black leader to address black suffering. Historians and biographers attempt to assess historical events in his psychological development with a mixed emphasis on Malcolm the man and Malcolm the leader. Malcolm X's public discourse raises further possibilities for examining Malcolm the adult educator of African Americans.

## Religious Leader

Scholars attempting to asses Malcolm's religious ideology in the context of (1) his Christian upbringing, (2) his conversion to the Nation, and finally (3) his acceptance of a more orthodox form of Islam. Religious doctrine was important in providing a basis for Malcolm to preach or teach about social issues for African Americans. Theological training provided a foundation for Malcolm to examine world (secular) events in the context of the Biblical and Koranic (sacred) text. Then Malcolm disseminated the information through his public lectures (and sermons), infusing history, culture, and politics into a social analysis. When we examine him from these areas of research, we observe that each serves as a basis for Malcolm's examination of the world.

Since his death in 1965 there have been a number of books written on Malcolm X from these positions, resulting in an ongoing debate on his legacy for African Americans. Both conservatives and liberals have laid claim to aspects of Malcolm's ideology and accordingly exhibit a wide range of views about Malcolm X's impact.[13] The unstated position of both sides is that there is something important for us to learn from Malcolm X and that his ideas are worthy of further investigation.

The fact that Malcolm X tried to address society's impact on black life underscores three key points. First, Malcolm lived a life that was educational, and we can learn something valuable from his experiences as a black international figure overcoming racism and segregation. Second, he served as an educator for and about the African American experience and thus was a proponent for the study of African American history as a way for Blacks to combat adverse conditions resulting from the acculturation process. Third, as an advocate for black concerns, he used cultural conditions as a useful tool for critical analysis of society through examination of U.S. history and social policy. His public lectures served as a vehicle to inform African Americans about the serious problems in society and to investigate how African Americans had been affected. Malcolm X became an advocate of educating adults from a cultural perspective through his community involvement.

Though Malcolm X's legacy and life have been explored from a wide range of angles, his educational impact on the African American community requires a closer examination through the examination of his intellectual views.

## Statement of the Problem

Racism was manifested in the institution of slavery and was later perpetuated in the practice of segregation, which has led to discrimination in employment, housing, and education for African Americans. This range of discrimination has had severe negative consequences on the quality of life for African Americans.[14] There has furthermore been a failure to resolve problems of race relations in America. This results in (1) failure to acknowledge the contributions of African Americans in society, (2) failure to examine African American life in a cultural context that recognizes traditions and customs, and (3) gross historical misinterpretation of the African American experience. An extension of this in the field of adult education has been a failure to appreciate the educational contributions of African Americans.[15] This has resulted in an incomplete picture of both the field and practice of adult education and of the African American practitioners who serve it. Thus, the educational contributions of prominent African Americans such as Malcolm X have virtually not been explored. Peter Bailey, a former assistant of Malcolm X's says, "Malcolm was a master teacher" whose loss to the black community is significant because few individuals have the prestige and ability to generate a rhetoric of black liberation.[16] Bailey asks the question, What in the African American experience makes the role of nontraditional education so important? What really was the educational impact of Malcolm X for the African American community? Has the scope of Malcolm X's contributions to adult education versus his intellectual thought been explored? In this study I will conduct an investigation of Malcolm X as an intellectual aesthetic who advanced the concept of adult education through his actions. Malcolm X's intellectual discourse versus his pedagogical approaches to African American social issues present further avenues of exploration. By discovering linkages in the fields of adult education and Black Studies, perhaps this could provide a well-balanced understanding of the axiological basis of culture and education for African Americans.

## Evolution of Adult Education for African Americans

Adult education has been an integral part of the African American experience. In their book *The Education of African American Adults,* Leo Mcgee and Harvey Neufeldt (1990) discuss the historical evolution of various forms of adult education in the United States. The teaching of slaves in any manner was limited and prohibitive in the early years of the United States (only 5 percent of the slave population had any form basic education—reading and or writing).[17] The difficulty of obtaining formal education for slaves resulted in concentrated educational efforts (for freeman and slave) by churches and literary societies. The advent of the abolitionist movement provoked a more hostile climate for educating slaves and freemen alike, limiting the "approved" educational opportunities from the 1830s up to the Civil War.[18] During the Civil War and after, black churches primarily, joined in part by the U.S. government, took the responsibility for educating African Americans.[19] Many southern black churches led by self-educated free Blacks established schools in the wartime South through the existing structure of black churches.[20] At the same time former slaves were recruited into the Union Army and received military training necessary to form black troops.[21]

During the Civil War education was seen as a means for social control, in anticipation of black retaliation for slavery. Because of this the types of educational programs that existed varied in their emancipatory emphasis— depending in part on whether they were sponsored by black churches or white missionaries. Therefore the number of educational opportunities open to Blacks was limited and the quality of their educational programs was inferior.[22]

At the center of the examination of African American adult education is the issue of control. To what extent was there black control over educational activities? Traditionally, education for African Americans has been viewed as a way to combat hostile forces and has been a direct reflection of their needs. Given the importance of the post–Civil War era in shaping forces that led to segregation and racial and economic discrimination against Blacks, the need for black leadership to form organizations to combat hostility in society in the late nineteenth and early twentieth centuries became crucial in the quest for autonomy from societal oppression.[23] Given the well-documented history of de facto and de jure segregation leading to the unequal distribution of resources in U.S. public education, a need developed for African American community leaders to take action in analyzing problems, defining strategies, and implementing solutions for the very survival of black people.[24] This need meant understanding and redefining the role of Africa and African people in society through educational activities.

## Relevance of Culture for African American Adult Education

The call for African American adults to be educated about their history according to John Henrik Clarke goes back to the beginning of the twentieth century, when scholars such as W.E.B. DuBois and Carter Woodson took the position that the contributions of Africans in the diaspora were both important and worthy of further study.[25] Alain Locke, a proponent of African American adult education during the early twentieth century expressed the importance for African Americans in understanding their history and contributions to world civilization:

> The study of racial and group history of group contributions to culture, or even of specific group problems is sound and constructively educative. In fact, these emphases have been found to be magnets of interest and galvanizers of the adult education program groups.... Social education is an unavoidable aspect of adult education, and an inescapable obligation of adult educators.[26]

It becomes clear that the development of educational programs for African Americans should reflect their cultural experiences and needs in order to be successful.

Carter Woodson, like Locke, was an early twentieth century scholar-practitioner of education for African American adults; he maintained an intense desire to fight against the notion that black people made no significant contributions to American history. In his book, *Miseducation of the Negro* (1933), Woodson's criticism of education, particularly of that during the Civil War, points to an educational emphasis on Europe, on teaching a world history in which the contributions of Africans were negated.

> In history of course, the Negro had no place in this curriculum. He was pictured as a human being of lower order, unable to subject passion to reason, and therefore useful only when made the hewer of wood and the drawer of water for others.[27]

As an advocate for educating African American adults, Woodson believed in a form of education that should do more than just promote knowledge for knowledge sake:

> Real education means to inspire people to live more abundantly, to learn to begin with life as (people) find it and make it better, but the instruction so far given to negroes in college and universities has worked to the contrary.[28]

Woodson's statement addresses the deficiency of formal education available to African American adults at that time. Additionally he is calling for research that is culturally and socially relevant to black life. Decades after Woodson, it would be the misrepresentation of African American contributions to American history via miseducation in public schools that the Malcolm X and others vigorously addressed at the height of the Civil Rights era. Here the Nation of Islam, led by Elijah Muhammad and Malcolm X, carried the gauntlet laid down by Locke, Woodson, Garvey, DuBois, and others in advocating a reeducation of black people, recognizing their historical accomplishments and contributions while emphasizing the experiences of African Americans rooted in their own culture and traditions.

**Purpose of Research**

Malcolm X has been a major figure in African American thought and culture. Upon examining the existing research on Malcolm X, we find three emerging themes: Malcolm as a nontraditional teacher, Malcolm as a community activist, and Malcolm as the precursor to the Afrocentric perspective. From these themes what must be examined is the overall educational impact of Malcolm X for African American adults. The following questions are raised to uncover a comprehensive educational understanding of Malcolm X. What was the impact of education on the life of Malcolm X? And what were his intellectual contributions as Muslim minister, community activist, and international figure in the context of his struggle to have the issues and concerns regarding African Americans recognized? Since Malcolm X existed outside of the formal structure of an educational institution, he has not been viewed as an adult educator. The examination of nontraditional education and culture provides a unique contribution to academic literature, breaking ground for further research.

**Thematic Schemes**

For the examination of Malcolm X, I will examine primary data to assess his views on education. The thematic schemes extracted for this study are based on a preliminary review of literature and relevance to Malcolm's educational contributions.

## Nontraditional Education

Malcolm X's life was indicative of nontraditional and self-directed learning in the context of environmental conditions. Having been formally educated during childhood in the public school system of Lansing, Michigan, Malcolm X dropped out and received what he called a "bachelor's degree" from the streets of Roxbury, Massachusetts, and New York City in the early 1940s. After several years of living a life of petty crimes, Malcolm X was caught and sent to jail in 1946. While in jail he embarked on a course of self-directed learning, utilizing an extensive prison library system. While in prison Malcolm read extensively on a variety of subjects—history, philosophy, and religion, including biographies on Shakespeare, Gandhi, W.E.B. DuBois, and Nat Turner.[29] In his pursuit to educate himself, Malcolm was introduced to the teachings of Elijah Muhammad and the Nation of Islam. After his release from prison, Malcolm continued to learn the basic tenets of the organization through participation in adult education programs for new members. Malcolm's ascent through the ranks of the Nation eventually led to his becoming head minister of the New York Mosque and later national spokesman for the organization. It is with the Nation of Islam that we see Malcolm's role as educator take shape, as his intellectual and theological studies become an important vehicle for him to represent the organizational goals related to Black Muslims and then to surpass them by addressing the issues facing non-Muslim African-Americans, using an international forum.

## Community Activism

Through his work with the Nation of Islam and later with the Organization of Afro-American Unity, Malcolm X sought to have many issues affecting African Americans addressed. Throughout his life Malcolm sought to mobilize African Americans in communities across the country to join the Nation of Islam. In his autobiography he mentions the founding of many mosques in various parts of the country.[30] These same organizational skills he would later use in founding the Organization of Afro-American Unity, for which Malcolm X sought to create a cadre of intellectuals and activists who would work together to generate a social, political, and economic network. Information could then be discussed and analyzed so that solutions could be presented to black community residents in Harlem, New York. In this way Malcolm sought to effectively address issues of public policy that affected not only African Americans but ultimately Africans in the diaspora. In a 1988 lecture, Dr. John Henrik Clarke, one of Malcolm's advisors, said of him: "Malcolm X tried to show us where we were in relation to the power focus of the world."[31]

## Precursor to the Afrocentric Perspective

At the crux of Malcolm's concerns were the negative conditions and representation of African Americans in society. As a result, Malcolm X was an advocate for black cultural expression and Pan-Africanism. Adopting a philosophy of Black Nationalism, Malcolm X's position for African Americans was to employ a knowledge of self by rediscovering African culture and using this as a way of life. Alex Haley, author of *Roots,* who assisted Malcolm with writing his autobiography, gave credit to Malcolm as inspiration for his own seeking to discover his African heritage. In advocating a celebration and a holistic embrace of African traditional culture, Malcolm X sought to address common issues involving racial injustice and political and economic independence from colonial rule. Thus he provided an intellectual and practical ideology for African Americans to liberate themselves from the shackles of their environment.

## Malcolm X, Education, and Culture

To examine Malcolm X's view on education and culture, it is important to understand that his earlier experiences in elementary and middle school had an influence. Being the only black child in several of his classes, Malcolm reflects in his autobiography, did not hurt his popularity among white classmates or his grades, which were exceptional. Still, away from his classmates, he was seen as a social oddity—being black and, given social stereotypes, having his classmates look to him for expertise on dating and romance.[32] The most profound affect in school is his being discouraged from educational advancement by his eighth grade teacher.[33] Though Malcolm would later conclude that this ultimately did not deter him from escaping the oppression in his environment, he does discuss the pattern of miseducation that occurs in the teaching of black history, which has a direct affect on problems of racism in society. While in the Nation of Islam, Malcolm X would emphasize a knowledge of black history for black people to build self-worth in a hostile climate. After leaving the Nation in 1964, he would address the question of education at public meetings of his political organization, the Organization of Afro-American Unity:

Education is an important element in the struggle for human rights. It is the means to help [black] children and [black] people rediscover their identity and thereby increase their self-respect. Education is our passport to the future, for tomorrow belongs only to the people who prepare for it today. They don't understand Black people, nor do they understand our problems; they don't.[34]

Malcolm X goes on to say that African Americans should continue "every type of education available." He criticizes American public education for hurting black people because "teachers and administrators fail to grasp" the problems of teaching black children, because they do not understand the "unique qualities of Black life." Malcolm clearly views the role of his political organization to be giving assistance to black adult education through "self improvement":

We must establish all over the country schools of our own to train our own children to become scientists, to become mathematicians. We must realize the need for adult education and for job retraining programs that will emphasize a changing society in which automation plays a the key role. We intend to use these tools of education to help raise our people's to an unprecedented level of excellence and self-respect through their own efforts.[35]

Malcolm X's view of education for African Americans is one that urges changes in the curriculum, examining black people as subjects not objects (Afrocentric), and in which black community residents put political pressure on the educational system for improving existing problems (community organizing). He urges that there also be supplemental learning outside of the formal educational systems, based on the needs of black adults in a dynamic society (nontraditional education).

## Conclusion

The contributions of Malcolm X to adult education in addition to his leadership role as a public advocate for social, political, and economic advancement of black people are quite evident. Examination of available resources on this subject show that Malcolm X's intellectual contributions are rooted in the cultural concerns of black people. Literary author and scholar Sonia Sanchez, who met Malcolm X, reflects:

Malcolm had no formal Ph.D; he had a Ph.D. in Malcolmism, he had a Ph.D in Americanism, in what had gone wrong with the country, and he brought it to you; and for the first time many of us began to look at ourselves again, and to say, "Hold it, it's possible to work at a job and not sell your soul. It's possible to walk upright like a human being.". . . He taught me, and I's sure a number of others, that you are indeed worthy of being on this planet earth.[36]

Malcolm X's educational impact on black adults and a detailed examination of him as an educator of black adults remains fertile ground for further research.

## References

1. Lerone Bennett, *Before The Mayflower* (New York: Penguin, 1987), pp. 226, 233, 34, 479; John Hope Franklin *From Slavery To Freedom* (New York: Mc Graw-Hill, 1994), pp. 220–46, 247–54; Maulana Karenga, *Introduction To Black Studies* (Los Angeles: University of Sankore Press, 1994), pp. 144–47, 317.

2. Michael Dyson, *Making Malcolm* (New York: Oxford University Press, 1995), p. 146.

3. Malcolm X, *The Autobiography* (1965. Reprint, 1992. New York: Ballantine Books), pp. 1–3.

4. Ibid., pp. 3–7.

5. Claude Clegg, *An Original Man* (New York: St. Martin's Press, 1997), pp. 41–73; E.U. Essien-Udom, *Black Nationalism: A Search for an Identity in America* (Chicago: University of Chicago Press, 1962), pp. 7, 257–58, 269–70; Malcolm X, *Autobiography,* p. 162.

6. M. Karenga, *Introduction to Black Studies*, pp. 175–76; George Breitman, ed., *Malcolm X Speaks* (New York: Grove Press, 1965), pp. 21–22.

7. Karenga, *Introduction to Black Studies*, pp. 175–76.

8. Clayborne Carson, *Malcolm X: The FBI File* (New York: Ballantine, 1992).

9. Clifton Marsh, *From Black Muslims to Muslims* (Lanham, MD: Scarecrow Press, 1996), p. 49.

10. C. Clegg, *An Original Man,* pp. 149–57; Bruce Perry, *Malcolm: The Life of a Man Who Changed Black America* (Barrytown: Station Hill Press, 1990), pp. 207–12; E.U. Essien-Udom, *Black Nationalism,* pp. 177–78.

11. Peter Goldman, *The Death and Life of Malcolm X* (Urbana: University of Illinois Press, 1979), pp. 115–16.

12. Malcolm X, *Autobiography,* pp. 350–363; P. Goldman *Death and Life of Malcolm X,* pp. 206–208; John Henrik Clarke, ed., *Malcolm X: The Man and His Times* (1969. Reprint, Trenton: Africa World Press, 1990), pp. 215–16.

13. Lenwood Davis, *Malcolm X: A Selected Bibliography* (Westport, CT: Greenwood Press, 1984); Timothy V. Johnson, *Malcolm X: A Comprehensive Bibliography* (New York: Garland, 1986).

14. L. Bennett, *Before the Mayflower*, pp. 35, 40, 45–46, 56, 70, 76–77, 84–87, 261–62, 300–301; M. Karenga, *Introduction to Black Studies,* pp. 12, 127, 271–72, 292, 361; J. H. Franklin, *From Slavery to Freedom,* pp. 495–507, 262–63, 405–8.

15. Leo McGee and Harvey Neufeldt, eds. *The Education of African American Adults* (Westport, CT: Greenwood Press, 1990) p. vi.; Diane Buck Briscoe and Jovita Martin Ross "Racial and Ethnic Minorities and Adult Education," in *The Handbook of Adult Education,* ed. Phyllis Cunningham and Sharan Merriam (San Francisco: Jossey-Bass, 1990), p. 583.

16. *Malcolm X: Make It Plain*, PBS documentary, 26 January 1994.

17. Leo McGee and Harvey Neufeldt, *African American Adult Education* (London: Routledge, 1990), p. viii.

18. Ibid., pp. 18–19.

19. Ibid., p. 36.

20. Ibid., p. 37.

21. Ibid., p. 38.

22. Ibid., pp. 45–46.

23. L. Bennett, *Before the Mayflower,* pp. 255–96; J. H. Franklin, *From Slavery to Freedom,* pp. 264–94.

24. M. Karenga *Introduction to Black Studies,* pp. 151–60.

25. John Henrik Clarke, "Africana Studies: A Decade of Change, Challenge and Conflict," in *The Next Decade; Theoretical and Research Issues in Africana Studies* (Ithaca: Cornell University, 1980), p. 31.

26. Alain Locke, *Negro in America* (Chicago: The American Library Association, 1933), p. 89.

27. C.G. Woodson, *Miseducation of the Negro.* (1933. Reprint 1977. New York: AMS Press), p. 89.

28. Ibid., p. 29.

29. *Malcolm X: Make It Plain,* PBS documentary, 26 January 1994; Malcolm X, *Autobiography,* pp. 174–90.

30. Malcolm X, *Autobiography,* p. 222.

31. Videotape Lecture of John Henrik Clarke in New York City, 1988.

32. Malcolm X, *The Autobiography,* p. 30.

33. Ibid., p. 36.

34. Malcolm X, *By any Means Necessary* (New York: Pathfinder, 1970), p. 43.

35. Ibid., p. 45.

36. David Gallen, ed., *Malcolm X: The Man and His Ideas* (New York: Carroll Graf, 1992), p. 42.

# 14

# Dr. James Emman Kwegyir Aggrey
# of Achimota

## Preacher, Scholar, Teacher, and Gentleman

### *Daniel Boamah-Wiafe*

Born on Monday, October 18, 1875,[1] into the Fante[2] ethnic group of the former Gold Coast,[3] young Kodwo Kwegyir Aggrey[4] grew up to become an internationally known educator, an advocate of racial harmony,[5] a noble Christian gentleman, and one of the beloved sons of Africa. Although his mother, Abna Andua, came from a royal family, Kodwo[6] Kwegyir, his father was neither royal family nor rich, but was a respected spokesman of the local chief[7] (Musson 1938, 9; Smith 1971, 15; Ofosu-Appiah 1968, 13).

As a child, Aggrey learned the legend of the Fante gods as well as the traditional Akan farming and folk-medicine practices. Neither of his parents received formal education, and both were illiterates in the Western sense. Determined that their son would not grow up unable to read or write, Kodwo and Abna enrolled young Aggrey in the Wesleyan School at Cape Coast. The Wesleyan School was an exclusive Christian school for boys, so his sister, Abonyiwa, could not enroll in that school. However, she joined the chorus and became the leader of the group. Aggrey loved school and learned so much and so fast that at the age of fifteen he was appointed a teacher at Abura Dunkwa, twenty miles away from his place of birth. He was in charge of teaching between twenty and thirty boys (Musson 1938, 11; Smith 1971, 31–32, 42).

On a visit to her brother at Abura Dunkwa, Abonyiwa assisted Aggrey by teaching new hymns to the children at Sunday school.

The cheerful sound attracted other children who happened to be wandering by, and they strolled in to see what it was all about. Before long, they too were joining in, and wondering at themselves for learning the songs so quickly. "Come again next Sunday," the girls said to Abonyiwa, when they gathered round her after Sunday school was over (Ofosu-Appiah 1975, 16).

After a year at Abura Dunkwa, Aggrey taught at the Wesleyan Centenary Memorial School at Cape Coast. Although he was only sixteen years old, he was allowed to preach. He had passed the Teachers' Certificate Examinations by the time he was twenty years old and was appointed the headmaster of the Memorial School. His students were exceptionally good and became famous for their examination results. Although Aggrey loved teaching, the young headmaster had a great urge for further education, so he continued to learn and work at the same time (Ofosu-Appiah 1968, 20).

## College Education in the United States

As luck would have it, Bishop John Bryan Small of the African Methodist Episcopal Zion Church, a native of Barbados, arrived in the Gold Coast from the United States on a mission (Ofosu-Appiah 1968, 22–23). Part of Bishop Small's plan was to recruit qualified young men from the Gold Coast to be trained for missionary work in the colony. Kwegyir Aggrey accepted Bishop Small's offer for further studies in the United States, so Aggrey left the Gold Coast for the United States, and in July 1898 he enrolled in Livingstone College in Salisbury, North Carolina. Livingstone College was one of the schools established for the descendants of the former black slaves. At Livingstone College Aggrey enrolled in the Classics Department, where he took all the courses required of the freshman class. He believed that it was important for him to enroll in courses that he liked, so Aggrey continued beyond the required courses. Among the ancients, he read Xenophon, Cicero, Virgil, Homer, Livy, Demosthenes, Juvenal, Horace, Plato, Aeschylus, and Tacitus. The courses that he took at Livingstone College included English literature, mathematics, German, theology, philosophy, astronomy, modern history, surveying, and navigation. Except for philosophy, he did well in most of his courses (Ofosu-Appiah 1968, 26).

With a Bachelor of Arts degree, Aggrey graduated with honors, at the head of his class, in 1902. In 1912, he received a Master of Arts degree, also from Livingstone College. Through additional studies and examinations, he received a Doctor of Divinity degree from Hood Theological Seminary (Smith 1971, 61). Because the authorities at Livingstone College thought so highly of Dr. Aggrey, they requested that he joined the faculty. Although Aggrey wanted to return to his native land as a missionary, he could not pass the opportunity of giving back to the institution that had given him so much. Initially, his intention was to teach for a few years in the United States, to gain some experience before returning to the Gold Coast to help his people. But Dr. Aggrey's work at Livingstone College lasted nearly twenty years. He was not only a lecturer, he was also the registrar and financial secretary as well. As a financial secretary, he was able to assist many financially disadvantaged students who were unable to pay their fees. Dr. Aggrey loved good music. He formed an orchestra for the college. The music in the college was so good that sometimes white people used to close their Sunday services early to go and hear the students sing. The people enjoyed the performances of the orchestra so much that Aggrey became popular (Musson 1938, 16–17).

After two years as a lecturer in North Carolina, he met his future wife, Rosebud Douglass. On November 8, 1905, Dr. Aggrey and Miss Rosebud Rudolf Douglass were married at Portsmouth. The Aggreys enjoyed a happy marriage (Smith 1971, 67, 71; Ofosu-Appiah 1968, 32). As a husband, Dr. Aggrey rejected the practice, common in certain parts of West Africa, of expecting married women to work very hard and yet be treated as subordinate to their husbands. Instead, he loved his wife very well and treated her with respect. Dr. and Mrs. Aggrey set up a loving and happy home; and within five years of marriage, they were blessed with three children. Their first child was a girl born in January 1907 and named Abna Azalea after Dr. Aggrey's grandmother. The couple's second child, who was a boy, was named after Aggrey's grandfather, Kodwo Kwegyir. The last child was a girl, born in July 1910, and named Rosebud after Mrs. Aggrey's mother (Musson 1938, 18–19; Smith 1971, 72; Ofosu-Appiah 1968, 32–33). Their children were nurtured and motivated to work as hard as they could. The children's love for their father "was without any fear, and so they often played friendly tricks on" Dr. Aggrey (Musson 1938, 19).

His life as a college professor, happy husband, father, and minister of religion was a very busy one. Ordained an elder in the Zion Methodist Church in 1903, Aggrey became busier when, in 1914, he took over the pastorate of two small churches, Miller's Chapel and Sandy Ridge, both near Salisbury, North Carolina. Dr. Aggrey delivered unique sermons, unlike those of other ministers. He preached about chickens and sometimes about goats,[8] and at times his theme was simply food to eat and clothes to wear.

Although Aggrey chose strange subjects for his sermons, the congregation found them very interesting and got so excited about them that they used to say in the middle of the sermon: "That's right, sir," or "Yes, sir," or "Thank God," or "Amen." And when they talked after the service they used to say: "There's gravy in his sermons; plenty of good strong meat, but gravy to make them savoury" (Musson 1938, 19–20; Smith 1971, 85; Ofosu-Appiah 1968, 26–29).

Dr. Aggrey had a very special reason to deliver the unusual sermons to his congregation, for the people of his two small churches were so poor that they did not often have enough to eat nor appropriate clothes to wear in cold weather. He sincerely believed that to bring the church members close to God he must help them to live more comfortably. As such, Dr. Aggrey taught them how to raise chickens for a living and how to drain the swamps so the mosquitoes would be killed. In this way his people would be saved from water-borne diseases such as fever. He advised them not to exhaust the land of its nutrients, but to adopt appropriate farming practices to ensure that the farms would remained rich and fertile. Aggrey explained that adopting soil conservation measures and proper farming techniques would also increase output and thus improve chances of increasing their prosperity (Musson 1938, 20–21).

**Return to Africa**

It was not until Aggrey was forty years old when the opportunity to return to his native Gold Coast came. The trustees of the Phelps-Stokes Foundation, in cooperation with the Board of the American Baptist Foreign Missionary Society, decided to appoint a commission to study African education. The intention was to find out how they could effectively help improve education in Africa. Dr. Jesse Jones, a Welsh immigrant to the United States who had surveyed black education in the United States, was appointed to lead the commission. Dr. Jones knew that in order to understand the needs of black Africans, he must have a black man as a member of the commission. Being certain that no one could help the commission members understand Africa better than Aggrey, Dr. Jesse Jones invited him to join the Phelps-Stokes Commission to Africa. Dr. Aggrey was glad to take advantage of the opportunity to use his experience, wisdom, and skills in the service of his fellow countrymen (Musson 1938, 23; Ofosu-Appiah 1968, 40–41).

The voyage to Africa first took him to England and then to Freetown, Sierra Leone, where he received a pleasant welcome. In Sierra Leone, Aggrey delighted the students of the Fourah Bay College with a stimulating address that surprised some of them (Ofosu-Appiah 1968, 46). He explained to them that although the courses they were taking at the institution were good, they needed to know more about life in Africa. To be happy, useful, and prosperous, there were other lessons that the students had to learn. He told them about the members of his poor congregations and about his unique sermons. Continuing, Aggrey said that because the members of his churches listened to the strange sermons and took his advice, they improved themselves, their homes, as well as their lives. He emphasized to the students that if they wanted satisfactory results, they had to learn more than the usual English and Western subjects. They had to find out what Africa needed most and to prepare themselves accordingly, so they could become useful to their people after graduation. His speech, which was interjected with Latin quotations impressed the students. After his speech, the students told him that some of their parents were farmers. Dr. Aggrey responded by advising them to study very well so they could become even better farmers than their parents were (Musson 1938, 24).

The members of the Phelps-Stokes Commission stopped in the Republic of Liberia on their way to the Gold Coast. Dr. Aggrey had sent letters to his friends and relatives of his impending return to his native land before the commission left the United States. In the letters, he informed them that he was returning with some white men who were friends of Africa. News of Aggrey's impending return to his native land spread like a wild fire. Aggrey never anticipated the tremendous welcome that awaited him on the Gold Coast. People crowded station after station to welcome him, wherever his train stopped. Some of them were his old friends; however, others were people who did not know him and were there to see Aggrey for the first time. At one place, the stationmaster was a former student. In the major towns, traditional leaders and important people met and gave him a public welcome. The Fantes, in particular, gathered in great numbers to welcome Aggrey and to show how proud they were of him in the evening meetings (Musson 1938, 26).

Dr. Aggrey received his greatest honor at Anomabu, his birthplace, where his old mother and some of their relatives still lived. As the car in which Aggrey was riding approached the village, it was unexpectedly stopped and he was taken to a house. His white colleagues were kept waiting for such a long time that they wondered what had become of him. After a while, he reappeared, dressed in a gorgeous Fante costume and followed by a group of people. He was taken to the parade ground, where all the chiefs and their subjects had gathered to give Aggrey a royal welcome. He was presented a beautiful ebony and gold staff and installed into the honorable traditional office of the *okyeame* (Musson 1938, 26).

The Fantes, particularly the people of Anomabu, would have liked for him to stay longer than he did, but they were also aware that other Africans needed Dr. Aggrey and understood that he could not stay. From the Gold Coast, Aggrey's party went to Nigeria, Angola, and some places in Southern Africa before they returned to the United States. Three years after his return to the United States, Dr. Aggrey accepted an invitation to join another Phelps-Stokes Commission to Africa. The itinerary of the second Phelps-Stokes Commission to Africa included Malawi (formerly Nyasaland), Zimbabwe (formerly Rhodesia), and South Africa. From Cape Town in South Africa, the Aggrey party sailed once again for home (Musson 1938, 26–27; Ofosu-Appiah 1968, 40–71).

## Black Pride and Positive Race Relations

Aggrey used stories and symbolism to explain his beliefs and thoughts on life in general and on race relations in particular. The practical stories he told and the symbolism he used enabled his audience to understand him better—even when he dealt with very difficult and complex issues. He practiced his beliefs, teachings, and rhetoric. He sincerely believed that black and white people are alike in their judgment as to right and wrong, the desire for knowledge, and their search for God and willingness to serve Him. He affirmed that Blacks and Whites could, and should be good friends. To help his audience understand his thoughts on race relations, he used the keys of the keyboard as a symbolism. The piano Aggrey explained has both black and white keys. The finest music is played on the piano when the black and white keys are combined appropriately. In the same way, both black and white people are needed, not separately but together in order to make the whole world a better place to live (Musson 1938, 28).

At times, Dr. Aggrey used humor to explain his thoughts on sensitive issues in such a way that his critics and people who had been rude to him could not help but like him. To a white person who told him that only white people would go to heaven, Aggrey responded by proposing that only "colored" people would go to heaven. Quoting the Bible, he argued that on the last day, the sheep will be on the right, and the goats would be on the left. God would say to the goats to depart and to the sheep, "Come, ye blessed." But the white man retorted, "What does that have to do with the black folks getting to heaven?" And Aggrey responded that blacks are of the only race on the earth that has anything on its heads that reminds one of the wool of a sheep (Musson 1938, 31). He continued that white people have done many wonderful things and that they have every right to be proud of their achievements; however, Whites have no right to despise Blacks because they have not done as much as the white race. He compared Africa to the "Sleeping Beauty" and was confident that some day the continent and its people will wake up to claim their worth in the comity of nations (Musson 1938, 32; Ghana Association of Writers 1975, 16).

He told Blacks that because God was responsible for their dark skin pigmentation, they should be very proud of it, just as people with white or yellow skin color. Whether black, white, or yellow, every human being has special duties to perform for the good of humanity—as such, people of all races must be proud of the nature of their pigmentation (Musson 1938, 28).

## Contribution to Education in the Gold Coast

Before the devoted Canadian became the governor of the Gold Coast, Sir Gordon Guggisberg was the head of the Survey Department in Nigeria. In the Gold Coast, his administration was responsible for constructing a modern harbor at Takoradi and for the development of railways in the colony. In addition, 3,000 miles of new roads were built, 1,300 miles of roads resurfaced with "tar macadam," telephone and telegraph systems were installed, and the Achimota College (also known as the Prince of Wales College) was opened. Together with the first principal of the Prince of Wales College, the Reverend Fraser and Governor Guggisberg, Aggrey played a major role in establishing the institution, which was staffed by both European and African faculty. Dr. Aggrey became a good friend and advisor of Guggisberg. It was also largely to Kwegyir Aggrey's efforts that, for the first time, a real understanding evolved between the British colonial administration and the people of the Gold Coast (Nkrumah 1971, 16; Dei-Anang 1964, 115–16).

Guggisberg believed that the best way to serve Africa was to improve education. Although the elementary school system in the Gold Coast was considered very good by African standards, secondary and higher education were practically nonexistent, so many qualified students had to get further education outside the colony. Secondary education in the Gold Coast began on the initiative of the natives themselves. Supported by nationalists such as John Sarbah, J.P. Brown, and W.E. Pieterson, the Wesleyans established a secondary school for boys at Cape Coast in 1876. However, as Ofosu-Appiah explains, the lack of

> funds led to the closing down of the school in 1889, but it was reopened through public subscription and the contribution of John Sarbah, J.P. Brown and J.W. de Graft Johnson. J. E. Casely Hayford became its principal for a short time. By 1904 a new School under the Fante Public Schools Ltd. had been founded and named Mfantsipim School—the oldest Secondary School in the Gold Coast, and the one destined to help Achimota achieve its aims of university education in the 20th century (1968, 72).

In his first address to the legislative council, Governor Guggisberg announced that education would be the main focus of his administration's policy. He was convinced that there was the need for a radical reform in the colony's education. Not long after he assumed his post as the governor of the Gold Coast, in September 1919, Guggisberg received the report of a committee on education appointed by his predecessor. However, the new governor did not think the report went far enough, so he set up a new committee whose report was presented before the arrival of the Phelps-Stokes commission in October 1920. The Commission's visit stimulated the Guggisberg administration's interest in education and emphasized the need to adapt education to the real needs of the people of the Gold Coast (Smith 1971, 226–27).

The main proposal of the new committee was the building of a new secondary school and a teacher training college. The report of the Phelps-Stokes Commission supported the governor's desire to establish a new secondary school in the Gold Coast. The salient part of the report was as follows:

> If the new ideas of education are to find expression on the Gold Coast, a new school, different from any school now in existence, must be built. A great deal of money will have to be spent on it, but, more important still, men and women who understand and believe in the new ideals must be found to staff it. (Musson 1938, 37)

The establishment of a new government secondary school was due almost entirely to the vision of Sir Frederick Gordon Guggisberg. A hillside property, eight miles north of Accra was chosen as the site for the school (Ofosu-Appiah 1975, 74). The place destined for the new institution, which was near Accra, was also once a hiding place for runaway captives during the slave trade. The hillside location got its name, "Achimota," (meaning "Do not mention the name") from the Ga language. Today, Achimota Secondary School is one of the finest post-elementary institutions in Africa and the name that once could not be mentioned is now well known throughout the world (Ofosu-Appiah 1968, 74).

In accord with the recommendations of his committee on education, the governor agreed that the success of the new institution depended on the quality and dedication of the staff who would run it. Sir Gordon Guggisberg was, therefore, determined to obtain a staff who would make Achimota not only a seat of learning in the Gold Coast, but a major character-forming institution. His immediate plan was to recruit a principal and an assistant. After consultation with the advisory committee at the colonial office in London, several names were considered to head the new school. The governor decided to recruit the Reverend A.G. Fraser to be the new principal. However, Rev. Fraser was still the principal of Trinity College in Ceylon and so could not take the job right away. Next, Sir Guggisberg selected Dr.

Aggrey, whom he had met before, for a position on the faculty.[9] Although he was considering two job offers from elsewhere in Africa, the Achimota position was the most appealing to Dr. Aggrey. He was interested in the job and wanted to accept the offer immediately; however, he declared that he would take the Achimota position only if the Reverend A.G. Fraser was appointed to head the new institution. Both men accepted their appointments to work at Achimota. In October 1924, under the supervision of these two men and four other recruits, the Prince of Wales College at Achimota was opened (Musson 1938, 38–39; Ofosu-Appiah 1968, 74–75; Smith 1971, 227–28).

Initially, the natives were very supportive of a new public secondary school in the Gold Coast. However, the attitude of many natives in the Gold Coast suddenly changed when details of the new institution were released to the public. They had hoped that Achimota School would not be a secondary school, but a higher institution of learning such as Oxford or Cambridge, where graduates would receive college degrees. Also, the fact that a major part of Achimota's mission was to study local conditions did not appeal to the local elite, who were more interested in "universal subjects" such as science and technology. Some of them complained that

> "We do not need Englishmen to teach us the vernacular; we know it, and besides there are no books in our languages; we want English." So they talked. The Africanism of the new school found many opponents. Echoes of the long educational controversy were wafted over from America. Many supposed that the fresh policy was a Machiavellian effort to palm off an inferior education upon the Africans—something that white people would not tolerate for themselves. They spoke as if education as practiced in England were the last word on the subject, not realising that Achimota was planned to give them education of a superior quality (Smith 1971, 237).

Attempts by the governor and the principal to explain their intentions to the natives were not convincing, so they turned to Aggrey for help. On his part, Dr. Aggrey had absolute faith and confidence in Governor Guggisberg, the principal, and their plans for the new institution. Aggrey knew and understood his people very well. He was confident that the people had misunderstood both the governor's intentions and the mission of the school. Because he was enormously popular and persuasive, his chances of explaining the rationale of the governor's plans for the school were good. Opposition to Achimota and the educational policy of the governor was strongest at Cape Coast, the intellectual center of the colony, and among his ethnic group. In several speeches, Aggrey explained the relevance of Achimota's mission to the Gold Coast and her people. After a two-week visit and thirty-three speeches and daily interviews, Aggrey was able to change the peoples' views on Achimota. Later, he was enthusiastically received in the western Fante districts (Smith 1971, 240).

## Influence on African Leaders and Views on Race Relations

In his autobiography, the future president and leader of the newly independent state of Ghana and a former student of the Prince of Wales College, Kwame Nkrumah,[10] wrote:

> But the figure to whom all Africans looked that day was Dr. Kwegyir Aggrey, assistant vice-principal and the first African member of the staff. To me he seemed the most remarkable man that I had ever met and I had the deepest affection for him. He possessed intense vitality and enthusiasm and a most infectious laugh that seemed to bubble up from his heart, and he was a very great orator. It was through him that my nationalism was first aroused. He was extremely proud of his colour but was strongly opposed to racial segregation in any form and, although he could understand Marcus Garvey's principle of "Africa for the Africans," he never hesitated to attack this principle. He believed conditions should be such that the black and white races should work together. Co-operation between the black and white peoples was the key note of his message and the essence of his mission, and he used to expound this by saying: "You can play a tune of sorts on the white keys, and you can play a tune of sorts on the black keys, but for harmony you must use both the black and white" (Nkrumah 1971, 14).

However, Dr. Nkrumah pointed out that he could not accept Aggrey's point of view as practical or realistic. He argued that harmony between the black and white races could only exist when the black race was treated as equals by whites. In Nkrumah's view, only a people with a government of their own can claim equality, racial or otherwise, with another people (1971, 14).

In spite of his untiring efforts to improve interracial relations and cooperation, Dr. Aggrey became an object of suspicion from the Criminal Intelligence Department (CID) of the Gold Coast for his alleged sympathies with Marcus M. Garvey and his Universal Negro Improvement Association (UNIA). Dr. Aggrey's beliefs and his teaching of racial understanding was regularly expressed in his famous symbolism about the harmony of the black and white keys of the piano. He explained that combined appropriately, the black and white keys of the keyboard make pleasant music; however, combined poorly the result is often noise (Crowder 1968, 413).

As Nkrumah recounted (1971, 15), he and a few Achimota students who remained on campus after the school closed for the holidays in 1927 were talking in the art auditorium when Dr. Aggrey suddenly walked in. The assistant vice-principal was excited about his leave and an impending visit to England and the United States. He joked with them and before he left he said: "Brothers, pray for me. So far I have been able to make you hungry but I have not been able to satisfy your hunger." From England, Dr. Aggrey went to New York, where he became suddenly ill and a week later died. As the future president of Ghana noted, following the sudden shock of the news about Aggrey's death,

> the gradual realisation that I had lost forever the guidance of this great man, sapped everything from me and I was quite unable to eat for at least three days. But it was during this period that I made the discovery that even on an empty stomach I seemed to have more than enough energy to carry on with my studies. This realisation proved invaluable in later years in America and England when, through poverty, I had to manage without food—to carry on not only with my studies, but also with the work which I had to do in vacations in order to earn money for university fees.
>
> It was because of my great admiration for Aggrey, both as a man and a scholar, that I first formed the idea of furthering my studies in the United States of America. My plan was to finish the teacher-training course, return to teaching for five years and endeavour to save the necessary passage money (Nkrumah 1971, 15).

In his autobiography, Nnamdi Azikiwe[11]—or Zik as the former president of Nigeria has affectionately been called—wrote:

> One day I listened to a sermon which saturated my whole being. I became spiritually electrified. It then dawned upon me that life had a meaning and I had a mission to fulfill; thus it was my task to make life worthwhile for my fellow men and to be a friend to struggling humanity. I was 16 years old; and the sermon was preached by the Reverend Doctor James Emmanuel Kwegyir Aggrey to a large congregation at the Tinubu Methodist Church (Azikiwe 1970, 36).

According to Zik, after Dr. Aggrey finished reading the text, which was taken from "Prophet Isaiah vi. 1–10," he delivered an inspiring sermon in a soft and melodious voice. As Nnamdi Azikiwe explained, the preacher's voice struck his soul

> with the force of a supernatural wand. Symbolic and suave, his message found my heart a ready soil for the dreams of a new social order. He proceeded to exegete his text, and asserted that Africans were ensconced in the wilderness of western materialism. Their ears were heavy; they heard but heeded not. Their eyes were shut; they seemed to see but they saw not.

Unless, therefore, there was a reorientation of values in Africa, that continent was certainly doomed. Dr. Aggrey spoke about his life, and said that when the time had come for someone to accompany the Phelps-Stokes Commission to Africa in 1921, he volunteered. And he had come to announce to us the glad tidings that "Nothing but the best is good enough for Africa." As he uttered these words, the scales fell from my eyes and I began to see a glorious future. His sermon ended in words like these: "If I, one of you, could go to the new world, and make a man of myself, then you can too. May God help you. Amen." (1970, 37)

Nnamdi Azikiwe explained that religious education gave him a positive conception of universal fatherhood and universal brotherhood. However,

Dr. Aggrey's sermon gave me intellectual curiosity, and Marcus Garvey's slogan, "Africa for Africans," gave me the ambitions to be of service for the redemption of the continent of Africa. These were sparks that kindled my spirit and made me seek avenues to articulate my feelings and desires. At the time when the National Congress of British West Africa was agitating for a better political status, the Anglo-phone-speaking colonies and protectorates in West Africa were advancing a transition within the constitutional self-government. Most of the West African elite could not appreciate what the Congress was battling against. However, they followed blindly, pinning their hopes on the integrity of the leaders of the movement (1970, 66).

Thus it was Dr. Kwegyir Aggrey's hope for a social rebirth and a new spiritual outlook among and toward Africans that, in part, inspired Azikiwe to pursue his college education in the United States and prepare for the leadership and the liberation of Nigeria.

## Influence on African America and the Civil Rights Movement

The influence of Dr. Aggrey's life, philosophy, and ideals was not limited to Africa and Africans. In a 1964 statement to the Ad Hoc Subcommittee on the War on Poverty Program of the U.S. House of Representatives, the former executive director of the National Urban League, Whitney M. Young Jr., noted that

We are asking you to say to those Negro kids and I say this in closing, what was best expressed through a story told by a famous African educator, Dr. Aggrey. He told of a farmer who went out in the woods to hunt and ran across a young eagle which had just been born. He brought the eagle back and put it in with the chickens. Some three or four years later a passing naturalist happened to observe this eagle being raised with the chickens and began to berate the farmer doing this. The farmer said in all innocence that he had not meant to do anything wrong and that for all intents and purposes, because the eagle had been raised since birth with the chickens, it was now a chicken. The naturalist offered to prove differently (Meier, Rudwick, and Brodericks 1971, 436).

Young continues that, after attempts to get the eagle to fly proved unsuccessful, one morning the naturalist in desperation took the eagle out and put it on top of a high cliff. He said, "Eagle, thou art an eagle. Thou were meant to fly in the sky and not work on this earth. Lift your wings and fly" (Meier, Rudwick, Broderick 1971, 436). The eagle trembled at first; however, as if new life had come to it, the bird lifted its mighty wings and flew off and did not return. Whitney Young explained what he hoped that the National Urban League and the other civil rights groups, churches, and hopefully his listeners would be saying to the black youth—that although they had faced barriers, discrimination, and had experiences that might have suggested that they were worthless, they were really worthy human beings. And although they had faced many handicaps, obstacles, and had been humiliated—and although some people may have suggested that the black youth were second-class citizens in the United States—they were really first-class citizens and fine human beings (Meier, Rudwick, Broderick 1971, 436).

Mr. Young pointed out that he was confident that the members of the Ad Hoc Subcommittee on the War on Poverty Program of the U.S. House of Representation were decent human beings, sensitive and intelligent. Because of that, he was hopeful that Congress would endorse the National Urban League's proposal and give the league the resources they needed for the job (Meier, Rudwick, and Broderick 1971, 437).

In honor of Dr. James E. Kwegyir Aggrey, the Phelps-Stokes Fund established the Aggrey Medal in 1986. The Aggrey Medal recognizes individuals whose accomplishments in education, interracial relations, and intercultural relations, international and human relations inspire and encourage scholars and activists. Honorees are selected from among qualified persons nominated by the Phelps-Stokes Fund Board (Phelps-Stokes Fund, 1997).

> The medal was designed by Chul Moon, a graduate student at Pratt Institute, whose design was chosen from a field of over two hundred entries in competition for the honor. The design represents Dr. Aggrey's strong commitment to and belief in education and his advocacy for interracial and international cooperation. (Phelps-Stokes Fund 1997)

The first Aggrey Medal, presented in 1986, was awarded to the Honorable Dr. Nnamdi Azikiwe, the first president of the Republic of Nigeria. In 1997, the honorees were David Levering Lewis, an author and a trustee of the National Humanities Center; David Rubadiri, an educator and the permanent representative of Malawi to the United Nations; and Susan L. Taylor, the editor-in-chief of *Essence* Magazine.

## Conclusion

In conclusion, I have to agree with Edwin W. Smith's (1971, vi) assertion that the late Dr. McDougal (1928) would have learned a great deal about Blacks in general, and black Africans in particular, from the life history of Dr. Kwegyir Aggrey if he had had the opportunity to know Aggrey or to read his biography. Dr. McDougal would then probably have refrained from making the statement that "the African race has never produced any individuals of really high mental and moral endowments, even when brought under foreign influences.... [I]t would seem that it is incapable of producing such individuals" (Smith 1971, 237).

## Notes

1. It is not known whether the name was Emman or Emmanuel. He was listed as Emmanuel by the Ghana Association of Writers (GAW) (1975, 14), but the majority of the sources consulted for this paper used Emman, which in the Fante dialect means "land or country."

2. The ethnic group called Fante, sometimes spelled *Fanti* is member of the Akan cultural group in Ghana and Cote d'Ivoire (Ivory Coast). Although the Akan dialects are structurally different from one another, they are often mutually intelligible. The Akan groups include the Asante, Fante, Akuapem, Akyem, Kwawu, Brong, and Ahafo.

3. In 1957, the Gold Coast achieved independence from Britain and was renamed Ghana.

4. It appears that he was born as Kodwo Mensa Kwegyir Jr. Among the Akans, *mensa* is a third-born male and *mansa* is a third-born female. On June 24, 1883, Aggrey was baptized into the Methodist Church and given James as his Christian name. His original family surname was Kwegyir before it was probably Anglicized as Aggrey (See: Michael Dei-Anang, 1964, 116; Ofosu-Appiah 1968, 13–14).

5. See Michael Crowder, *West Africa under Colonial Rule* (Evanston, IL: Northwestern University Press, 1968), 413.

6. Either Kodwo among the Fantes or Kwadwo among the Twis is the first name of an Akan male born on Monday. Fante, Twi, Akuapem, Kwawu, Asante, and Akyem are all Akans.

7. Like other Akans, the Fante chiefs rarely spoke directly to the people, but rather through a spokesman (*okyeame*) who was considered the "chief's mouth." The duty of the chief's spokesman was "to put into eloquent speech what the chief wished to say" (Musson 1938, 9).

8. See also Smith 1971, 87–89.

9. Because Aggrey did not have experience in administration, the Rev. R.C. Blumer, who had worked with Fraser before, was appointed vice-principal and Aggrey became assistant vice-principal (Smith 1971, 230).

10. Dei-Anang, 116.

11. It is important to stress that the first president of independent Nigeria was a postcolonial African statesman.

## References

Azikiwe, Nnamdi. 1970. *My Odyssey: An Autobiography.* New York: Praeger.
Crowder, Michael. 1968. *West Africa under Colonial Rule.* Evanston: Northwestern University Press.
Dei-Anang, Michael. 1964. *Ghana Resurgent.* Accra, Ghana: Waterville.
Fraser, A. G. 1938. "Foreword" to *Aggrey of Achimota.* London: United Society for Christian Literature, Lutterworth Press.
The Ghana Association of Writers (GAW). 1975. *International Centenary Evening with Aggrey of Africa.* December 5.
McDougal, William. 1928. *The Group Mind, a Sketch of the Principles of Collective Psychology, with Some Attempt to Apply Them to the Interpretation of National Life and Character.* New York: G.P. Putnam's Sons.
Meier, August, Elliott Rudwick, and Francis L. Brodericks, eds. 1971. *Black Protest Thought in the Twentieth Century Second Edition.* Indianapolis: Bobbs-Merrill.
Musson, M. *Aggrey of Achimota.* 1938. London: United Society for Christian Literature, Lutterworth Press.
Nkrumah, Kwame. 1971. *Ghana: The Autobiography of Kwame Nkrumah.* Reprint. New York: International Publishers.
Ofosu-Appiah, L.H. 1968. *The Life of Dr. J.E.K. Aggrey.* Accra: Waterville Publishing House, a Division of Presbyterian Book Depot Ltd.
Phelps-Stokes Fund. 1997. "An African Evening." United Nations Delegates Dining Room. June 12.
Smith, Edwin W. 1971. *Aggrey of Africa: A Study in Black and White.* The Black Heritage Library Collection.
Young, Whitney M. Jr. 1971. "For A Federal 'War on Poverty': A Statement of Whitney M. Young, Jr., Executive Director, National Urban League, Inc." In *Black Protest Thought in the Twentieth Century.* 2d ed. Ed. August Meier, Elliott Rudwick, and Francis L. Broderick. Indianapolis: Bobbs-Merrill.

# 15

# Bothersome Biography

## Emmett Jay Scott

### *Maceo Crenshaw Dailey Jr.*

A set of complex and compelling forces prompted me to select Emmett Jay Scott, Booker T. Washington's legendary private secretary, as my dissertation biography topic at Howard University in 1975. Malcolm X's statement "that of all our research history is best suited to reward all endeavors" was the reason I indeed remained at Howard University to struggle with the biography on Scott, enduring even arrest after my one-person protest demonstration in the president's office. A student of the remarkable 1960s, caught in the vortex of change and continuity of the 1970s, I had turned Malcolm's statement into a preoccupation with biography to shake the tree of history for intellectual, developmental, and personal fruit.[1]

I wanted to understand, through the life of Emmett Jay Scott, Booker T. Washington and his movement, from the vantage point of my own frustrations with the 1960s and the fears of the 1970s. I was convinced that a moment of progress in one era was being turned into a mountain of problems in the other with the collapse of the Civil Rights Movement; with the deaths of the Kennedys, Malcolm X, Martin Luther King, and Medgar Evers; with the flight from the country of Stokely Carmichael; with the incarceration of H. Rap Brown and Angela Davis; with the fizz-out of the student movements (white and black); with the election of Richard Nixon and Watergate. The velocity of historic change was leaving me feeling disappointed with the pace of progress for African Americans, and biography turned, amidst these circumstances, into a search for meaning and alternatives. History hinged, in my youthful mind, on helping people through the maze of Americanism and difficulties they faced, and I anxiously accepted the challenge of bothersome biography in focusing on the long and productive life of Emmett Jay Scott.[2]

There were the four quaint ditty phrases echoing in my mind as I began my research—ones I recalled having heard as child and young adult as the "dozens" (i.e., artistic craftsmanship of trivia joke swapping) were played by African American historians, intellectuals, activists, and others, caught in the throes of struggle and the horns of dilemmas:

"NAACP stands for The National Association For Certain People"
"UNIA stands for the Ugliest Negro In America who was Marcus Garvey"
"A black communist is an overeducated West Indian"
"B.T. in Washington's name stands for 'Bad Taste'"

It was the last charge with which I grappled in my examination of Booker T. Washington, Tuskegee Institute, and the Tuskegee Movement. The approach would be in studying the secondary and tertiary individuals in the Booker T. Washington movement, to raise questions related to their gravitation to the great African American leader, the nature of their involvement and support, and their endeavors in the aftermath of Washington's death in 1915.[3]

Emmett Jay Scott was an easy choice, though I had to expend enormous intellectual energy getting acceptance for the fact that he was worthy of a dissertation. This difficulty, though seeming at one point insurmountable, was mild compared to the problem of constructing Scott's life once I went to examine the primary data. There were the myriad private letters in the Booker T. Washington Collection reposed in the Library of Congress, the two hundred boxes of Emmett Jay Scott Papers housed at Morgan State University, the numerous secondary sources of newspapers, magazines, and pamphlets, and the increasing volumes of biographies and other scholarly syntheses on the subject of Washington and ancillary issues. These made my task indeed a daunting one. I sought quick solutions as I importuned my Ph.D. advisor, Dr. Arnold Taylor, to let me do a limited version of Scott's life for a quick exit with full credentials from the graduate school: a political biography or a first-part biography covering the first half of Scott's life. He, however, was a staunch believer that Howard University indeed had to live up to its reputation as the "capstone of Negro education," as well as of African American elevation, so I received a resounding no to all of my proposed intellectual panaceas for a prematurely awarded Ph.D. I learned one valuable lesson that I quickly impose upon my students anxious to write biography as a means of understanding the past and other possibilities: if you must write the biography, pick someone who made a few profound contributions and had the good sense and grace to die young. Emmett Jay Scott did not accommodate me in either of these regards. He lived to the age of eighty-four and did so much and embarked on so many varied activities that one wonders that he had not found his way into print much earlier in a biography—no matter how inchoate or however much based on secondary sources or hearsay. So I went to work on his life, trying to unravel the many mysteries.[4]

My quest was to be as imaginative in my biographical construction as my mentor and history professor Dr. Benjamin Quarles had been in his opening lines of his Frederick Douglass biography, where he wrote, "Douglass seemed to be a man destined for the pulpit or platform, six feet tall and a baritone voice."[5] I had a similar pithy, if harsher, statement on Scott, given to me by former Howard University historian Dr. Charles Wesley and archivist Dorothy Porter as I dined with them one evening in Washington, D.C.: "Scott was the only man who could walk on snow without leaving footprints." This presaged my exploration into the life of an African American who was neither fully hero nor villain, but rather perceived by many contemporaries as a sneaky person, devious in his devotion to Booker T. Washington, and, therefore, too dangerously powerful for a Negro. Setting out to examine Scott's life led me into backwaters and bedrooms to explain the developments of a black community from Reconstruction to the Civil Rights Movement and, more especially, during the Booker T. Washington era and legacy.

I learned foremost, through the life of Emmett Jay Scott, what a determined group of African Americans had achieved behind the troubling and now un-American wall of segregation; that separation had compelled African Americans of an earlier era to be straightforward about their difficulties and had fostered a rare brand of dedication, duty, and diplomacy. Scott was the personification of all this. His Houston, Texas, birthplace, where the Klan and other white reactionaries swaggered across the stage of history, was a place where Blacks had found agency (to use the new word in the lexicon of many African American intellectuals) in their resolve to build survival and progressive institutions and organizations. Perhaps I was too keenly aware of the accomplishments of black Texans owing to my disappointment with what should have been a better legacy of the Civil Right movement of the 1960s or with what seemed to be lackluster leadership and confusion in the aftermath of Martin Luther King's assassination. As I studied deeper into the realities of both periods—Scott's and my own—juxtaposing the two in my mind and not immediately on paper, I began to understand the extent to which the African American community was driven by charismatic leadership, and that if individuals of the status and ability of the

Douglasses, Truths, Tubmans, Booker T. Washingtons, W.E.B. DuBoises, Martin Luther Kings, and Malcolm Xs were not on the scene or horizons as prominent national leaders, there stemmed the belief that not much was happening to deal with or ameliorate racial conditions.[6]

I found, however, an interesting pattern, explaining the trajectory of the black community from 1860s to the 1960s. The initial phase and important period of the pattern were the decades between 1865 to 1895, an era of profound organizational and institutional growth and development in the black community. The institutional and organizational developments on the local-community levels gave rise to a remarkable and visible second stage where extraordinary leadership bestrode the black community from 1895 to 1915—essentially the age of Booker T. Washington, Ida Wells-Barnett, Anna J. Cooper, Mary Church Terrell, T. Thomas Fortune, and W.E.B. DuBois, who were preoccupied with institutional and organizational structures for African American progress. With the formation of the NAACP and the National Urban League (NUL), two of the more prominent organizations, came the third stage of organizations and institutions, from 1909 to post–World War II. Out of this came the fourth period of leadership of the Civil Rights Movement, from 1945 to 1968; Martin Luther King Jr., and the array of black students emanating from African American colleges of the South. In alternating and symbiotic periods (one age fueling the other) of heightened activities by institutions and organizations, followed by stunning leadership personalities, I found the problematic pattern of progress for the black community. When strong, powerful black leaders were not found on the national level, the historian's gaze was best directed to the local black communities, where local leaders were subsumed by and functioned primarily within organizations and institutions. They may not have been as strong or charismatic as those rising to national fame and prominence, but they were in the trenches, inching the black community along the way to reform and development by their emphasis on institutions and organizations and poised to attach themselves at some point to stronger black leaders on the national level—should such individuals appear. More than likely, those local institutions and organizations (where leaders of lesser ability were to be found) proved to be training, ethos-instilling grounds for leaders of the next stage.[7]

Hence the importance of Scott, a product of the local institutional and organizational developments in the small enclave of Houston's black community and his being propelled out of such a neighborhood and era to hitch his wagon to the Booker T. Washington glory train. Scott understood so well what Washington was trying to achieve, owing to his experiences in Houston. He had pulled himself up from poverty through family, church, and community, all part of the institutional and organizational structures and the chorus of commitment and creativity that were dealing with the race question. He attended college, started a newspaper, and earned the reportage title of "Get Together Scott" for his editorials exhorting Blacks to unity. The lesson here was a simple one that explained Booker T. Washington's "cast down your buckets" and "separate as the fingers of hand"—shibboleths as the progressive views of black leadership, not conciliation and compromise.[8]

Booker T. Washington's popularity in the black community and his sudden rise were explained to me through the prism of Scott's life as an important by-product of the cadre of African American local leaders who saw and heard in the Tuskegee principal's platform and plans many ideas consistent with their own as they sought to build and strengthen institutions and organizations in their hamlets, neighborhoods, towns, cities, and states. They were driven almost to obsession with this, and saw a means of elevating their struggle to a national level, a national movement in the persona of Booker T. Washington. Where two or more met and identified a problem, there were later inchoate rumblings of movement—in Florida, Mississippi, Alabama, Texas, Georgia, North and South Carolina, Tennessee, and Maryland. These were the troubled states of the South, where they had been so "buked and scorned." Their heroes and heroines were people of dignity and of so much culture that they became the "Black Bourgeoisie" to white and black scholars and people trying to conceptualize and understand them. Those African Americans of the late nineteenth century had come to know their Plato and Bach in their preoccupation with African American talent and competency. They too were building a civilization: Afro-Saxons, perhaps, but riveting in its purpose and charged with the concept, as the black theologian Alexander Crummell stated most challengingly: "You have got to organize a people who have been living nigh two hundred years under a system of the most destructive mental, moral, and physical disorganization the world has ever seen." Against this backdrop I began to understand the black men and women of the nineteenth century: their determination, exuberance, and quest for excellence in forging the field, factory, and flower of life into a flotilla of advancement for black folk. Their lives when captured in prose almost had the power to burn the pages as we read of African Americans distancing themselves from slavery, moving through segregation, and shaping the society of the future. How was all of this possible, I merely had to look at the life of Scott at Tuskegee.[9]

Emmett Jay Scott, who lived from 1873 to 1957, maintained an almost impossible regimen of work as he labored incessantly and indefatigably to sustain Booker T. Washington. Responding to letters, traveling as emissary, gathering intelligence, signaling out foes to be dealt with, encouraging

Booker T. Washington in moments of lull and loss, Scott somehow managed, along with his wife Eleanora (née Baker) Scott, to keep his family intact and on line for progress. The five Scott children were well trained; two attended elite white colleges and became part of the "Talented Tenth," which black scholar W.E.B. DuBois saw as the salvation of the black race. Scott also succeeded in writing four books, numerous essays, and newspaper articles; enjoying a brief affair with Alice Dunbar Nelson; going to Liberia to try to save the country from financial ruin; and carrying on the feud with W.E.B. DuBois as they both moved through the first half of the twentieth century. Serving as special assistant on Negro affairs to Secretary of Army Newton D. Baker from 1917 to 1919, as secretary-treasurer/business manager of Howard University from 1919 to 1932, and as secretary of the institution until 1938, and moviemaker, adviser to Republican Party until the early 1950s, and investor in business ventures in both white and black communities, Scott was a man of many talents and was involved in numerous activities for the promotion of African Americans and his own self-aggrandizement. He seemed blessed with a blissful marriage, although on at least one occasion he did break his vows of loyalty to his much-esteemed and admired wife Eleanora, who died in 1939. His wife's death brought closure to the larger and most significant phase of Emmett Jay Scott's life.[10]

Scott himself died a man of achievements and distinction in the late 1950s, though his death went mostly unnoticed by African Americans. He was clearly another conundrum in the historical interpretations of the Booker T. Washington movement. His life reveals in many ways the often-quoted phrase by the savant Santayana that those unaware of their history are doomed to repeat it. In the instance of African Americans, however, ignorance of history meant being locked in a time warp without either a past or future possibilities. A significant African American reading of Booker T. Washington and his movement, instead of confusion and scholarly name-calling, might have placed Blacks in a better position to make meaning and promise of their status as American citizens. In this sense, the nervousness that others shared about the importance of Scott as a biographical subject seemed very misguided. His life opened for me many fascinating vistas of African American history and consciousness. To read about the machinations of those at Tuskegee Institute as they sought to wend their way through the complications of life in the deep South and maintain their professional demeanor was intriguing indeed.[11]

To explore subsequently Scott and a similar group of African American politicians, educators, and activists in the Washington, D.C.—then believed to be the "Black Man's Paradise"—offered another extraordinary profiles. Certainly there was the element of plebeian and bourgeoisie synthesis in

Scott's life. He was not the one-gullah black Southerner recognizable to most who know the history of Booker T. Washington; nor was Scott comfortable in the DuBoisian camp of northern African Americans, those formally educated Blacks arrogantly aware of their abilities. Scott was, however, a bridge between the two factions, working for Booker T. Washington, but yearning for the sophisticated company, status, and breeding of New England–trained black intellectuals. At Tuskegee Institute, he walked and worked among farmers and persons of "practical affairs." At Howard University, he sought to be a force sustaining the great Negro university as that universal educational point of piety and progress in the black community.[12] Neither plodder nor intellectual, Scott was, however, a striver with a modest but important record of achievements among activists, business individuals, and intellectuals alike. The great Howard University biologist Ernest Just is reported, in his request for funds for a culture of amoebae, to have received a Scott reply that the campus could not have the species "swarming like a herd of elephants." It is unlikely that Scott did not know of amoebae; it is more probable that he meant it as a joke, if indeed the quote is really his. Scott was clear about having at Howard the kind of faculty it ultimately came to have in the brilliant cadre of scholars of the 1930s and 1940s. He merely thought that they should all be Republicans and submissive before administrators—an impossibility even given the marginal job opportunities for black scholars at a university constantly struggling for funds and resources. Scott spent the waning days of his life and career in a remarkable job as director of the Sun Shipbuilding Yard Number 4, where he showed the prescience and organizational skills that could only come, perhaps, from someone steeped in the ideological movement and behavior of Booker T. Washington, where the emphasis was on getting things done. In a shipbuilding yard that employed 10,000 African Americans at the height of its productivity, where a ship per month was completed and christened, Scott was scarred by his Washingtonian willingness to accept a segregated yard and labor experiment, despite the fact that his creditable claim of paying jobs, incomes, and opportunities outweighed apartheid at that moment in the employment sector. People without work and jobs and still in the throes of the Depression were being called upon then by the NAACP to bank on integration in the long run. This seemed risky business and not much consolation to the starving and unemployed.[13]

Scott's personal experiences in Chester, Pennsylvania, would have consequences evident in the Black Power movement and the Black Panther Party of the late 1960s and mid 1970s. Scott's son Horace, a physician and philanderer, fathered a child out of wedlock. The child, Elaine Brown, would later become consort to Huey P. Newton, provisional head of the

Black Panther Party, and author of her own remarkable autobiography *A Taste For Power*. Elaine used her grandfather's legacy and life as one of the builders of Howard University in a futile attempt to prod school administrators there to allow Huey Newton to speak on campus. The set of Scott genes are evident in the remarkable resemblance Elaine bears to her grandfather and her stunning capacity for recall, redolent of Scott's ability for memorization of details. Elaine's writing of her autobiography gave her a fuller appreciation of the importance of her grandfather's life, and she contacted me about certain phases of his career. She too was convinced that Emmett Jay Scott had marched shrewdly through the black community and rightly deserved a biographer. I, of course, marveled how Scott had managed well to hide his tracks frequently, embellish his reputation for public consumption, and add to the enigma of Washingtonian legacy.[14]

Biographical methodologies, paradigms, and theoretical perspectives were important to me as I tried to construct Scott's life, testing approaches of other scholars and reviewing what should be central issues in the examination of an individual's story. The requirements of narrative prevailed in just trying to follow Scott in his footsteps through the late nineteenth and first half of the twentieth century, and in using, as one attendee at Professor Kenneth Silverman's monthly New York University evening seminar and dinner affair (for those, scholars and lay persons, in the city working as biographers) cautioned me, "just good old-fashioned good sense and judgment."[15] My choices of graduate schools were clearly the best selections for me. Enrolling in the history department master's program of Morgan State University, I had the good fortunate to work with some of the greatest minds anywhere in academe: white or black, the United States or the world. The great Benjamin Quarles was there, and his classes were inspiring and informative. Another faculty member was the young David L. Lewis, who was bringing closure his biography on Martin Luther King Jr., and would go on to a stellar career, garnering most recently a Pulitzer Prize for his biography of W.E.B. DuBois. There also was Robert Johnson, a University of Wisconsin Ph.D. and brilliant lecturer in the classroom, who kept his students on the edges of their seats as he spoke with what seemed to be intimate knowledge of the follies and greatness of historical characters from Tudor and Stuart England. Roland McConnell could bedevil graduate students with his insistence for mastery of the skills of the historical craft, but he gave one a clear sense of the pedestrian demands of the profession. All of these individuals knew their history, but they also knew Negro America and understood that learning, laughter, love, lasciviousness, lechery, liberation, liability, and loss constituted the drama and dialogue of the human experience, and that African Americans did not have to make mystical cases for their successes or shortcomings because they, after all, were members of the human community.[16]

My Morgan mentors were not prepared to exempt Blacks from culpability or creativity by making some special or convoluted case for the specificity of African Americans. They understood that there were special instances of strategy, but the concluding sentences of their lectures and books centered on the issues of the human race. It gave the Morgan scholars their greatness and their capacity for motivation. Their students went forth with no special beliefs that they were better or worse than others, but they knew they had to take the journey of life and redeem themselves before their teachers, preachers, and parents who had carefully nurtured them. If there was any mysticism at Morgan, it was not rooted in any believed essentials of "blackness"—that would make for a lot of madness—but rather in a belief in testing the human spirit and capacity for achievement in spite of disadvantages. This concept drove me to Howard and later to the biography of Emmett Jay Scott. Benjamin Quarles was another reason I attend Howard University; he was insistent that it was the place for me given my interests. He frequently laughed at the many times our paths crossed in libraries in Baltimore and Washington, D.C.; some years later, when he had occasion to write a recommendation for me, he advised that I was a young scholar "who knew where the bodies were buried." Prior to enrolling in the Washington, D.C., fine institution of higher learning, I had taken only minor interest in the fact that Emmett Jay Scott had bequeathed his personal papers, letters, and books to Morgan State University, but at Howard University, I soon had many occasions to return to Morgan State to complete my dissertation biography and talk with a masterful biographer in the person of Benjamin Quarles.[17]

I could not have had a more intense learning experience than as a Ph.D. candidate at Howard University, thanks to the preceding, 1960s-generation of "Negro transformed into black student," who changed the institution so remarkably in those eventful years from 1967 to 1968. Writer Paula Giddings had it right when she observed of her student days there that "you walked into the Administration building, the switchboard now is taken over by students and was running much more efficiently than it ever had before." The students barged into poor Dean Snowden's office, and—in the words of one of them, Tony Gittens—the scholar and administrator "was quite shocked. He was absolutely shocked. He was shaking, he was trembling. And then we just told him that his time had come." When I got to Howard University as a graduate student in 1971, the administration had regained control, and the first words we were greeted with were "never would another class like those students of the 1960s be let into Howard because they damn near tore the university down." We were hardly encouraged by what they thought of us as students, but I believe we brought as much intellectual pressure to bear on our mentors as university student activists of the 1960s had in direct confrontation: James Early, Bernice Reagon, Rosalyn Terborg-Penn, Sharon Harley, Evelyn Brooks Higginbotham, and Gerald Gill, to name a few who have made their marks.[18]

Seeking a topic for the dissertation while completing my course requirements for admission to Ph.D. candidacy, I saw the remaining greatness of the Howard University of the 1930s and 1940s and the transformations of the 1960s that went to the core of African American achievement, sustaining an institution whose name was virtually synonymous with concerns for American democracy and commitment to racial reform. The names of Howard University faculty members of that era constituted the who's who of savants. Their body of literature and scholarship still remains mostly unsurpassed in understanding of race, class, and gender in America: Ralph Bunche, E. Franklin Frazier, Ernest Just, Charles Thompson, Rayford Logan, Sterling Brown, Arthur Davis, Dorothy Porter, and Doxey Wilkerson were indicative of those notables at the university. I had the great pleasure of studying with Professors Arthur Davis and Rayford Logan, interviewing Mordecai Johnson, Charles Wesley, Dorothy Porter, May Miller Sullivan, Charles Thompson, and Doxey Wilkerson. They gave me clues, gossips, and facts about Howard University and what they thought of Emmett Jay Scott. They essentially sensitized and frightened me with the difficulty of my task; they sent me forth with the view that I had no other choice but to do my best.[19]

I think in some instances they must have laughed and admired my youthful zeal and perhaps foolishness in trying to tackle, as a graduate student, such a complex, awesome, colossal, and difficult project as a biography of Emmett Jay Scott. Indeed, in some of my interviews, especially the one with Charles Thompson, I was the one essentially interviewed, and he at one point asked me directly what led me to believe that I had the ability to bring the biography to closure with the appropriate scholarly cogency. Professor Thompson had spent many summers trying to make sense of the Booker T. Washington movement and legacy. In the early 1930s, he had complained to Emmett Jay Scott, then at Howard University as secretary-treasurer and business manager, of the difficulty of gathering all the information at Tuskegee and giving it some order for better understanding of that era. His unpublished manuscript has still not been turned into a book, so Professor Thompson was not too optimistic about my succeeding with the Scott biography.[20]

What Howard University and Morgan State University provided for me were laboratories for grappling with African American personalities and individuals who studied or were a part of the struggle for advancement, as well as a glimpse of the lives of individuals who were a part of the great dramas in the black community. I had occasion to talk with individuals at those institutions who knew the greatness and follies of many of those remarkable scholars and professors at the African American colleges. While seeking to gather data on Scott and writing the biography, I felt privileged by that exposure and excited by the contacts my education was providing. I was a member of the black educational community and functioning within a compressed and intensive segment of a larger environment and world that I was desperately seeking to make sense of. I was in the crucible. I had presumed to study Scott's life at the same time that it impacted upon my life as an African American and graduate student. I had the opportunity to experience an historical continuum and to interact and interview many of the characters that connected one era to another. Sent from Howard University for oral interviews, I traveled to the North Carolina Mutual Insurance Company in Durham for a meeting with its president; to Atlanta, Georgia, for discussion with Morehouse College president emeritus Benjamin E. Mays and Emmett Jay Scott's sister (who ordered me from her home five minutes into the interview); and to Houston, Texas, to see other Scott family members. Crystallizing in my mind was the fact that my research agenda was beginning to parallel my life, and the biography was beginning to consume me to the extent that my wife and children began to speak of the fact that I was working on the life of "Uncle Emmett," when I could not be found or was off on a research junket. My more cruel detractors were questioning whether I would bring the biography to completeness, either as dissertation or book.[21]

Aware of such cruelties, I resorted to reflections on the childishness and instances of professorial pubescence I have witnessed or heard mentioned in the university: from seeing one scholar chase another around the speaker's platform, to hearing of another rebuke his audience of harsh critics with the retort "your mama," to reading a statement of Congresswoman Shirley Chisolm remarking that she had never understood how vicious politics could be until she taught in college. These thoughts amused me and made me forget outside distractions. I adopted the philosophy of my friend, jazz saxophonist and artist Marion Brown, who once stated, "As long as I know what I am doing, I am cool." Yet for all the travail and the occasional conviction that one is in a profession that comes all too close to pugilistic threats to underscore the validity of scholarly points, still one cannot find a more rewarding form of employment. The crude part of the profession, of course, is the quest for publication. Here politics can surface in the most cruel and disconcerting ways—most graduate schools should actually offer courses in navigating one's early professional path to publication and tenure: a "how to do it" course. I could have profited from such a course.[22]

My biography was submitted to the University of North Carolina Press in the 1980s. I received telephone information and confirmation that the press's in-house review had produced an extremely favorable assessment and that the manuscript would be forwarded to only one reader for comments and criticisms. This small thing seemed all that was required, given the evidence of several statements vouching for the quality of the manuscript and the importance of it for publication. The follow-up response was a devastating one for me, and maybe a blessing in its resounding *no*. The anonymous critic/reviewer was alluded to as someone too powerful to offend or not heed the judgment of. There was no need, so I was told by the letter of refusal, to question the "accommodationist" stance used to interpret the Booker T. Washington movement or the activities of his followers and subordinates. I resolved to return to the biographical drawing board and produce a work that no one could refuse. This, of course, was a mistake. The best strategy would have been to mail the manuscript to multiple publishers, finding one courageous enough and determined to work with me to produce the best possible rendition of Scott's life. I am not too disappointed in my decision at that moment and have been glad that I have done more homework on Scott's life. I shall be mailing the manuscript to potential publishers at the end of this summer. One needs to know when to release a project. If it is, as one pundit put it, a monstrous thing to try to write a biography about someone you have never known and with whom you have never lived, it perhaps is a worse sin not to know when to release the subject from your scholarly grips and into the world, casting it off, so to speak, for it to sink or swim.[23]

Bothersome biography, to say the least, led to a beleaguered scholarly life and an odyssey for me in my determination to comprehend, actively and intellectually, the great American racial drama. Many rewarding moments of my life have been spent struggling with the enigmas of Mr. Emmett Jay Scott. The window of his life opened a verdant pasture to the promises and problems of the black community. Later teaching stints in the North and South gave me first-hand exposure to the worlds in which W.E.B. DuBois, Booker T. Washington, Mary Church Terrell, Anna J. Cooper, and Emmett Jay Scott inhabited, seeing there the remnants and sometimes casualties of great struggles and the ashes of what could have been a more important legacy. I learned, most significantly, that at the level of life as an African American there were many great examples of honor, decency, and brilliance in the black community and that all of this had to be turned into building blocks. I learned of the extraordinary work ethic of a preceding generation of black giants in social movements and scholasticism; I learned of the cruel mangling of bright blacks too sensitive to survive their critics, white and black; I learned foremost that we could do much better than the spate of leaders guiding us post-1968 and that there were still great questions needing to be addressed under the rubric of race. I learned also that in writing biography, one is writing, to a great measure, autobiography: problems and promises of your own life that you may project on historical characters. This is a good thing, though you should not be surprised if the answers do not come forth readily and with crystal-clear meaning. For me, the central question has been what does it really mean to be black in America, and I sought to resolve that in examining Scott's life. The revelations, the ride, and the rewards have been well worth the wait at the publication gate.

## References

1. See Malcolm, X, "On Afro-American History." Unable to pay my student bill at the end of the semester, I was barred from having my transcript mailed to the SUNY-Brockport's African and African American Studies Program, where I was being considered for a one-year appointment. After a day of tossing myself on the mercy of Howard University administrators and pointing out that the policy for withholding of transcripts had been rescinded, my frustration, probably owing to the Washington, D.C., heat and humidity, prompted me to march into the president's office with an ultimatum that "they would have to mail my transcript or arrest me." A faculty trustee, Professor Harold O. Lewis, was kind enough to extricate me from the city police retention center and, strangely enough, I, from this rash act, endeared myself to some of the old-guard faculty members, who admired my moxie.

2. Having lived through the sixties, I strangely have to rely on my notes when I endeavor to teach that period. It gives much credence to Arthur Schlesinger's thesis of the impact of the velocity of history on the human organism. I still am awaiting the cogent ground-level book that will really capture the essence of that era: its music, poetry, politics, and possibilities. *Eyes on the Prize* is indeed a good effort, but one comes away from the book and videos believing that "something else," as Ornette Coleman would have it, needs to be said.

3. My schooling in Baltimore with the great "griot" Mary Carter Smith was my introduction to Africa. My elementary school teacher, Mrs. Carter Smith made trips to Africa in the 1950s and returned to educate us about the realities of the continent. She wore clothing and jewelry from Africa, and we students were stunned by her beauty and eloquence. She was walking "Afrocentricity" in the 1950s. Many of my professors, friends, and activists would regale us with these little ditties. Community pundits and preachers also added to the folklore, and Howard University and Morgan State University continued the learning experience of what was said from the "down and under."

4. Maceo Crenshaw Dailey Jr., "Emmett Jay Scott: The Career of a Secondary Black Leader," Ph.D. diss., Howard University, 1983.; see also the works of Professor Louis R. Harlan on Booker T. Washington: *Booker T. Washington: The Wizard of Tuskegee, 1901–1915* (New York: Oxford University Press, 1983); *Booker T. Washing-*

*ton: The Making of a Black Leader, 1856–1901* (New York: Oxford University Press, 1972); and *Booker T. Washington Papers* (Urbana: University of Illinois Press, 1972).

5. Benjamin Quarles, *Frederick Douglass* (Englewood Cliffs, NJ: Prentice Hall, 1968); interview with Charles Wesley and Dorothy Porter, 14 October 1977, Washington, D.C.

6. See Dailey, "Emmett Jay Scott," for this discussion.

7. Ibid.

8. Ibid.

9. Ibid.; see also Wilson Moses, *The Golden Age of Black Nationalism* (New York: Oxford University Press, 1988); Benjamin Brawley, *The Negro Genius* (New York: Biblo and Tannen, 1966), 105.

10. Dailey, "Emmett Jay Scott."

11. Ibid.

12. Ibid.

13. Ibid.; Kenneth Manning, *Black Apollo of Science: The Life of Everett Ernest Just* (New York: Oxford University Press, 1983), 225.

14. Elaine Brown, *A Taste for Power* (New York: Pantheon Books, 1992), 50–55; 284–85; Dailey, "Emmett Jay Scott."

15. I had a one-semester appointment at New York University, and there had the opportunity to participate in the extremely rewarding evenings in the seminars and in Village restaurants, where we continued our discussions on many evenings. Professor Silverman was a jolly fellow in organizing and guiding us to think more critically about biography.

16. This information is based, of course, on recollections of my graduate career.

17. Benjamin Quarles to Robert Hill, 8 August 1980. A copy of this letter is in possession of the author of this paper.

18. Henry Hampston and Steve Fayer, *Voice of Freedom: An Oral History of the Civil Rights Movement from the 1950s through the 1980s.* (New York: Bantam Books, 1990), 424–49.

19. See Rayford W. Logan, *Howard University: The First Hundred Years* (New York: New York University Press, 1969) for the best synthesis on the richness and importance of the university. My dissertation footnotes cover the many interviews, so I shall only list a few places, dates, and names here: interview with Arthur P. Davis, Washington, D.C., 2 August 1978; telephone interview with Mordecai Johnson, Washington, D.C., 21 July 1975; interview with Charles Wesley and Dorothy Porter, Washington, D.C., 14 October 1977; interview with Rayford Logan, Washington, D.C., 2 April 1975.

20. Interview with Dr. Charles Thompson, Silver Springs, Maryland, summer 1977.

21. Dailey, "Emmett Jay Scott," 1–10; interview with Benjamin Mays, Atlanta, Georgia, 27 July 1977.

22. My attendance at various scholarly conferences has led to some experiences that give credence indeed to the thin line between love and hate, and sanity and insanity. People who use words and thoughts to do in their foes are often more cruel and surgical than those who use the rapier. A colleague once left a session where he was discussing his research and remarked joyfully to me that no one in the room had "laid a glove on me." This, needless to say, was a learning experience for me, for I had not yet developed the requisite mentality for survival in the academy.

23. Anonymous reviewer to Iris Tillman Hill, editor-in-chief of the University of North Carolina Press, 1 October 1985. A copy of the letter is in the collection of the author of this essay.

# About the Editor and Contributors

**Robin B. Balthrope,** Assistant Professor of History at California State University at San Bernardino. She holds a Ph.D. from The Ohio State University. She has published articles in the *Journal of College Student* and other ethnic and historical journals. Her research area of interest is African American history and American history.

**Earnest Norton Bracey,** Professor of Political Science at the Community College of Southern Nevada. He holds a Ph.D. in public administration and public policy from George Mason University. He is he the author of the following books: *Black Samurai; In the Light of Day; Choson;* and the coauthor of *American Politics and Culture Wars.* Also, he has published articles in the *Nevada Historical Quarterly; Research in Race and Ethnic Relations;* and the *NCO Journal.*

**James L. Conyers Jr.,** Chair and Associate Professor of Black Studies and Sociology at the University of Nebraska at Omaha. He holds a Ph.D. in African American studies from Temple University. He is the author of *The Evolution of African American Studies;* the editor of: *Black Lives: Essays in African American Biography; African American Historiography; Africana Studies: A Disciplinary Quest for Both Theory and Method;* and *Charles H. Wesley: The Intellectual Tradition of A Black Historian.* He is coeditor of: *African American Sociology;* and *Africana History, Culture, and Social Policy.*

**Maceo Crenshaw Dailey Jr.,** Director of African American Studies and Associate Professor of History at the University of Texas at El Paso. He holds a Ph.D. in history from Howard University. He is the author of numerous articles, which have been published in: *Review of Black Political Economy; Atlanta History; Contributions in Black Studies;* and *Freedomways.*

**Olga Idriss Davis,** Assistant Professor of Performance Studies at Arizona State University. She holds a Ph.D. in communications from the University of Nebraska at Lincoln. She is the coeditor of a forthcoming book titled *Communication and African American Women: Studies of Rhetoric and Everyday Talk.* Also, she has published numerous articles in scholarly journals such as *The African American Review* and *Women's Studies in Communication.*

**LaVerne Gyant,** Director of the Center for Black Studies and Assistant Professor of Black Studies and Adult Education, Northern Illinois University. She holds an Ed.D. in adult education from Pennsylvania State University. She has published numerous articles and book reviews in the *Journal of Black Studies, Marriage and Family Review,* and the leading journals in the field of adult education.

**Mitchell Kachun,** Assistant Professor of History at Southeast Community College in Lincoln, Nebraska. He holds a Ph.D. from Cornell University. He has published journal articles in *Pennsylvania History* and the *Journal of American Ethnic History.*

**Clement B. G. London,** Professor of Education at Fordham University Graduate School of Education at Lincoln Center. He holds an Ed.D. from Columbia University. He has a prolific record of publishing and is the author of five books: *History and other Disciplines; Through Caribbean Eyes: Reflections on an era of Independence; On the Wings of Change; Parent and Schools;* and *Three Turtle Stories.* Additionally, he has published numerous articles in the leading journals in Black studies, ethnic studies, and education on a national and international level.

**Calvin A. McClinton,** Assistant Professor of Theater and Dance at Kent State University. He holds a Ph.D. from Wayne State University in Detroit. He is currently working on a biography of *Vinnette Carroll,* which is under review.

**Owen G. Mordaunt,** Associate Professor of English at the University of Nebraska at Omaha. He holds a Ph.D. from Indiana University. He has published numerous articles in *TESOL Journal; TESOL Reporter; Afrika Focus; Nebraska English Journal;* and *Educational Studies.*

**Gloria T. Randle**, Assistant Professor of English at Michigan State University. She holds a Ph.D. in english frpm the University of Chicago. Her Research interests focus on examining the works of Toni Morrison. She is currently coediting a book titled *Meditations on the Jazz-Blues Aesthetic.* She has published articles in the *CLA Journal* and the *African American Review.*

**Ralph A. Russell**, Assistant Professor of Music, Grinnell College. He holds a Ph.D. from the University of California at Santa Barbara. He has written numerous articles on contemporary classical music and jazz.

**Andrew P. Smallwood** is Assistant Professor of Black Studies at the University of Nebraska at Omaha. He holds an Ed.D in adult education from Northern Illinois University. His research area of expertise is African American history, psychology, and policy studies. He has published articles in the *Western Journal of Black Studies.*

**Julius E. Thompson,** Director of Black Studies and Associate Professor of Black Studies and History at the University of Missouri at Columbia. He holds a Ph.D. in American history with a concentration in African American history from Princeton University. His books include *Percy Greene and the Jackson Advocate; The Black Press in Mississippi; Hiram Revels: A Biography;* and he has recently completed a literary biography of Dudley Randall and the Broadside Press, which is scheduled for publication in 1998 by McFarland Publishers.

**Daniel Boamah-Wiafe,** Associate Professor of Black Studies, University of Nebraska at Omaha. He holds a Ph.D. from the University of Wisconsin at Madison. He is the author of *The Black Experience in Contemporary America* and *African Today.* He has published numerous articles in the leading Black studies journals.

**Ida Young,** is an elementary school teacher in the Pennsuaken School District, in Pennsuaken, New Jersey. She holds a Ph.D. from Temple University in the Department of African American Studies. Presently, she has focused her attention on writing fiction books for children.

# Index